# Raising Resilient Children

# Raising Resilient Children

## 7 steps to help children thrive in the classroom and beyond

Gavin McCormack

*This book is dedicated to my mum, for holding my hand, telling me that she loved me and tucking me in at night. And also to Mr McKenny. Thank you for noticing me.*

RAISING RESILIENT CHILDREN: 7 STEPS TO HELP CHILDREN THRIVE IN THE CLASSROOM AND BEYOND

First published in Australia in 2025 by
Simon & Schuster (Australia) Pty Limited
Level 4, 32 York St, Sydney NSW 2000

10 9 8 7 6 5 4 3 2 1

New York Amsterdam/Antwerp London Toronto Sydney New Delhi
Visit our website at www.simonandschuster.com.au

A catalogue record for this book is available from the National Library of Australia

ISBN: 9781761429804

Cover design: Luke Causby/Blue Cork
Illustrations: Elizabeth Kerry
Typeset by Midland Typesetters, Australia
Printed and bound in India by Thomson Press India Ltd.

The paper this book is printed on is certified against the Forest Stewardship Council® Standards. Griffin Press holds chain of custody certification SCS-COC-001185. FSC® promotes environmentally responsible, socially beneficial and economically viable management of the world's forests.

# Contents

# List of figures

# Introduction

Life is a fleeting gift. We're granted, on average, a mere 4000 weeks to walk this earth. That's 4000 precious weeks to chase our dreams, craft a life we love, find fulfilling work, explore the world, nurture cherished relationships, leave a positive mark on the planet and become the remarkable people our parents envisioned us to be. Not a single week can be wasted, and if you're reading this book, there's a good chance more than 1000 weeks have already passed! But our journey of self-discovery and growth doesn't wait for the bell to ring on our first day of school; it begins the moment we take our first breath.

My story begins in the heart of one of England's largest council estates. When I was just a small child, my dad left. Just like that, it was my mum and me against the world. Luckily, she is a survivor. Raised as one of seven children, she has a fighter's spirit and a knack for tough decisions. She realised that to secure the best possible future for me, we needed to leave that grim environment. But escape didn't come quickly. We were still there when I was thirteen, stuck in one of those back-to-back houses, a tiny fence separating us from the drama of our neighbours' lives—from what I remember, it was a little bit like that TV show *Shameless*. By this time, my mum had remarried and I had two younger brothers.

I distinctly remember one sunny Saturday morning at thirteen years old, and meeting my friend Michala. Our friendship had blossomed from our shared passion for skateboarding. Being young entrepreneurs, we'd noticed some neighbourhood kids didn't have skateboards and came up with an ingenious business plan: we'd glue sandpaper to scavenged wood, attach wheels and sell them as 'skateboards'. They sold like hot cakes! Kids were practically throwing their money at us. Because my pocket money back then was a measly 25p, I felt like a millionaire. I was the master of my own destiny; it was empowering. I immediately started working towards making my dream come true: to own a Raleigh racing bike with 21 gears.

But a neighbourhood boy called Sean had taken a dislike to me—perhaps the sandpaper had come loose on the skateboard I'd crafted for his little brother, though I can't be sure. When I stepped outside my house one morning, he was waiting, fists clenched and ready. He punched me right on the nose. I ran back inside with blood pouring down my face.

My stepdad was furious. 'Come on buddy, stick up for yourself!' he said. 'Get back outside and fight back!' He even suggested that I should go find the kid and punch him harder—after all, I was the bigger one. But fighting wasn't my style. That wasn't how I envisioned success.

After we walked over to his house to tell his mother what he had done, thankfully, my mum decided that enough was enough; it was time for us to move.

Saying goodbye to the neighbourhood was bittersweet. My uncle came over with a truck and we loaded all our stuff in the back. As we departed, children lined the street—some looked sad, others waved, but most seemed indifferent.

A few hours later, we were settling into our new house in another part of town. While we were still in a council house, it was in the affluent part of the city. Grand old Victorian manor houses lined the streets, and some children wore straw hats and long socks to school. I wouldn't be attending that sort of school, though. I was headed to the local comprehensive. With 2000 students and lots of space to run around, it was a much better environment than my previous situation, but came with its own set of challenges.

I went from being a skinny, poor kid in a neighbourhood where everyone was struggling, to being a skinny, poor kid in a school where many people had wealth. I became acutely aware that my trousers were too short, my trainers were knock-off Nikes—Nick's—from the local discount store, and my packed lunch wasn't much to write home about. They never knew, though, because I usually ate in private, making some excuse as to why I couldn't eat with them.

On reflection, school is supposed to be about learning, but when you're in the thick of it, the reality can be quite different. You're not just absorbing academic lessons, you're learning how to survive in society, navigating life's social dynamics and political wranglings. Who sits with whom in the common room? Who has a crush on whom? What fashion trend is in or out this week? You're also trying to navigate the chaos to figure out who you really are and what you want to do with your life before heading out into the world. But despite the perils of school, through sheer determination and a good dose of luck, I managed to stumble through and survive.

At age sixteen, I was still in school, determined to keep going. The next challenge was choosing my A-levels. These were the key to my entire future, or so I was led to believe. Along with all the other spotty teenagers trying to find their way, I was handed a 100-question survey, designed to assist the selection process by revealing our future job prospects. Excited, we dutifully filled them out, and our surveys were shipped off to a 'futuristic' computer. (This was 1994—the Commodore VIC-20 was futuristic then!) Somehow, this machine was supposed to know me intimately; understand the 'future me'; comprehend how the local, national, and international economies and job markets worked; and reveal my true destiny.

A month later, my personal report arrived at school, prompting a meeting with the careers advisor. I was so excited to discover what the universe had in store for me. By then, I'd been through some changes. I'd experienced my first kiss and grown my hair long. I'd also taken on a whopping three jobs! I was a paperboy every morning, evening and weekend. On Thursday nights and every Saturday, I worked at a supermarket checkout, and on Saturday nights, I scrubbed pots in the local restaurant. Somehow, I'd climbed a rung or two on the social ladder at school. While I was nowhere near the top, I had a few good friends to my name. What's more, I now wore real Nike trainers and could afford my own tuna sandwiches from the canteen. I'd grown in confidence and was feeling good about my future job prospects. As I waited outside the counsellor's door, I envisioned my future. What was I going to be? A doctor, architect, engineer? The world was my oyster.

I walked into the room and took a seat, the anticipation buzzing through me. The careers advisor arrived, clutching my results in her hand. She was tall with long blonde hair; she looked like a lady from a 1980s fitness commercial. Rustling through some papers, she said the computer system had come back with two jobs that suited my personality.

*How exciting!* I thought.

My first option was a driver's mate. *What?!* That's a person who accompanies long-distance lorry drivers to stop them from falling asleep. In my survey, I'd said I loved talking and dreamed of travel. But a driver's mate? Was that really what the future had in store for me? The second option was even more laughable—a shepherd! Don't get me wrong, I like the countryside, animals and a bit of leadership, but this was ridiculous. I made my excuses, went back to the common room, lied to my friends to save face and got on with life.

It goes without saying that the futuristic job-seeking analytical systems of the 1990s were spectacularly wrong. I didn't become a driver's mate. Or a shepherd. Clearly, the system was flawed. Did my teachers really believe these were my best options? Couldn't they offer their own insights and advice, based on their impressions of me? Did they even know me?

The one person who really knew me was my mum. When it came time to decide what to do after high school, I turned to her for advice. We sat in the living room of our council house, the UCAS book resting on my knee, discussing which university course to take and where to study. At the time, I was running a football training club for little kids after school, and Mum had noticed the sparkle in my eyes whenever I returned from coaching them. She suggested I become a teacher. That way, I'd always be working for people and serving my community, and

I could make a positive impact every single day. We talked about the reality of teaching, but Mum managed to convince me it was the most meaningful way to make a difference in the world—not to mention the fantastic holidays! I was sold. Teaching it was.

I was soon faced with a new hurdle—actually getting into a teaching college. My grades weren't predicted to be that great, but I loved geography and had a teacher who cared. His name was Mr McKenny; he looked a little like Art Garfunkel, had a huge smile permanently etched on his face, and he taught everything with passion. Gorges, volcanoes, plate tectonics—he made every lesson feel like an exhilarating adventure. Mr McKenny could see I needed some words of encouragement, so one day, he asked me to stay behind after class. Convinced I was in trouble, I braced myself for the worst. To my surprise, he sat me down and told me he wanted me to get into university. With a C in geography, I might be able to scrape into a teaching degree at Sheffield Hallam University.

That was all the encouragement I needed. I had a newfound purpose. Mr McKenny gave me some invaluable guidance on what to study and how to study it. He assigned research tasks, coached me on answering exam questions and taught me how to draw diagrams. I went home, set up a little table in my bedroom, relocated a lamp from the living room and got to work. Fuelled by his belief in me, I followed every bit of his advice. I'd never worked so hard in my life. Six weeks after the exams were over, the results came back. Mr McKenny was right. I had done it. My C in geography was just enough to get me a preliminary interview at Sheffield Hallam University.

My mum was so proud of me, although she wanted me to attend the local university so I'd be close to home. I couldn't think of anything worse. It was time to fly! With my hard-earned C in geography clutched proudly in my hand, I attended the open day alongside 500 other hopeful students, nervous but excited. After participating in some preliminary workshops where the lecturers observed us, I received the news that would change the trajectory of my life; I was accepted into Sheffield Hallam University's teaching degree. I was going to be a teacher!

University was a fresh start, a chance to hit the 'master reset' button and reinvent myself. I could wear whatever I liked, say whatever I wanted and become the person I knew I had the potential to be. Freedom, however, came with a hefty learning curve. I had to cook my own food, wash my own clothes and make my own bed. I had no idea how to do any of those things, but I soon learned the ropes.

It wasn't until my first practicum that I realised I was on the right path. I'd been assigned to a kindergarten class at a school on the outskirts of Sheffield, predominantly filled with Pakistani children. Some children were refugees, starting their lives in a new country. For a month, I was going to be their teacher. They were so tiny, and I had been entrusted with a monumental task—teaching them the alphabet, basic maths skills and how to hold a pencil. I was also acutely aware that I was, in a small way, nurturing their growth and shaping their future. I was determined to spare them the challenges I'd faced in school—they'd already endured so many hardships. I decided I was going to be the teacher who cared. I was going to be Mr McKenny. I would strive to be the kind of educator he was—someone who prioritised connection over curriculum.

Teaching wasn't just a job, it was a calling, and I was all in. It didn't feel like work. I'd start the school day early and stay up late into the night, preparing my lessons, attempting to be as inspirational as possible. And the kids? They loved it. I'd stumbled my way to the front of a classroom, with 60 eyes looking at me for the answers to life and its mysteries. I was a teacher! This was my chance to prove that even a skinny kid from the council estate could make a difference. Mind you, this wasn't just about me; it was about the potential in every face staring back at me. It was about changing the world, one lesson, one child at a time.

Looking back on my formative years, it took some serious luck, a lot of tears and some bloodshed before I finally found my way. When I did, I was practically a man. What had those nineteen years amounted to? Was it merely about survival? It certainly felt that way. It seemed like such a waste of time. Weren't those supposed to be the years I soaked up knowledge like a sponge, mastering languages and absorbing information at an exponential rate? So why was 'bonjour' the extent of my French vocabulary? And why did so much of my childhood revolve around trying to fit in, stay afloat and not be bullied or excluded?

Mr McKenny had managed to motivate me and it felt amazing. But why did it take so long? If I'd felt this kind of compassion sooner, maybe I'd be fluent in French by now. This experience taught me that we can't expect children to flourish until they feel connected. The curriculum is important, but connection should always come first. When children feel acknowledged, appreciated and understood, they thrive.

Maybe you're wondering what qualifies me to speak on this matter? Well, after graduating, I embarked on a teaching journey that spanned multiple countries: England, France, Spain, Australia, India and Nepal. After fifteen years in the classroom, I retrained as a Montessori teacher with the Montessori World Education Institute. I then became the principal of Farmhouse Montessori in Manly, Sydney. In 2018, I was appointed Montessori Australia Ambassador. In my efforts to improve the education system in the Himalayas, I've built numerous schools and established three major teacher-training centres, which have trained hundreds of Nepalese teachers. I've also authored children's books and Montessori parenting guides, and trained thousands of teachers and parents worldwide on what I call 'purposeful education'.

To further my mission, I recently co-founded the website Upschool.co, which provides free education to hundreds of thousands of children across the globe. And to inspire them, I've embarked on incredible journeys to some of the world's most remote areas, including Antarctica, the Arctic and Mount Everest Base Camp. In these locations, I film lessons on various cultures, values, and wildlife such as rhinos, polar bears, blue whales and orcas. Through these experiences, I've gained insights into childhood and education from nearly every possible angle. So to the parents, teachers and anyone else reading this book, I ask:

*How can we empower children to uncover their passions and purpose as early as possible during their 4000 weeks on Earth? And how can we redefine the concept of educational success, ensuring our children feel engaged and fulfilled while also preparing them for the world of tomorrow?*

Let's find out!

# Step 1

# Modelling the behaviour you wish to see

## Actions speak louder than words

In teaching and parenting, non-verbal communication is a powerful tool. When we want our children to learn a valuable lesson or be generous with others, we may plead, 'Come on, Jonny, share your toys with your sister.' But more often than not, children learn from watching what we do, not what we say. Children are incredibly perceptive about our body language, facial expressions and tone of voice. While the spoken word does play a part, non-verbal communication is the key to helping us get our message across effectively.

For example, if you tell a child to stay calm but your tone is harsh and your body language is tense, the child is more likely to mimic your stress rather than your words. Or saying 'I'm fine' to a child while crossing your arms and avoiding eye contact—or pretending to be interested in their day at school while looking at your phone or smartwatch—can send conflicting signals. We need to align our verbal messages and non-verbal signals to effectively communicate meaning to everyone in our lives, especially our children.

According to Dr Albert Mehrabian, a psychologist who researches non-verbal communication, 93 per cent of communication is non-verbal. When communicating with each other, we use 55 per cent body language, 38 per cent tone of voice and only 7 per cent of actual spoken words. With every wave of the hand, raised eyebrow or subtle shift in tone, we're sharing our message.

Although effective communication is an important core life skill, when we're also mindful of the interplay between language and actions, we can appreciate the profound and lasting impact it has, not just for our children but for everyone around us. Sometimes, our actions and words can influence another person's behaviour, their perception of us, our relationship with them, or even the culture and beliefs of a group of people.

In 2007, I was teaching at a school in Lakemba, Sydney. I hadn't been exposed to Montessori education yet, but I'd always tried to be the teacher who taught slightly differently. I was assigned a Year 6 class filled predominantly with Bangladeshi and Lebanese children. Some had come to Australia as refugees and most spoke English as a second language. The classroom was always a place of laughter and excitement as I aimed to make every lesson engaging and ensured the children had as much agency as possible by letting them choose the direction of the lessons.

At the time, student wellbeing was a relatively new concept, and after attending a professional development course on the subject in the city, I was feeling inspired. To integrate and cater to student wellbeing in my classroom, I allowed the children 30 minutes of free time after lunch where they could choose from some options I believed would positively impact their wellbeing. It was also a chance for me to gather my thoughts after a busy lunchtime doing playground duty, dealing with grazed knees, completing photocopying and attempting to eat my lunch—all within a 30-minute window.

After lunch, I gathered the class together and informed them of the new initiative. They were so excited about having the opportunity to choose. Before I could even inform them of the details, they were already whispering about where they'd sit and with whom they'd work. Now, it wasn't completely free choice—that would be ridiculous.

I offered them a choice from a predetermined list; it's freedom within limits. They had a selection of five activities:

1. **Quiet art:** Each child had an art pad and they could draw and colour anything they liked.
2. **Meditation:** Children could find a comfortable spot in the room, close their eyes and think.
3. **Continued classwork:** Children could continue with any classroom activity they were passionate about, but they had to work in silence.
4. **Listening to music:** Children could listen to music using headphones.
5. **Silent reading:** Children could read quietly to themselves.

The next day, we were off. The children had enthusiastically told their parents about the new activity. Some brought in cushions, cuddly toys, art pads and colourful pencils, eager to participate. How exciting would this wellbeing activity be? We were all looking forward to finding out.

For the first week, I observed as the children embarked on this new journey. They loved the freedom to choose. Interestingly, most chose silent art, which proved to be an excellent and therapeutic choice. However, I really wanted the children to adopt silent reading—I knew how relaxing it could be and how it would improve their language and comprehension abilities. Plus, that would let me tick off a significant part of the curriculum—a requirement in the school—thus freeing up more time to teach the things I loved. Crucially, I didn't want to enforce it upon them, because that would go against everything I believed in and I knew it wouldn't work. So, I decided to choose silent reading myself, thus modelling something I wanted them to follow. While the children were undertaking their chosen wellbeing activity, so would I.

In Week 2, after lunchtime, I picked up a copy of *Harry Potter* and wandered over to the quiet area to read my book in silence. With one eye on the words and another on the children, I could see a lot of interest in what I was doing. I wasn't at my desk marking books, I was reading for pleasure. It didn't take long for my plan to start working. The children soon noticed I was really enjoying reading; I looked purposefully relaxed and emphasised how great reading the book was: 'Wow, I feel so great after that time reading!'

At the beginning of Week 3, a girl joined me in the quiet area with her own copy of *Harry Potter*. Later, as we packed away our things to get ready for the afternoon's lesson, we chatted briefly about Hagrid and the evil teacher at Hogwarts. The class noticed we were having fun reading and had things in common to talk about. Just like magic, by the end of that week, every single child was reading a book each day—either at their tables, in groups or sitting on floor cushions. I hadn't said a word about my preference, I simply modelled it.

While some may think I manipulated them and removed the choice, freedom and agency I advocated for earlier, that's not the case. I simply modelled the behaviour I wished to see, and in two short weeks, the students followed suit. Because, when we're mindful of how we're acting, in combination with the words we use or the passion we show towards something, being able to guide the children in our care without pressure or verbal persuasion becomes our greatest superpower.

## What we are, they will become

Our children are constantly observing us and will attempt to mimic our actions, eventually incorporating these behaviours into their own lives. We know it the moment we accidentally curse in front of a child, only to have them loudly repeat the word at a friend's dinner party. We also see it when our children try to haggle over bedtime and chores, just like they've heard us bargaining at the local market. These instances are a reminder that our children are always watching and learning from our example, for better or worse.

Maria Montessori aptly called teachers 'guides' for a reason. While some aspects of the curriculum require explicit teaching, the most crucial life lessons cannot be taught—they must be modelled. You can't teach confidence or determination with a worksheet, expecting to say, 'Well done, everyone, for filling in that worksheet on confidence. You're now all confident people.' However, we can certainly create environments that naturally foster these skills, allowing them to grow organically.

And so, if we cast our minds towards the future, considering how to shape the behaviours, thoughts and actions of the children under our guidance, we should ask ourselves:

*What kind of leaders do we want shaping our world in 20 years, and how can we empower our children to become them?*

Contrary to the often grim portrayal on the news, the world isn't so bleak; most people are lovely, kind and generous. That being said, I'm sure you'll agree that **fostering more empathy, love, determination, conviction, humility, kindness and compassion can only enhance our society**. These virtues are timeless and transcend technological advancements. They will always be in demand, making our world a better place.

Our overall objective should be to nurture children's arithmetic, comprehension and reading fluency, but also their moral compass; ability to think with their hearts; and capacity to perceive the world with love, empathy and compassion.

Even as an adult, every moment is a chance to learn something new. The lessons that stand the test of time often appear in the most unassuming moments. When I was 21, I set off on a road trip with a friend from university. She was driving me to a concert in Bournemouth, five hours away in the south of England. Her old, beat-up Volkswagen Beetle had a sticker on the window saying, 'If you can be anything, be kind.' It spoke volumes about the kind of person she was.

On the way to Bournemouth, someone abruptly pulled out in front of us at a roundabout, bringing us to a sudden halt. While I almost jumped out of the sunroof in fright, she calmly brushed the hair from her eyes, put her hands back on the wheel and whispered, 'They must be in a rush. Maybe they're going to the hospital. I hope they're okay.' Then we carried on driving and listening to the Rolling Stones.

Although it was more than 20 years ago, this moment of empathy and understanding changed my perspective on 'rude drivers'. You never really know what somebody else is going through. Being able to see the world through their eyes isn't a skill you can learn. But it can certainly be modelled, as it was modelled for me that day. To this day, I think of what she said whenever somebody pulls in front of me.

Now, imagine you're driving to work with your children in the backseat. They're listening to every word you say and watching every movement of your hands and feet. They're learning how to do everything you're doing, storing it in their ever-expanding knowledge base for when they'll need it. Then someone pulls out in front of you, cutting you off without warning. You respond by hitting the steering wheel with your fist and yelling, 'What the ——?! Are you blind?!' The lesson for those sponge-like brains sitting behind you is clear: 'When somebody gets in the way of my plans, I yell, scream and get angry.' A lesson I'm sure none of us wants our children to learn.

Once we understand that everything we say and do will be etched into our children's behavioural patterns for their entire lives, we see our actions have the greatest influence on who our children will become and what values they will hold dear. Although our words and actions can be extremely powerful, our children have five senses. How we deliver our actions can have countless interpretations.

One winter morning in Sydney, I stood in line for a coffee at my regular spot. The air was crisp and cold, visible with each breath. As I glanced around, I noticed a mother and her two children standing nearby, waiting for a table—a two-year-old in a stroller and an older sibling, maybe five years old, holding her hand. Several families of a similar size were waiting in line; most parents were engrossed in their phones while the children stood by their sides. But this mother stood out; she reminded me of my own mum. As she waited for a table, she stroked her daughter's hair and kissed her, letting her know she was loved. It was beautiful to watch—children lock away these behaviours in their core memory bank to recall over a lifetime. I wanted to go over and tell her how amazing it was to see such a touching display of care and love. I didn't, because that would be creepy, but as a teacher, these interactions are more than just words; they signify acceptance, unconditional love, safety and security. As we will come to learn in this book, when our children feel safe and secure, it significantly enhances their ability to learn and absorb the values we want to instil in them.

By fostering a sense of safety, security, love and open communication, as well as embracing everyday experiences as opportunities for learning, we empower our children to become lifelong learners who thrive.

In the classroom, the teacher's relationship with children is different from that of parents. Ideally, home is a place of unconditional love and children know that. But in the classroom, the rules of engagement differ. A child's tantrum at home will end with hugs, kisses and 'I love you', whereas at school, the child could wind up in the principal's office. But there are many ways to make a child feel safe in a space like the classroom—while being mindful that some children unfortunately don't have that unconditional love at home.

As teachers, we're constantly thinking of ways to stay connected with our students because when they feel welcome, safe and secure, their ability to learn grows exponentially. Just like parenting, every teaching moment counts. You've probably seen those viral videos of teachers greeting students at the door with high fives or fist bumps. It seems like a lot of effort just to say 'hello' to your class, right? Well, there's more to it than meets the eye.

On my first Montessori teaching practicum back in 2014, I stood at the door, eagerly awaiting my new class to arrive. My teacher mentor stood over my shoulder and gave me some precious advice:

*In a Montessori classroom, every child is greeted at the door upon arrival with a handshake. Make sure you look each of them in the eye and say 'good morning' with a smile.*

I didn't think too much of it at first. Because the methodology was created more than 100 years ago, I thought it was just an archaic pleasantry that had stood the test of time—a bit like how my posh friends say 'indeed' instead of 'yes'.

The children arrived and off I went, shaking each of their hands, bending down low to look them in the eyes and saying 'hello' with the biggest smile I could muster. Thirteen years later, and I haven't missed a day of standing at the door each morning, shaking the hand of every child as they enter my school or classroom. But it wasn't until a few months ago, when chatting with the brilliant MIT neuroscientist Professor Mark Williams, that I grasped the power of that simple moment and the profound effect our actions can have on others.

As we sat in a café in Sydney drinking coffee, Professor Williams explained to me that human brains can recognise when our skin comes into contact with another person's skin. This primal reaction is etched deep in our DNA. Your skin recognises that it's touching skin, but the skin isn't yours—it belongs to someone else who is close enough to you to be in physical contact for a prolonged period.

The touch, in turn, alerts your body that you're safe; otherwise, why would you be so close? Where there was only one of you, there are now two; you are thus 100 per cent safer than before. And because you're now safer, your brain can alter your emotional state almost immediately. Within seconds of a child shaking your hand and saying 'hello' at the door, their blood pressure drops, their heart rate slows and a hormone called oxytocin (the cuddle hormone) is released into their body's systems, letting them know they're safe and secure. So that handshake at the door of every Montessori classroom, that little touch? It's not just a 'hello' or ceremonial greeting. It's lowering anxiety and calming heart rates. Those handshakes are like a big warm hug (without the hug!) saying:

*Welcome! You're safe here and*
*you're ready to learn!*

Ever wondered why the car salesperson shakes your hand before trying to sell you that new Mazda? Well, now you know!

## The rise of still face syndrome: A growing concern

When children are young, every sight, sound and touch presents an opportunity to learn something new. As they explore the world and act independently, they engage in various actions, both positive and negative. But how do they learn what is appropriate?

Children rely on us to navigate these boundaries. Imagine a child gently tugging on a cat's tail while sitting on the rug. As they do, they glance up for feedback. If you respond with a playful smile and shake your head, they learn two things: first, tugging the cat's tail isn't encouraged but isn't serious enough to cause upset, and second, they associate that specific expression with actions of this nature.

This process is essential for developing emotional intelligence. Through mirror neurons, children are wired to mimic those closest to them, using facial expressions as emotional cues. By mirroring our expressions, they reinforce social bonds and emotional learning, which are crucial for survival and social development.

The problem comes when parents and caregivers spend excessive time on their smartphones. A 2022 study by the Global Web Index reported that the average person spends nearly seven hours a day on their phones, primarily using social media, video content and messaging apps. This constant distraction deprives children of vital face-to-face interactions. According to Dr Jean Twenge, an expert on the impact of technology on child development, this 'over-reliance on digital devices' means children miss out on critical social and emotional cues.

So when little Tommy tugs on the cat's tail or helps his sister up after a fall, instead of receiving a lesson in emotional intelligence, he may be met with a blank, distracted face. This leads to a loss of micro-interactions, preventing Tommy from learning how to read and respond to emotions.

This phenomenon is linked to what psychologists call 'still face' syndrome, a term introduced by Dr Edward Tronick. In his landmark 'Still Face Experiment', Tronick showed that when caregivers suddenly stopped responding to their babies' emotional cues, the infants became distressed and disconnected. 'When the mother makes that still face,' Tronick explains, 'the baby starts to lose the emotional connection to the mother.'

Today, instances of still face syndrome, often due to smartphone overuse, are leading to similar emotional disconnections between children and caregivers, especially in developed countries like Australia. In response, special classes and schools are emerging worldwide to teach children how to read facial cues, express emotions and understand how others feel.

To prevent still face syndrome from affecting your children, the solution is simple: when your children are present, put your phone away. Engage with them, be present and let them learn from your expressions. While Facebook reels and YouTube shorts may be entertaining, they're certainly not worth your child missing out on important emotional cues that will shape their ability to connect with the world around them.

# Educating the whole child

This approach to education—often called 'educating the whole child'—fosters children's overall development. It's about creating a community that nurtures their emotional wellbeing, builds essential skills and supports academic growth. And although I come from a Montessori background, my goal in writing this book isn't to promote any specific methodology. Instead, I want to highlight something universal: our children are constantly observing us. They're watching every move we make and soaking up every word we say. Every adult who interacts with children, whether for a moment or a lifetime, plays a role in guiding them. **Through our words, actions and reactions, we help to shape the path they'll take**. Our job is to model the best version of ourselves, both at home and school, so they have the modelled example they need.

To prepare our children for the challenges of tomorrow and help them become well-rounded individuals who will positively impact the world, they need to learn a broad array of life skills. They must understand how to share their space and belongings, manage criticism and learn to persevere when the going gets tough. Furthermore, they need to learn how to see the world from perspectives other than their own.

But how do we instil these critical lessons in the receptive minds of our beloved children without resorting to lengthy lectures or threats like 'Wait until your father gets home' or 'One more warning and you'll be sent to the principal's office'? It doesn't take a rocket scientist to understand that an environment saturated with threats, punishments and rewards breeds anxiety and fear, and I'm sure we all know the detrimental effects these emotions can have if they're a constant presence in a child's life.

# The power of observation

One of the key principles in my Montessori training is the importance of observation in supporting children's academic, emotional and social development. While Montessori teachers may be a small percentage of educators globally, anyone who works with or spends time around children can embrace these observational skills.

However, a common concern I hear from teachers is that they simply don't have the time to observe. They feel overwhelmed by the demands of a packed, outcome-driven curriculum that leaves little room for anything else. And while I totally understand where they're coming from, my response is always the same: independence creates freedom—not just for the child, but for the teacher too. When schools focus on developing independence in children as a success criterium, classrooms become a place where children have freedom to learn and teachers have time to observe.

## 1. In the classroom

As a school principal, I took great pride in this aspect of our school. Every fortnight, I'd give school tours to families interested in enrolling their children. After discussing the fees and operational details, I'd take the families into classrooms so they could see the learning in action. Many were surprised at what they saw. The rooms were always filled with voices and movement—some children eating a snack in the corner and chatting, others working at a group table building a volcano from cardboard, and still more working diligently on their mathematics. The teachers were often out of sight—perhaps huddled on the ground teaching an individual child or observing from afar. All this was possible because the school focused on fostering independence and had prepared an environment filled with trust and self-regulation.

When we begin to foster independence in the classroom, the teacher's role shifts from direct instruction to careful, insightful observation. The students engage with their various projects, lessons and social interactions, while the teacher remains a watchful, supportive presence. In these moments, they're observing essential skills, otherwise known as 'soft skills', which cannot be taught using a textbook or manual, but can only be learned through experience.

The teacher observes the children working, arguing, debating, and experiencing boredom or frustration and moments of breakthrough. They watch from a distance, taking notes and only intervening when absolutely necessary. As the children work, the teacher (or 'guide', in the Montessori system) looks for the essential skills such as leadership, compromise, care, empathy, negotiation, humour, humility and persistence. Interestingly, these are precisely the skills the world desperately needs. I mean, wouldn't it be great if our leaders followed through with their promises? Or if CEOs of major companies considered the environment before agreeing to build the next coal mine? So it's vital we develop individuals with the skills and values that will make our world a better place for everyone.

Imagine receiving a report from your school that not only listed your child's academic achievements, but also included careful observations of their personality and the fundamental human qualities they demonstrate on a daily basis.

When Elon Musk hires new employees for top engineering or executive roles, he doesn't focus on their resumes or grades. Good grades don't necessarily equate with being able to handle life's complexities and challenges. Instead, he asks them a simple yet profound question:

*Tell me about your life from beginning to end,*
*and explain some of the problems you faced*
*and how you overcame them.*

Why does he do this? Musk wants to understand how these potential employees will navigate the intricate issues that might arise on the launchpad at Starbase or in the Tesla factory. Skills like problem-solving, resilience and adaptability will equip our children for a future we're still trying to fully understand.

## 2. In the home

Parents play the most influential role in shaping their children's future. Think about this: the average child spends roughly 140 hours a month at school but a staggering 540 hours at home. Of course, many of those hours are spent sleeping, but even so, they're still in the home environment. That's a powerful reminder of how crucial family life is in the holistic development of our children. The question is:

*How can parents use observation as a tool to understand what their children need—not just academically, but emotionally and socially?*

### The BBQ test

You have countless opportunities to observe your child and see how they behave and respond socially and emotionally. We might think we know our children inside and out—after all, we spend so much time with them—but we often look at our children through rose-tinted glasses, and that's only natural.

But to gain similar insights as the teacher in the classroom, parents can try this: take your children to a party or BBQ where adults and children are mingling. Instead of joining the adults and discussing the latest rugby game or your weekend activities, spend 30 minutes quietly observing your child as they interact with the other children. Take note of what they do well—are they sharing, caring, helping and waiting patiently? More importantly, identify areas where they struggle. Are they being overly bossy, demanding their preferences are prioritised, or showing signs of aggression? After this honest observation, you'll gain a clearer insight into which skills your child has mastered, as well as areas you need to work on together.

Both teachers and parents can harness observation to prioritise the skills we model for our children. If it becomes apparent that our children are struggling with compromising or sharing, this could indicate an environmental issue or our own modelled behaviour. Once we identify the skills requiring improvement, we just need to shift our focus to enhance opportunities for these skills to develop naturally.

*'When a flower doesn't bloom, you fix the environment in which it grows, not the flower.'*
*—Alexander den Heijer*

If our children are the flowers, we're responsible for positioning them in the sunniest spot.

## How children learn empathy

*'Nobody cares how much you know until they know how much you care.'*
*—Theodore Roosevelt*

One of the most important skills we can impart to our children is empathy. This is where mirror neurons can play a leading role.

In the early 1990s, researchers studying macaque monkeys discovered brain cells they termed 'mirror neurons'. These specialised cells activate both when an individual performs an action and when they observe someone else performing the *same* action. These neurons have since been found in humans and help us understand other people's actions, intentions and emotions. They are pivotal in developing empathy, allowing us to mirror the experiences of another. For example, when children see an adult comforting a crying child on the playground, they can feel the emotions the crying child might be experiencing. Similarly, when they see someone gently move a snail out of harm's way on a cold, rainy day, they can sense the relief the snail might experience.

As adults, we have the power to activate our children's mirror neurons positively, but how do we go about it? The answer is delightfully simple: by walking through life with kindness and caring for everyone and everything we encounter. Our children will naturally pick up on these actions and start mirroring them. Who would have thought changing the world could be so enjoyable? The next time a spider appears in the house, for example, no matter how uneasy you feel about its hairy legs or scuttling movements, resist the urge to squash or spray it. Instead, calmly place a glass over the spider, slide a piece of paper underneath and say aloud in front of your child: 'Off you go, little guy—your family must be wondering where you are.' Just like that, you've planted the seed of empathy, showing them how to treat even the smallest creatures with care and respect.

## The joy of doing good for goodness's sake

In many classrooms and homes, reward charts for good behaviour, special privileges for the so-called 'golden child', points for answering questions or extra playtime for acts of kindness are commonplace. I must admit, I've used these methods myself and while they can help maintain order, they fail to reflect the realities of the world—and therein lies the problem. If our children only act for the sake of a reward, we've missed the purpose of instilling these values.

Life doesn't hand out stickers for holding the door open or extra playtime for helping a neighbour in need. Certain moments, like stopping to help a stranded motorist or guiding a family of ducks safely across a busy road, remind us of the inherent goodness in doing what's right simply because we can—not because someone is watching or there's a treat to be gained. These selfless acts, though often unnoticed, hold the power to shape the kind of world we all want to live in.

Albert Bandura, one of the world's leading psychologists, coined the phrase 'social learning theory', which promotes the opposite of the reward chart. Like Maria Montessori, Bandura influenced many of my school policies when I was a principal because he argued that learning can take place naturally when direct reinforcement and punishment are absent. His research proved children learn from observing others' actions and the consequences of those actions. Consider the child who offers to help the teacher clean their desk. The child happily puts away the pens and pencils, wipes down the table and tidies the books into a neat pile. Then they sit down on the carpet during circle time, feeling proud they got to do 'adult work'. The other children observe this and soon they all want to feel the same way—a revolution starts in the classroom and they all begin to help each other whenever they can!

The goal for us as adults is to help children learn—not from getting a sparkly red sticker or extra pocket money for finishing their homework, but through the emotional response and feelings they experience from behaving a certain way.

A good teacher friend of mine named Jack is the kind of person who, if you called him in the middle of the night to help you move a fridge up ten flights of stairs, would get out of bed, put on his shoes, drive over and assist you. Not because he expects a biscuit afterwards or for you to post a selfie on Instagram with the hashtag #kindness, but because he has the capacity to help and feels it's the right thing to do. Whenever people talk about Jack, they say, 'Oh, I love Jack, he's such a great guy.' And he truly is. Because of that, he leads a content life, exuding kindness and composure. He's the kind of friend anyone would be lucky to have. Wouldn't it be lovely to hear the same said of our own children?

The important lesson from Bandura's research is that we need to create environments and set expectations for our children—and ourselves—where we do good for its own sake, so our children follow in our footsteps. As adults, we have the responsibility to set the gold standard for behaviour through our actions, so our children act first out of compassion and love, rather than for words of praise or rewards. **Once our children feel how good it is to do good in the world, that's all they'll want to do.**

## The importance of being human

It was the beginning of a new term in the spring of 2020. As the school principal, I had been sitting in my office for most of the day, preparing for an upcoming school excursion. Permission slips, bus timetables and brochures were strewn all over the place. Needing a break, I decided to pop into one of the classrooms and say goodbye to the children as they left. As I walked down the corridor, I saw two kindergarten girls standing by the cloakrooms, packing their bags and getting ready to head home. They were whispering and talking behind their hands. As I walked by, I managed to overhear their conversation:

The first girl, pointing at the bathroom: 'I think I just saw the teacher go into the toilet.'

'Teachers don't use the toilet,' said the second girl.

'Maybe she's cleaning it,' suggested the first.

'Probably,' they agreed, as they walked back to class.

For any teachers reading this, they'll know our children often think we're not real humans. They imagine we live in a cupboard in the back of the classroom and that we don't go shopping, use the toilet, or have friends and fun! They see us only in one context: standing at the front of the class every day, neat, tidy, prepared and ready—the oracle who delivers the knowledge. If we think about this reaction on a deeper level, it tells us a lot about what's missing in any adult–child relationship.

Modelling our humanity in front of our children is critical for them to develop their emotional intelligence. Each morning in my classroom, I'd start the day with circle time. And while we often associate 'circle time' with preschool environments and Alcoholics Anonymous meetings, circle time was sacred and pivotal in developing a sense of connection and trust with my classes.

If we want our children to be able to healthily share their emotions from an early age into adulthood, our biggest challenge lies in creating spaces where sharing feelings openly is just something we do. In the classroom, this might be during circle time or while collaborating on projects. At home, these moments can occur anywhere—in the car

## Circle time

Circle time is a moment for sharing what has happened in the eighteen hours since we last saw each other and how we felt about it. We all sit on the ground—at equal height, with equal opportunity and each voice holding equal importance.

To get the ball rolling, I'd ask, 'Does anyone want to share their evening with us? Did anything exciting, unusual or meaningful happen last night that you'd like to share?' The responses would vary, especially at the beginning, and could often be superficial. When I had a chance to speak, I'd tell them about my running club or going rock climbing. I'd even share if a mosquito had been buzzing in my ear all night, I hadn't had a great sleep and was exhausted. I always tried to be honest with a particular focus on how I felt and why. I wanted them to understand I was human and it was possible for me to be tired—I wasn't some robot who'd swallowed an encyclopaedia and lived in the cupboard! I had feelings and thoughts, and so did they, and they were all equally valid and important.

You might wonder why I bother with this when there are worksheets to complete, content to cover and algorithms to learn. Well, this sacred time each day has allowed me to forge a strong connection with nearly every class I've taught. For children, this time is an opportunity for them to share who they are, what they feel and what they need, ensuring everyone can be heard. It helps us all understand that life can be challenging, including for the adult in the room, but when we're surrounded by a group of friends who truly care and listen, there's no need to be afraid. The worksheets can wait!

on the way to school, around the dinner table or even at bedtime. Our children are ready to connect with us, and just like the questions I ask during circle time, the questions we ask may help our children open up to us.

Many parents I've met often complain that when they pick up their children from school and ask, 'How was your day?' or 'What did you do today?', the response is usually 'boring' or 'nothing'. But maybe we need to ask different questions:

*What was the best part of your day, and what made it so special?*

*Was there anything that made you feel uncomfortable or worried today?*

*Can you tell me about a time you felt proud of yourself today?*

*Did anything or anyone make you laugh today? What was it?*

*How did you help someone today, or how did someone help you?*

Once we get the questions right, hopefully our children will begin to ask us things like 'Did you feel special today at work, Dad?' or 'What did you have for lunch today, Mum?' And when challenging moments arise, we don't need to pretend that everything is okay all the time to show our strength and leadership abilities. **Having the courage to be vulnerable in front of our children is, in fact, a significant demonstration of strength**.

Maintaining a façade of invulnerability is not only completely unrealistic but can lead to mental exhaustion. Remember, children are extremely astute, so pulling the wool over their eyes is next to impossible. They'll notice the bags under your eyes after a 60-hour work week and your lack of patience at the dinner table after you've pulled an all-nighter at the office. So, having the courage to share our true thoughts, feelings and emotions with children not only lets them care for us but also teaches them that it's okay for them to be not-okay.

If they do share their feelings, we'll listen to their stories without interrupting or finishing the story for them, then we'll respond with empathy, love and kindness. This approach of collective sharing and caring helps create an environment of emotional openness and honesty. Everyone, including our children, can feel confident in their ability to demonstrate love, care and compassion for others, and in so doing, they develop a profound sense of purpose and fulfillment from caring for others in their time of need.

## Collective community values

After talking to hundreds of parents as a teacher and principal, I've found most parents want their children to be academically sound, but more importantly, they want their children to be happy and mentally well. 'I just want them to be happy', they'd say. So how can modelling collective community values help?

A 2023 Gallup survey found that 29 per cent of Americans have been diagnosed with depression—a staggering figure in a population of 333 million. While many factors contribute to this condition, having a range of coping mechanisms against mental health issues are essential. Research by Mezulis, Hyde and Abramson in 2006 highlights the role of cognitive vulnerability in developing depression, particularly during adolescence. They concluded that when adults express emotions, model healthy coping strategies and communicate openly, they provide children with essential positive behavioural examples, helping to prevent negative cognitive styles that predispose them to depression. So when we create conditions at home and school where emotions are shared, discussed and reflected upon, we can help our children to avoid developing negative thought patterns that lead to self-blame and low self-esteem, and to be more resilient against these debilitating conditions.

## The classroom constitution

I'm sure we've all seen classroom rules alerting us to dangers such as 'Don't run', 'No shouting' and 'No violence'. While these rules provide clear boundaries, they are limited in fostering a sense of belonging and collective responsibility. An authoritarian approach to rules and red lines can sometimes inspire rebellion—there will always be a few who want to cross the line. And then, what do we do? We punish those who break the rules, perhaps by publicly humiliating them in front of the class, removing some stickers from their reward chart or, worse still, sending them to the principal's office.

Quite often, children who break the rules are experimenting, trying to be noticed or calling for help, which should spur us to pay more attention. **Sometimes, those who need the most help ask for it in the most inappropriate ways, and in no world does punishing these children result in positive outcomes.**

According to Bandura, enforcing external or teacher-created rules on children and punishing those who break them serves no purpose. When rules are enforced upon our children, rather than being negotiated collectively, they have no investment in them. As much as possible, our classrooms and homes should resemble the real world. In a democracy, we vote for leaders who hold similar values to us in the hope that society will reflect our notion of right and wrong, so why can't our homes and classrooms do the same?

The fact is, children perform best when they have a say in how their life plays out. And although it may take more time to set freedoms and limitations if our children need to have a say in what they are, once agreed upon, children are more understanding when it's time to put the iPad away or turn the lights out, because they played an active part in making the rules and now it's time to follow them.

In countries, we find constitutions—guiding principles for our behaviour—while companies have workplace culture. For instance, at the head offices of Canva, the design platform with more than 120 million users, workers can choose whether to come into the office or not. They're trusted to do what meets their needs, which fosters a positive work environment. As a result, Canva receives a whopping 300,000 job applications a year and, once hired, almost nobody leaves. On several occasions, it's been voted as the best place to work in Australia. Why? Because they have established a deep level of trust with their team. Small changes can lead to significant outcomes.

*'Employees come first. If you take care of your employees, they will take care of the clients.'*
*—Sir Richard Branson*

In Japan, we find a similar story. Many areas of Japanese culture are deeply rooted in respect. In many schools, children spend the last fifteen minutes of each day cleaning their classroom. They sharpen the pencils, tidy the library and even clean the floors. This isn't a punishment; it's part of the school culture and prepares the classroom for the next day. If the pencils aren't sharp, or the classroom is dirty, then someone else will need to do it—but why should they? The children created the mess, and the same children will use the space in the morning.

At the 2022 FIFA World Cup held in Qatar, Japanese fans cleaned the stadium stalls before leaving, while fans from other countries left their rubbish behind. Their inherited cultural values and compassion for others meant they couldn't conceive of having somebody else clean up their mess, and rightly so. If only we all had the same mindset, maybe the oceans wouldn't be filled with discarded fishing nets, our beaches cluttered with plastic and our rivers polluted with waste chemicals from factories.

## Putting the classroom constitution into practice

Actions that may seem insignificant, such as cleaning your classroom or trusting who you work beside, have profound long-term effects on our attitudes and values. The same applies to the rules in our homes and classrooms. What if the rules weren't rules at all, and what if they weren't concocted by the teacher during the school holidays? What if we decided on our very own classroom culture? What if, on the first day of the school term, the teacher asked the children, 'When other people are talking about our class in the staffroom or on the street, what would you like them to say?'

What would the children say? Perhaps the conversation would go like this:

*'I want them to say we are kind,' says one child.*
*'I want them to say we are good friends,' says another.*
*'I want them to say we work hard,' adds another child.*

Based on that conversation, the children decide on their values and jot them down. They've just written their own collective constitution—their mantra—and instead of authoritarian rules, they now have a class culture. **This is who we are, and these are the values we uphold**. The sign on the wall may read something like this:

*In 5K, we keep our promises, we always try our best, and we always try to share and help when we can.*

The classroom mantra heads home, too. Parents try to emulate it at home and discuss it at the dinner table. It's even reported in school newsletters and student reports. The children, teachers, school principal and parents are all working towards the collectively decided values of the children they care for. Imagine a school where the way in which our children show up each day is just as important as demonstrating what they remember about the maths or science lesson. **Imagine the adults who would be leading our world in 20 years**.

**Figure 1.** Our class rules

## Establishing a growth mindset

One of the first things I did as a school principal was to shake up our traditional student reports. I teamed up with one of my amazing teachers to come up with a plan: no more grades, rankings or test scores. Instead, parents would see a holistic view of their child's progress. We wanted to focus on how much they'd grown, not just what they'd memorised.

We started holding one-on-one 'conferences' with each student. The children booked 30-minute chats with their teachers to talk about what they wanted to focus on. It was all about what they were interested in, not just the curriculum. (Our job was to build the curriculum around them.)

Of course, we still reported on their academic progress, but we also talked about their social and emotional skills, personalities and the values they were developing. Their goals reflected not on *what* they wanted to be in the future, but *who* they wanted to be—empathetic, compassionate, resilient, determined, brave. We were attempting to move towards a growth mindset approach to learning, assessing and reporting on our children.

Establishing a growth mindset begins once we've answered key questions like:

*What matters to me?*

*What do I care about?*

*What kind of person do I want to be?*

These reflections set the foundation for a growth-oriented approach to life, giving us clear direction and purpose.

Russ Harris, a renowned author and therapist specialising in acceptance and commitment therapy, offers a valuable strategy for children and adults striving for success. Known as the 'choice point', his concept involves understanding what values matter to us and what kind of people we want to be—akin to setting a personal or classroom constitution. Whenever we're faced with a decision or experiencing a thought or emotion, whether big or small, this method prompts us to pause and consider:

*Will the action, thought or feeling I'm about to engage in lead me away from who I want to be, or towards it?*

This straightforward yet powerful tool encourages children to foresee the potential consequences of their actions, and consider how their choices might impact themselves and others. It's also a useful reflective tool for adults to respond thoughtfully if a child makes a poor decision:

> *Tommy, do you think that only letting boys play your game on the playground, and not allowing Stephanie to play because she's a girl, takes you away from or towards who you want to be?*

This tool helps guide children to make decisions that not only foster their own growth, but also positively affect those around them. I use it regularly with children, friends, family and myself. I often find myself looking at menus in restaurants, thinking, *Hmm, choice point! That cheeseburger looks amazing, but what direction will it take me?* 'I'll take the chicken salad, please!' The choice point approach simplifies the growth mindset idea, making it more accessible

**Figure 2.** Choice point

and actionable. With children, this approach is transformative. You'll often hear one child chime in 'choice point!' as another teeters on the edge of a decision they might later regret. It empowers children to pause, reflect and choose a path that aligns with their goals and values.

## Trust and consistency

When my two brothers and I were kids, we had a strategy whenever we wanted something new or out of the ordinary. We never went to my stepdad—he was a tough sell. Instead, we'd head straight to Mum. She was more likely to say 'yes', and we knew it. The problem? Mum was clever. Just as we thought we were about to win her over, she'd hit us with: 'You better wait until your dad gets home and ask him!' And just like that, our plans were foiled. Needless to say, we rarely got what we wanted. It taught us something valuable though: trust and consistency go hand in hand. Even when we knew Dad's answer would probably be 'no', we also knew it would be fair and unchanging. While frustrating at the time, that consistency gave us a sense of stability that we came to rely on.

Trust is a crucial element in the relationship between children and adults. The strongest relationships are founded on trust. For a child, trust is synonymous with consistency. It's about the adult being a stable presence in a world where everything is in flux. Change is the only constant for a child—their classroom peers are ever-changing, their moods are constantly shifting, their bodies are evolving rapidly and the external world is moving faster than ever. So, being a constant and consistent figure in a child's life offers them a moment of calm and predictability. They think, *When I approach him or her, I know exactly what response I'll receive.*

I have two pet cats. I found them on the street, and they are always hungry. They'll eat anything from anyone without a moment's thought. If it's on a plate, they'll hoover it down like it's their last meal. But one day, about a year into our daily feeding ritual, I decided to heat their food in the microwave. I wanted them to have their first hot meal. My heart was in the right place!

But I'd accidentally made it too hot. As usual, my tabby cat went to wolf it down. The poor guy burned his mouth. Don't worry, he wasn't seriously injured, but something significant happened that day. He lost his trust in the food on his plate. Was he going to get burned every time from now on? Ten years later, he still paws at the food before eating it, just to make sure it's not too hot. Poor guy.

You're probably thinking, *Why is he telling me about his cat, and how is this relevant to child development?* Because this is what happens to our children if we're inconsistent in the way we act, respond or behave when we're around them. It only takes one moment of inconsistency to make them hesitant to share how they feel, or what they want or need from us.

*'Trust takes years to build, seconds to break,*
*and forever to repair.'*
*—Dhar Mann*

Of course, we all have bad days—perhaps we haven't slept all night, or life's challenges are piling up—and we inevitably slip up. Maybe we promise to keep calm, then lose our temper, or we set a boundary, then let it slide. So, what happens when we fall into the trap of being human and accidentally break our children's trust? Will it really take forever to mend?

Thankfully, no, it won't. But mending trust does require patience, sincerity and accountability. Like many adults who work with children, I've made this mistake countless times. And while it doesn't happen overnight, trust can always be rebuilt if we're willing to admit our mistakes and make amends.

Here's a simple four-step plan to help anyone who has accidentally broken trust with their children:

### Step 1: Acknowledge and apologise

Admit your wrongdoing! Sit in a quiet area, get down low, make eye contact with your child, and be sincere in your actions and words. Remember, children know when you don't mean it; they learn these skills as soon as they can see faces and hear voices.

### Step 2: Explain why it happened

Without making excuses, discuss that, as humans, we sometimes make mistakes and act out of character or instinctively. This validates to your child that mistakes are okay, and we'll all make them at some point in our lives.

### Step 3: Set expectations

Explain to your child how you will try your best in the future and what they can expect from you. Give them the power to hold you accountable.

### Step 4: Follow through

Keep your promises. Over time, you'll find that trust is restored, and when it is, your relationship will be stronger than ever.

## Avoiding hypocrisy

One of the most frequently used phrases by children, especially when they're upset, is 'It's not fair!' At first glance, this may seem like a mere objection to a request or rule. But this phrase holds a deeper meaning.

Often, we expect children to perform adult-like tasks—washing the car, helping a sibling with their coat, answering the door or running an errand alone. We frame these responsibilities as privileges and, indeed, they are. Children love doing the chores we hate. Give a child the chance to vacuum the house and watch as they beam with pride. It's plain for all to see as they puff out their chests and hold their heads high, entrusted with adult responsibilities. These moments signify our trust in them and nurture their independence and responsibility. However, this brings a significant caveat: if we treat them as our equals in these tasks, we must also treat them as equals in all respects, particularly when making decisions and listening to their thoughts and feelings.

The question then arises: where does hypocrisy enter the equation? Consider the rules we set collectively at home or in the classroom—the constitution of our mini-society. These rules might include:

*We never bring phones to the dinner table.*

*We always remove our shoes before entering the house.*

*We always leave the classroom tidy.*

*We always use a calm voice in the classroom.*

These rules all sound well and good, but for them to truly take hold, everyone must adhere to them—including teachers and parents. If you don't believe me, just try banning phones at the dinner table and then taking a call in front of your children while tucking into your chicken salad. Or instruct your children to tuck their classroom chairs under the table to keep people from tripping over but leave yours sticking out. They'll notice, and the response won't be pretty!

If we fail to live up to our own standards, the cry of 'It's not fair!' is not only expected but justified. Even if the child doesn't say it out loud, they'll remember that you broke the rules and use it as evidence later. 'But last week, you had your shoes on in the house, so why can't I?'

Whether in our homes or classrooms, we all share these spaces and their associated responsibilities. If an adult decides they are above performing simple tasks like sharpening pencils or putting away the dishes, they shouldn't be surprised when confronted with accusations of unfairness. Because, indeed, it isn't fair.

## The bridge between home and school

Many mystical phenomena exist but can't be seen—like the Earth's gravity, magnetism or true love. But the most mystical of all is that invisible line between the classroom and the outside world. In the classroom, children understand this is a place where learning occurs; they keep their books tidy, slide their seats under the desk neatly and gather their belongings quietly at the stationery corner. Holding hands with their partner, they line up at the door for playtime. Calendars, schedules, timetables and clear expectations define the space. It's orderly and efficient because the environment was designed with the teacher–child relationship in mind.

Three o'clock comes around, the bell rings and it's time to go home. As we say goodbye, the children cross that invisible threshold and something happens. The child enters a new world, where the rules of engagement are different. For starters, ideally, there is unconditional love out there. To the child, it doesn't matter what happens now: the gloves are off. No matter what they do, their parents will always love them, which gives them the freedom to express themselves however they wish. It could be the silent treatment with grunts and groans, a tantrum when soccer training is cancelled, an excited hop and skip, or a big warm hug and kiss. Each day is different.

This also poses a problem. Because of the inherent difference between the environments of home and school, the child has to dance between the two, sometimes blurring the lines and forgetting what the expectations are. To counter this problem, as a school principal, I made sure the families in our school were well aware of how the classrooms worked and what our expectations were, so they could model these at home, too.

Each term, I invited parents to school and into the classroom in the evening, to sit on the carpet and be taught just like their child. They'd attend lessons with the teachers based on the subjects the children would be learning next term, they could sit where they liked, make things from card and use scissors. They absolutely loved it. 'I wish I'd

**Figure 3.** Home versus school

gone to a school like this,' they'd say. Even better, they'd adopt some of the methodology into their homes, thus building the bridge between what happens in the classroom and at home.

When you do activities like these, you'll see it's essential for parents and teachers to collaborate closely to harmonise these spaces and merge the boundary between home and school. At home, just like at school, children should enjoy comparable freedoms and responsibilities, underscored by clear, non-negotiable collective rules. At school, children also need personal spaces—a cubby hole for their belongings when younger, evolving into a locker when older. The secret is in the communication and openness between the school and the students' families.

And if we imagine the community as an orchestra, every instrument, regardless of size, position or melody, contributes a unique sound to the overall composition. Likewise, children feel integral when they understand their role, whether it's playing a simple rhythm or a complex solo. Their contribution adds to the harmony of the whole.

Ultimately, the magic lies in forging a seamless connection between home and school, ensuring children feel equally valued, safe and understood in both. By aligning our expectations and recognising each child's individuality, children learn that school isn't solely where we learn, and home isn't merely where we play—both provide rich opportunities for academic, emotional and social development. Through open collaboration and allowing children space to grow, we cultivate an environment where these essential skills flourish naturally.

## Four fundamental principles to building connection

In my early years as a teacher, I genuinely believed a quiet classroom—where every child was busy with a task I had assigned—was the pinnacle of success. Orderly schedules, perfectly straight lines of children marching to recess and an air of control seemed to symbolise what being a 'good teacher' was all about.

But as time went on, particularly after completing my Montessori training and exploring alternative schools and methodologies, my perspective shifted dramatically. I realised that true success in education wasn't about maintaining control; it was about creating an environment where children could flourish—socially, emotionally and academically.

Through years of observing colleagues, children and leaders like my former mentor Dr McKeith, I've distilled the art of connection into four core principles.

### 1. Actively listen—the 30-second rule

When a child enters a space—whether it's your classroom or the kitchen—acknowledge them. Pause for a moment, get down to their level, smile and make eye contact. Let them know you see them and that they matter. Aim to acknowledge every child within 30 seconds of them entering the room. It's a habit I call the '30-second rule'—a small but powerful way to build connection and show children they're valued. Once you've locked eyes, ask them how they feel or what their plans are for the day. If they share something with you, really listen. Put your phone away, close the laptop, face them and listen to understand, not just respond. No matter what they tell you or how long it takes, let them finish. As adults, nothing is more offensive than finishing someone else's sentence, ignoring them when they enter your space or speaking down to them, so why do this to our children?

## 2. Share your time

Time is one of the most precious gifts we can offer. For a child, shared time represents love, interest and value. This could be a shared hobby, a planned experience or simply sitting down together with no agenda other than being present. In a classroom, it means getting to know each child individually. At home, it's about carving out moments that are entirely theirs, with no distractions or interruptions. If you have multiple children, this one-on-one time becomes even more important, making each child feel uniquely cherished and leaving lasting imprints on a child's heart and mind (for more on this, see Chapter 6).

## 3. Be positive and hopeful

Children flourish when surrounded by positivity and optimism. When a child shares an idea with you—no matter how impractical or far-fetched—respond with genuine excitement. Even on days when your own outlook feels clouded, their hope could be the spark to shift your perspective. Knowing you believe in them will empower them. After all, what we think is impossible often isn't. As you'll discover throughout this book, I've seen children achieve extraordinary feats simply because someone believed they could. Belief is a powerful catalyst, and your encouragement might be the first step towards their extraordinary success.

## 4. Walk the path together

We're all on a journey of self-improvement, striving to learn, grow and do better—whether it's mastering a new skill, cutting back on screen time or exploring the world more. And while we walk this path, our children are watching. They see our triumphs, but also witness our struggles. By sharing your journey openly, you invite them to celebrate your wins just as you cheer for theirs. Let them see you stumble, fall and rise again—because sometimes, they'll be the ones helping you back up. Growth is a shared experience, whether in the classroom or around the dinner table. And the journey? It's infinitely better when taken hand in hand.

## The impact of stress on learning

When I was in secondary school, I rarely got into trouble. I kept my head down and tried to stay out of the spotlight. Yet every Monday morning brought a moment of dread. The principal, Mr Philp, would stand before more than 1000 children and call out the names of those who were to report to his office immediately after assembly. Although I'd done nothing wrong, my heart would pound and a bead of sweat would trickle down my back as I braced myself for the possibility of hearing my name. In those moments, I felt unsafe and uncertain.

When children feel emotionally and physically safe, the amount of stress in their bodies is significantly reduced. **Children flourish when they feel safe**. Stress, on the other hand, can derail the learning process entirely. Whether it's fear of being told off, punished, ridiculed in front of peers or even having test scores announced publicly (which is all too common), these stressors create an environment that inhibits growth. A 2019 study published in the *Journal of Neuroscience* highlights that a stress-free brain has up to 50 per cent greater capacity for memory retention and critical thinking. So, it's clear that if we want children to embrace learning with curiosity and enthusiasm, we must reduce unnecessary stress.

# What happens if our children are stressed

## 1. Fight-or-flight response

It's natural to want to avoid the unknown. Think about introducing a new sport at school—some children will instantly try to opt out. Or consider offering a child a food they've never tried before; suddenly, they're not hungry. When we're faced with unfamiliar or challenging situations, the body's fight-or-flight response kicks in. This ancient survival mechanism floods the system with stress hormones like cortisol, preparing us to either confront the threat or flee from it. But although this response is useful in dangerous situations, it can be a barrier to growth in environments that feel unpredictable or unsafe.

For children, this stress can accumulate long before they encounter the unknown situation itself. A classroom lacking structure, a new activity sprung on them without warning or an environment where they feel unsure of expectations can trigger a cascade of avoidance behaviours. These include refusing to participate, withdrawing socially or displaying outbursts of frustration.

## 2. Limited learning

Have you ever tried to concentrate or learn something new when extremely stressed? Imagine attempting to grasp a complex concept while your car's broken down and you're stranded on the side of a busy freeway, surrounded by honking cars and chaos. It's almost laughable to even consider it.

However, this scenario is all too common in the lives of our children. You see, when a child experiences high levels of stress, their brain's ability to process and retain information diminishes significantly. Elevated cortisol levels, triggered by fear or anxiety, impair the hippocampus—a critical part of the brain for learning and memory. As neuroscientist Professor Mark Williams explains, stress inhibits the brain's synaptic plasticity: its ability to adapt and form new neural connections. And prolonged stress hinders neurogenesis, the creation of new neurons in the hippocampus, further stalling the capacity to absorb and integrate new knowledge.

When a child is worried about making a mistake, being ridiculed or facing unpredictable consequences, their ability to connect new learning with prior knowledge becomes severely limited. It's not that they're unwilling to learn; their brains simply can't function optimally in such an environment.

## 3. Memory is affected

Picture this: you're the keynote speaker at a prestigious conference. The room is packed with 1000 eager faces waiting for you to begin. You glance down at your laptop, only to realise it's logged you out and your carefully prepared presentation is no longer visible on the big screen. All you need to do is type in your password, but in that moment, with every eye on you, your mind goes blank. The password—something you've entered hundreds of times before—is suddenly out of reach.

Why does this happen? Stress. When we're under pressure, our ability to recall information, learn new concepts or navigate simple tasks becomes impaired. The surge of stress hormones overwhelms the brain's prefrontal cortex, responsible for higher-order thinking and memory retrieval. This disruption affects cognitive functioning, leading to forgetfulness and difficulties with problem-solving and retaining knowledge.

For children, this can be particularly detrimental. Whether it's recalling a maths formula during a test or trying to follow multi-step instructions in class, stress diminishes their capacity to perform. It's not a matter of intelligence or effort; their brains are in survival mode, prioritising immediate safety over memory and learning.

So the next time a child is having a tantrum before school, refusing to step out of the car, struggling to recall lessons from class, finding it hard to focus or grappling with overwhelming emotions, some underlying issue might be making them feel uneasy, unsafe or afraid.

What can we do? Start by acknowledging and validating their feelings without judgement. Create a safe, open space where they feel comfortable expressing themselves. Then work together to find a solution, reassuring them that you're there to support them if the feeling resurfaces. The good news is, we can work collectively to minimise the stress in children's lives.

## Minimising stress

School routines and practices might not seem stressful at first glance. But if you take a closer look, you'll notice echoes of the industrial revolution—markers originally designed to prepare students for factory or mine work—still embedded in today's schools. Bells ring loudly, interrupting moments of deep focus. Charts and scores are displayed for all to see, adding unnecessary pressure and comparisons. Children often sit in rigid rows facing the front, only allowed to speak when the teacher gives permission.

These far too common, outdated practices do little to foster the kind of safe, nurturing environments that let children thrive. While every home and school is unique, we can all take steps to empower young minds and support them in becoming everything they dream of being.

### 1. Establish predictable routines

When children know what is coming up, they feel more confident and, as a result, their stress levels are significantly reduced. This could be a simple chart where children can see the full day ahead of them on the fridge door or their learning schedule posted on the classroom wall. With a visual roadmap, unexpected bumps become smooth sailing and anxiety takes a backseat.

### 2. Validate feelings

When a child tells you they feel a certain way, first listen then validate their feelings as real. Their explanation may not be entirely factual—if a child says they have a stomach-ache, it could mean they're anxious about an upcoming activity or event. Our task is to listen, validate and investigate until we uncover the real reason behind the emotion.

## 3. Be consistent with discipline

Just as children can immediately spot hypocrisy, they also notice consistency. Children love to know where the boundaries lie. If we say the TV goes off at 6 pm, then we need to ensure it happens without fail at 6 pm. Children will test you to see if they can get five more minutes, but giving in is risky. They've identified a weakness in your resolve, and soon, that house of cards will come tumbling down. What we say, we must enforce and maintain.

## 4. Empower children through choices

Giving our children choices in how their day unfolds allows them to feel validated and builds their confidence. Simple tasks, such as allowing your child to choose their clothes from a predetermined selection, or having a democratic classroom vote on which sport to cover in Term 2, involve children in the decision-making process. This tells them their voice matters and is important.

## 5. Teach coping skills

While the skills for the future cannot be taught directly, coping skills for stressful situations certainly can. We can model these skills ourselves when we face challenging moments. Teaching skills such as deep breathing, meditation and relaxation techniques provide our children with remedies for unexpected situations they may encounter. Knowing they can help resolve their own problems helps them feel safer, regardless of what might lie ahead.

## 6. Encourage social connections

Imagine a lone meerkat standing guard, on the lookout for predators. It seems vulnerable, right? But meerkats live in close-knit groups called mobs, with complex communication and shared responsibility for raising their young. While one stands guard, keeping an eye out for danger, others forage for food. Just like the meerkat mob, our children thrive when they have strong social connections. By joining clubs, having secret languages, creating imaginary worlds, playing role-playing games and working together, children feel supported, safe and valued, which fosters a sense of belonging within their community.

## 7. Maintain a safe physical environment

When we feel threatened or scared, our natural instinct is to retreat. But what if there's nowhere to go? When we feel trapped and there's nowhere for flight, we fight. In our classrooms and homes, children must have a safe space to retreat to—a place they can call their own. This can be as simple as a cubby under the stairs fashioned with soft lights, cushions or familiar toys to create a calming environment where the child can remove themselves from any perceived danger. Once the child feels safe, they can use their coping strategies, which then lets us approach and listen to what's happening and help to resolve the issue.

## 8. Model emotional regulation

Emotions are normal and everyone experiences them. As adults, we mustn't hide these feelings but express them in a healthy manner. I remember seeing my father cry for the first time when I was fifteen. His mother had passed away, and I had never seen this other side of his personality before—a humbling moment. Getting emotional is the perfect time to demonstrate that it's okay to cry, laugh or feel deflated, or even feel angry. The sooner they can see this in us, the better.

## 9. Provide reassurance and support

When a child needs help, they'll show you. The child who causes the most trouble in your class often needs the most love. When a child reaches out to us, whether through an emotional breakdown or by hunching their shoulders and retreating, we must first acknowledge them and reassure them that everything will be okay: 'I hear you, I'm here, I'm not going anywhere and I'll help you get through this.'

## 10. Cultivate self-esteem

A child comes home and proudly announces to her father that she scored eighteen out of twenty on her maths test. The father, putting down his cup of tea, responds with those all too common words: 'Let's sit down and go through the two you got wrong.' But the child, with wisdom far beyond her years, counters, 'No, Dad, how about we go through the eighteen I got right?' And she's spot on.

*

Once we start to implement and build these strategies into our everyday routines and overall mindset, we create an environment where children feel supported, understood and empowered. If we want to raise children with a strong sense of self-worth, self-confidence and the conviction they can accomplish anything, we must shift our focus from their shortcomings to their efforts, accomplishments and improvements by whispering statements such as:

*I'm so proud of you for working so hard, you've made so much progress.*

Here, we're maximising the impact of positive talk, a powerful tool we should use generously, especially when children are stepping outside their comfort zones, trying new foods or daring to think creatively. How we respond to their attempts, regardless of the outcome, not only lays the foundation for their self-esteem but also nurtures their resilience and determination. When we focus on their efforts and celebrate their bravery, we empower them to approach the world with curiosity and courage, and there is nothing more powerful than a child who is willing to give everything a try.

## Conflict resolution

Conflict often gets a bad reputation. Many see it as something to avoid at all costs, but it's a vital part of learning and growth. When managed thoughtfully, conflict can teach invaluable lessons to our children. Resolving conflicts independently requires anyone, especially children, to practise an array of important skills. They need to communicate, listen, negotiate, compromise and understand different perspectives to find a resolution. And if we adults step in too soon, we can inadvertently stifle the development of these skills.

Compromise and negotiation aren't learned from adults intervening but rather through the natural challenges children encounter as they grow. Our role is to observe quietly, provide guidance only when necessary and give them the space to learn through experiencing situations they'll face in the real world.

When I was a child, my father would get furious with me for answering back. Seeing me and my brothers arguing over who would be in charge of the television remote control, he'd confiscate it and turn off the television, stating that now nobody was allowed to watch it. But he had no idea that we'd created a pact—the first one to wake up in the morning had control, and my brother wasn't following the rules! Why didn't he know? Because he didn't give me 30 seconds to explain the situation. I wanted to be heard, and when I wasn't allowed to get my point across or if I thought the decision was unjust, I would rebel, answer back and get into even more trouble.

Adults often step in too quickly to resolve children's conflicts. We say things like, 'Alright, what's going on here? Why is everyone shouting? You two, move apart—I don't want you sitting together for the rest of the day,' or 'Go to your rooms!' But what if, instead, we paused?

By allowing a situation to unfold—within reason—we give children the opportunity to resolve issues on their own. It might take time for tensions to settle, but with enough space and a supportive environment, they can work things out. In doing so, they practise and refine essential skills like communication, empathy, compromise, reflection and negotiation, setting the stage for their emotional and social growth.

In the classroom, teachers have many ways to resolve conflict. There's the good, the bad and the ugly and, trust me, I've tried all of them—from separating children who are arguing in class to punishing the whole class for one child's actions. While these may work in the short term, it wasn't until my Montessori training that I was exposed to a unique method you can implement at home or in any classroom.

## The Peace Rose

In a typical Montessori classroom, teachers try to avoid intervening in conflicts. Instead, we equip children with tools and skills to resolve their issues independently. One of my favourites is the Peace Rose. This simple yet powerful resource is designed to help children as young as three navigate disputes on their own. Here's how it works:

In the classroom, disagreements are inevitable—someone's taken another's seat, someone feels left out or, heaven forbid, someone is using another's pencil. When things get heated, and without instruction, an older child may step in with the Peace Rose. Like a magical wand, it signals the beginning of meaningful conversations, compromise, negotiation and understanding.

The children involved in the conflict step aside. The rose is handed to the first child, who expresses their viewpoint. Then the rose is passed to the other child so they can speak, and so on until they reach a resolution and 'peace' is restored. No teacher involvement is necessary. The children develop strategies to resolve any issue through dialogue, compromise and active listening, building skills that serve them for a lifetime.

When we talk about preparing our children for the future, this is what we envision—akin to how staff members might resolve conflicts in an office, perhaps with HR mediation. Executive functioning isn't just for executives; it can take place in kindergarten classrooms. While the Peace Rose might not be appropriate for children of all ages, it demonstrates that when children are empowered to solve problems for themselves, we set them up to handle any kind of difficulties they may face in the future.

**Figure 4.** The Peace Rose

We're not just teaching them conflict resolution skills—we're allowing them to organically develop grit, resilience and problem-solving. Sure, it can get a little loud and messy at times, but that's all part of the process. **After all, the real world doesn't come with a handy teacher's aide to break up every squabble. Better they learn to work it out themselves now while the stakes are low.**

With so many of our world leaders resorting to armed conflict and war to resolve their differences with other nations, I can't help but wonder if the Peace Rose approach might actually be useful at the United Nations (UN).

## Follow the child

When I moved from being a classroom teacher to becoming a school principal, some people thought it might be an unwise move—myself included! As a teacher, I could clock off at 3 pm, head to the beach for a swim and relax for most of the evening. Yes, I had to plan a few lessons here and there, but like anyone who has worked for more than 20 years in the same profession, it had become almost second nature.

The reason I took the jump was not because of money or power, but influence. My mum had promised me that teaching would let me make a difference, and yes, I had taught many children, worked in various countries and influenced some great things in my classrooms—but what if I had a whole school to work with? What if I was the navigator of a ship filled with hundreds of students? After a few conversations with people I trusted, it was time to take the plunge and lead a whole school.

By this time, I'd been building schools in Nepal for several years—more on this later! While I normally relied on my friends and the online community to help with this mission, I now had a whole school of passionate children and parents to work with. In my first term at the school, I was very much a hands-on principal, teaching classes and working with the children.

One day, in an attempt to make a connection with one of the classes and inspired by Maria Montessori's mission for world peace, I decided to share my Nepalese adventures and future school-building plans. I wanted to show the children a problem that existed in the world and hopefully inspire them to help the Nepalese community establish a new school. But I didn't want to tell them what to do; I wanted to let them use their critical thinking, empathy and experimentation skills to try and help me solve the problem.

I sat down with the Stage 2 children (six- to nine-year-olds) and showed them some pictures of the community I was headed to next—the children they'd be helping, their current school (which looked more like a prison cell than a classroom) and a map of the location.

The Nepalese community in question is in a place called Nawalparasi near the Indian border—a dusty village with rice fields, buffalo in the gardens and smiling people cycling in the hazy afternoon sun, carrying bits of wood or building materials on their backs. I could tell the images painted a new perspective for these children. Once I finished telling them about the mission ahead, I opened the floor to questions so they could gain more context.

The children asked questions like:

*What kind of food do they eat?*

*What do their houses look like?*

*What language do they speak?*

The children wanted the full picture, and I did my best to paint it. 'They mainly eat rice and lentils,' I told them. 'Their houses are usually very bright in colour—often greens and pinks—but for many people, the kitchen floor is made from cow poo! When it's cold, they don't have a heater, so villagers bring the buffalo and goats into the downstairs part of the house while the humans stay upstairs. The warmth from the animals heats the house so everyone can keep snug. There are tigers in this area, too, so keeping the animals in the house is much safer for them.'

'Tigers!' they exclaimed. Immediately a flurry of questions came up about living with tigers.

I could see they were invested as I had cleverly used what some teachers call 'the educational hook'. Through their questions and my responses, I believed they had gathered sufficient context. Before I left the room, I reminded them one more time that although I had done this before, I was bamboozled by this job. It was a big task to renovate a whole school, and if they had any ideas on how they could help, I would be more than willing to listen.

Although I could have actually done it without them, I needed to show them I was vulnerable and human. I didn't have *all* the answers, and the job would be much easier if we could do it as a team. As the children prepared to go home, I could hear the gentle chatter of ideas being shared on the carpet. On leaving the classroom, I could hear them telling their parents about the school, the tigers and the buffalo living in the houses. I was hopeful about the coming days.

The next morning, a student aged seven appeared at my office. Carrying a suitcase in his hand, he said, 'Gavin, I went through my bedroom last night and collected all the things I don't use or need any more in this suitcase. I want you to take them to Nepal.' Inside it were books, some shoes, a woolly hat, some board games and paints. One of the items was a bunch of old, half-used colouring pencils with an elastic band around them with a little note attached that read 'Nepal'. He had thought carefully about this and he genuinely wanted to help. I thanked him for the amazing gesture and told him I would take these items to the children who needed them the most. I called his mum to make sure he hadn't taken the items from his father's office or his brother's bedroom, and I placed the suitcase in the corridor outside my office.

Like a ripple in a pond, it began. Almost immediately, the other students started asking questions about the suitcase. What was inside, who had donated it? Within one week, and as if by magic, I had ten suitcases filled with everything a child could dream of—clothes, hats, shoes, books, pencils. It was as if the child who donated that first suitcase had started a movement—a movement of kindness and empathy.

Seven weeks later, I flew to Nepal with almost fifteen suitcases filled with everything you could possibly imagine. We renovated the small school and stocked it with the donations the children had collected. It looked beautiful. So beautiful that the head of the local municipality called it the most beautiful school in Nepal. On the grand day of opening, I cut the ribbon to let the children inside. With a buzz of excitement, the students bustled into their new school, mouths hanging open and eyes wide with joy. They walked over to the shelves in awe, grabbing books, games and toys, and started engaging with learning. It was one of the best moments of my life.

I could have watched that scene all day long. Then, in a moment of serendipity, I noticed as one boy picked up the little bundle of colouring pencils wrapped in an elastic band. He carried them carefully to his new classroom table, took a piece of donated white photocopier paper and began to draw his first-ever picture. With a heart filled with happiness, I watched as he drew a picture of his house with a tree by its side. It was a moment I will never forget.

When he had finished, he walked over to me and asked, 'One paper more?'

A week later, I returned to school in Sydney to show the children what they had achieved. I had taken before-and-after photos with this moment in mind. The children couldn't believe it. They had changed the world, and it started with one child having an idea and modelling a behaviour the rest of the school would come to follow.

*

During this chapter, we've spoken a lot about observing the child and modelling behaviours to assist them in their quest to become the person they want to be. But the role model we all need does not have to be the oldest, tallest or wisest. A true role model in any community is someone who dares to tackle the impossible without hesitation or fear of failure. They are the ones who care for everyone, no matter the circumstances, and strive to understand the world from every perspective while making the most of the resources they have. This time, it just happened to be a seven-year-old boy with a half-filled suitcase who showed us the way.

## Be the change

We're all on this journey together, trying to become the best versions of ourselves. It's a breeze for some, a slog for others, and that's okay. It's the effort, not the outcome, that matters. By tuning into our children, understanding what they need and figuring out how we can help, we can guide them to be the best versions of themselves. We're showing them the way, not merely telling them.

Our children need a guiding light, and guess what? We are that light. When we learn just how much our actions shape them, it's a game-changer. Sure, grades and test scores matter, but they don't tell the whole story of who our children are becoming. By being good role models, giving them our full attention, really seeing them for who they are and being true with our emotions, we're setting them up for success on so many levels.

Our job isn't to boss them around; it's to show them how to live—how to face challenges head-on and embrace the world with open arms. A child who is resilient has the tools to handle whatever life throws at them. Our job is to show them what tools to use and when to use them. Imagine your grown-up child looking back and saying, 'They were always there for me and they truly cared.' That's the kind of legacy we all want.

*'Every child is one caring adult away from being a success story.'*
*—Josh Shipp*

There's no better feeling for our children than having someone believe in them as they navigate the ups and downs of childhood. And let's be real, we're not perfect. We'll mess up and get things wrong, and that's okay! What matters most is being the best example we can be for our children. Our words and actions are like seeds we plant in them, which they'll carry with them for a lifetime.

**What you are, they will become**. It's a simple truth, but it's a powerful one.

# Step 2

# Skills over scores—five essential skills every child needs

Many of us consider school the place where we lay the foundations for life, but our learning capacity is shaped long before we step into a classroom. Some estimates suggest that 70 per cent of everything we'll ever learn is already in our brains by age seven, while research by Rishi Sriram (2020) indicates that about 90 per cent of brain development occurs by age five. Between birth and age seven—what Maria Montessori famously called 'the sensitive periods'—millions of neural connections are formed every single second. During this time, children absorb almost everything they see, touch, hear and feel. Simultaneously, they learn vital lessons for life: emotional regulation and how to absorb, process and integrate new information.

These early lessons equip children with the ability to learn and adapt to the array of new subjects thrust upon them throughout their school years. But perhaps even more importantly, these formative years lay the groundwork for the lessons of life itself—lessons that help them live safely while navigating the world in all its complexities, including being able to get what they want, express their emotions, show love and care to those around them, and persist when things get difficult. They also include reading body language; picking up on non-verbal cues such as facial expressions, tone of voice and intonation; and developing a sense of intuition.

And although you may not have been aware of it, these skills were imparted into your beautiful, spongy brains long before you sat at any table and opened a textbook. Unbeknown to you, as your parent wheeled you around in the pushchair, sat your highchair next to the dinner table or let you pat the dog, you absorbed these core skills all day, from all angles and from merely being in the environment and taking in everything through all five senses. No wonder babies sleep so much; they must be exhausted!

Those early years pass in the blink of an eye. Before you know it, you can walk, talk, use the toilet, tie your shoelaces, zip up your coat and grasp how the world works—or at least the basics. As the sensitive periods draw to a close, your parents start thinking about the next big step: school. They embark on endless school tours, comb through countless websites and join parenting Facebook groups to see what others are doing—all in the hope of giving you, their child, the best possible start in life. And this effort isn't misplaced. Choosing a school feels like one of life's major decisions, up there with picking a baby's name or—dare I say it—deciding which colour to respray your car (a nod to any car enthusiasts reading this).

From the moment you hang your hat and coat on a peg for the first time and take those tentative steps into a classroom, everything changes. It's the start of phase two, where you begin to learn an entirely new set of skills, setting you on a path of discovery that will shape the rest of your life.

The classroom door opens, the teacher welcomes you to the place where you'll spend the next twelve months and, suddenly, you're thrust into an environment filled with absolute uncertainty. Billions of variables are at play in the average classroom and, to survive, you have to evolve quickly. There are lots of other faces to look at and analyse—some have eyebrows raised; others have tears running down their cheeks; some are folding their arms; others don't want to talk; and some want to hold your hand, take you to the reading corner and be your friend.

With so many choices to make, things to understand and problems to solve, school is a whole new ball game. Each of the challenges you face and decisions you make adds a new layer of experience, building you into the person you'll eventually become.

Your new home, the classroom, is like a mini version of society outside, and the skills you learn within those four walls will prepare you for the real world that awaits in twelve years or so. Just like new lava drying on the side of a volcano creates new layers of basaltic rock, each experience in the classroom is a new lesson for life, eventually forming a formidable mountain that can stand up even during the fiercest of storms. Each layer is a new skill that will equip you for what the future has in store. The more skills you have a chance to develop, the easier you'll find it to ride the storms the future will inevitably bring.

In educational circles, these skills are often referred to as essential or soft skills; to me, they are the bedrock of everything we call *education*. They are skills like learning how to share, looking after our belongings, making decisions and showing care when a friend is hurt. Without them, life becomes harder, small tasks feel insurmountable and our dreams can seem impossibly distant. Yet, despite their importance, these skills are often overlooked because they can't be neatly graded, don't feature in any textbook and certainly won't boost a school's standing in the national league tables, where academic results reign supreme. To the bane of every teacher out there who entered the profession to change the world through education, life skills are put on the backburner and sidelined as academic scores, rankings and exams clutter the timetable.

## A caveat for you

I want to make it clear that even though, when I ran my own school, one where we had no scores, points, rankings and grades, this doesn't mean I'm against teaching and learning traditional academic subjects such as maths, English and science. These are fundamental to success in our ever-changing world. If you can't read, it's going to be difficult to succeed at anything. My argument is that children should learn these traditional subjects in unique, individualised ways, assessed not only through tests and scores, but also through observations and progress made. And they must be taught in environments that allow children to develop essential life skills as they learn.

I'd also like to clarify that I'm not criticising the way we teach or parent our children. Everyone is doing their best. What I intend to do with this book is challenge the current system, which, in my opinion, is based on academic competition and comparisons among our children, schools and even countries.

Let me explain further: the reason why standardised tests, grades, rankings and scores are so prevalent in our schools is because countries are ranked against each other academically using the Programme for International Student Assessment (PISA) scale. PISA is an annual worldwide study conducted by the Organisation for Economic Co-operation and Development (OECD). It evaluates educational systems by measuring fifteen-year-old students' academic performance in reading, mathematics and science.

The OECD releases an annual list of the top academic countries in the world. In 2022, Singapore was ranked as the highest-achieving country for academics, closely followed by Taiwan and Japan. However, other OECD studies reported that students in high-performing East Asian countries, including Singapore, showed higher levels of anxiety about schoolwork and tests than their peers in other regions—and we know all too well the impact that stress has on our children's wellbeing. High-achieving students with outrageous levels of anxiety? That doesn't sound like success to me. Clearly, something needs to change.

Sadly, the relentless global push for academic excellence, driven by standardised tests and scores, seeps into schools worldwide. Schools vying for top spots in national and local league tables strive to attract parents looking for the 'best' education for their children. The result? Children endure a barrage of meaningless and often stressful tests, year after year—sometimes even term by term—all to demonstrate that the teachers and school are performing admirably. It's a grim picture.

So what can we do about it? Well, for starters, we should allow teachers to do the job they are trained to do, trusting in their expertise and freeing them from constant micromanagement, endless test rehearsals and rigid, prescriptive syllabi. Teaching is, after all, a profession that thrives on passion and creativity. If we empower teachers and give them the freedom to inspire, then surely their enthusiasm, wisdom and passions would trickle down to students—not the stress and pressure of achieving high grades or rankings to prove we are 'worthy' educators.

In an ideal world:

*Students should be working on tactile, real-world projects that inspire them. They should be guided by teachers delivering inspirational content that lets them live their dream of changing the world, one child at a time.*

My hope with this book—and the conversations it inspires—is to propose meaningful, holistic changes to our current educational system. These changes must prioritise the balance of academic, social and emotional education for our children, recognising home and school as the primary environments for learning. We must start viewing education through a different lens—one that focuses on preparing children not just for today's tests, but for tomorrow's opportunities, where true educational success is raising well-rounded, resilient and capable individuals ready to thrive in the world.

**Tomorrow's future sits in the classrooms of today. Our job is to decide who we want the guardians of tomorrow's world to be.**

## Finding purpose

When you look at how schools, the media and especially social media frame it, success is all about grades, scores, rankings, high-paying jobs, fancy houses, luxury holidays and maybe even a Lamborghini boot stuffed with cash. Okay, maybe I'm exaggerating a little, but these messages are everywhere, quietly shaping how we think.

You could argue that striving for top marks, getting into the best schools, landing high-paying jobs and making loads of money is the path to purpose. But from what I've seen, it's quite the opposite. Chasing these things often keeps us from discovering what makes us come alive. We're like a hamster on a wheel, running endlessly in circles, while the cage door is wide open, offering the freedom to roam the fields, feel the breeze and munch on barley.

I've seen it time and again: people who wait until retirement to start asking themselves what really matters. If you need proof, take a walk along the beaches of Goa. You'll find plenty of 65-year-olds fresh out of an ashram, wearing baggy trousers and sporting a new earring, staring out at the ocean, wondering why they spent decades in a career that didn't fulfil them.

It's a sad picture, isn't it? But that's why this book exists—to help ensure our children discover their true purpose as early as possible, so they never end up wondering 'what if' later in life.

**Figure 5.** Wouldn't it be better if our children discovered their purpose earlier?

I've always been the type to say 'yes' to new ideas and opportunities. While that might sound overwhelming to some, this instinct has led me to switch jobs more times than I can count and move all over the world. And it's opened doors I never knew existed.

In 2016, the principal at my school trusted me enough to let me complete my final Montessori practicum in Kathmandu, Nepal. That small act of faith changed the course of my life. Nepal was like nothing I'd ever seen—towering mountains, humble villages, and schools made of mud and cow dung filled with the most incredible children, who were eager to learn despite having next to nothing. Those children, coupled with the awe-inspiring presence of the Himalayas, ignited something in me. Despite having zero experience in construction or fundraising, I felt overwhelmed by the need to help these children access an education that could rival the rest of the world's.

With my newfound purpose, over the next seven years, I poured everything I had into building schools and libraries across Nepal. I ran marathons dressed as a granny to raise money, rallied my friends for support and learned as I went along. The projects grew larger and more ambitious with time. I spent countless nights coordinating concrete deliveries to remote villages, shipping tens of thousands of books to schools in the mountains, and negotiating with builders to make sure our schools were earthquake-proof.

Some schools were tiny and hidden away in the mountains; others were larger and located in Kathmandu's bustling streets. Each project came with its own unique challenges, but they were all driven by the same goal: creating spaces where children could learn, thrive and dream of a better future. We even transformed old bank buildings into Montessori training centres, giving women the chance to retrain as teachers. The best part? None of it ever felt like work—because I was fully invested.

Fast forward to 2021, during the chaotic early years of the Covid pandemic, when the world of education was flipped on its head. Suddenly, Zoom and other technologies became a teaching lifeline. This seismic shift got me thinking. Through countless conversations with my good friend Richard Mills, we started to explore the potential of technology in education—not as a substitute for connection but as a tool to enhance it. That realisation led me to take another leap.

I stepped away from my role as a principal and co-founded Upschool.co with my fellow teacher Richard Mills. Upschool is an online platform offering free courses aligned with the UN Sustainable Development Goals (SDGs). Each course inspires children to use their knowledge to make a positive difference and help create a better world.

Since its launch, Upschool has reached hundreds of thousands of students worldwide. It's also taken me on a teaching journey like no other. I've climbed to Everest Base Camp to teach about Sherpa culture, travelled to the Arctic Circle to discuss polar bears, stood among penguins in Antarctica and delivered a lesson on volcanoes in Iceland—while they were erupting! **These moments remind me that education isn't confined to classrooms; it's alive in the stories we tell, the places we explore and the connections we create.**

Through all my travels, one truth stands out. Sure, grades, rankings and flashy salaries might look like the path to happiness. But without a sense of purpose—without the feeling that we're making a difference—those things are just surface level. Real contentment comes from following your passions and using them to create a positive impact. If we want the same kind of fulfilment for our children, we need to help them uncover their unique talents and guide them to use those gifts to make the world a better place.

## A global perspective

As well as enabling children to develop a unique set of skills, we want them to understand where and how they can best use them. **Before a child can paint a masterpiece, they must first learn to hold a brush.** Through my work at Upschool.co, I've recorded lessons in front of some of the world's hidden wonders. Our aim: to bring these invaluable lessons into the classrooms and homes of children who might never have the chance to experience them otherwise. For instance, if you're a child living in landlocked Nepal, there's a strong chance you've never seen an ocean wave. So how could you consider taking care of something as abstract as the ocean, a polar bear or melting ice caps? We might as well be asking these children to protect Saturn's fifth moon.

By travelling to these exotic locations and bringing the lessons we create into as many classrooms as possible, we hope that when children see the same person (me) standing in front these features, they'll feel more connected and therefore compelled to protect them. We know that consistency in the classroom alleviates educational anxiety in children, so having me as a constant presence for them means they can have one consistent point of reference, regardless of the content being delivered. And for me? I get to live my dream, travel the world and follow my purpose. A win-win all around.

### Elephant Island and a story of resilience

In the spring of 2023, I was invited to join an expedition of naturalists and ice scientists on a voyage from Ushuaia in South America to Antarctica. During this unforgettable journey, I was exposed to a story that epitomises sheer determination and the importance of resilience, hence the title of this book.

The team and I met up in Argentina, ready to sail across the Drake Passage (one of the roughest seas on Earth) to the Antarctic continent and across to South Georgia—a small island in the southern Atlantic Ocean. We planned to travel to these locations with a film crew to record lessons about the wonders of the region.

During one especially windy afternoon, the captain called us out onto the deck to look at Elephant Island—a rocky mass surrounded by clouds with the Southern Ocean lashing at the shore. At first glance, it wasn't the kind of place any of us would survive on for long but, as historian Jeff Nagel told me, the island was the setting for one of the greatest survival stories of all time, which required a set of skills no test could measure, no teacher could teach, but that we all want our children to have.

The story starts in 1914 with a British polar explorer named Ernest Shackleton, who set sail aboard a wooden ship named the *Endurance*. He aimed to sail to Antarctica and cross the continent with his team of 28 men. After arriving on the Antarctic continent, his ship became trapped by pack ice—frozen seawater that halted the journey.

He rallied his men to try and release the ship by cutting through the ice with saws and metal tools, but to no avail. On 27 October 1915, the men were forced to abandon the ship and find refuge on the floating ice sheet that eventually crushed their ship before their eyes.

They spent the next five months floating on the pack ice with almost no hope of being found or rescued. Surviving on their reserved resources and their leader's spirit, the crew remained hopeful.

But the only way to survive was to move. Shackleton ordered the men to jump into the three lifeboats and row to the nearest landmass, Elephant Island. Although running low on food, and eating penguins for breakfast, lunch and dinner, the crew stayed optimistic that they would make it out. After four and a half months of eating penguins in the cold, Shackleton realised they weren't going to be found. The only way to save his men would be to risk his own life to save theirs.

He broke up the three wooden lifeboats and used the wood to build a bigger, stronger boat to withstand bigger seas. After rowing 1,600 km across one of the world's roughest seas, using only the stars for navigation, he and five of his men arrived in South Georgia, home to a whaling station named Grytviken.

But he landed on the wrong side of South Georgia! So he climbed one of the island's highest mountains and traversed a huge glacier to reach Grytviken. There, he borrowed an empty whaling vessel and, as promised, returned to Elephant Island. After nine months of living on the cold ice and munching unfortunate penguins, Shackleton saved every single man. Not one life was lost.

Shackleton arrived home to a hero's welcome in the UK. His determination, grit and resilience under extreme pressure had made him a national hero and turned his failure into success. The skills he demonstrated are unteachable, ungradable and unrankable. They not only saved his men but made him one of the world's most famous explorers and heroes.

Hearing this story of Shackleton, it all made sense: our children need an environment that allows them to solve problems on their own, think critically about what to do next, take calculated risks and work with their intuition.

**Education is not about 'what' our children become, but 'who'.**

## A focus on personality

While researching for this book, I dug out my old school report cards. I'm sure everyone reading this can relate to what I'm about to say next: the marks, grades, points and rankings stand out clearly, with capital As, Bs and Cs. (Who am I kidding? Mine are filled with Ds, Es and Fs! But let's not dwell on that ...) For hundreds of years, these have been the hallmark of success for parents:

*My Tommy is top of the class.*

*Sarah got an A in Geography.*

*Rachel is being moved into a special class because she's so smart.*

While these achievements are commendable and worth celebrating, they leave us asking a deeper question: what do they really reveal about the character, dreams, aspirations and hopes of the children themselves?

To truly find out what's going on, parents must delve deeper into the comments section to get a holistic understanding of their child's progress. They're expected to read between the lines, making inferences to gather information on how their child is developing as a young person. And while we may find comments about effort made, or a mention of kindness or hard work here or there, student reports and assessments generally focus on what we can measure rather than on what truly matters.

As I glance through my reports, the only skill mentioned in the three-page report card is 'effort':

*Gavin loves art and science and always makes an effort.*

That's nice to hear, but I'm sure there was more to me than that. What about my ability to share, communicate and negotiate? I have two younger brothers and was very good at these things. Do these executive functions not matter?

To be fair, the concept of essential or soft skills is more prevalent in educational discourse now than 20 years ago. However, with curriculum requirements, timetables and rigorous schedules imposed on parents and teachers, the development and integration of these skills often get lost. There isn't enough time in the day for our children to learn through real-world applications and experiences on top of completing a list of monotonous tasks set by the school system, not to mention societal pressures to achieve 'success'.

## The true measure of educational success

While on a trip to China recently, I toured the country with a young man, Mannie, who was working in schools around the country, helping them integrate new technologies. Mannie told me his father had made a lot of money in the cosmetics industry and was considered a successful businessman. But he had also died at an early age due to stress.

The fact that Mannie used the word 'successful' to describe his father, despite his early stress-related death, really struck me. We still have a lot of work to do when it comes to defining and understanding success.

Consider this: you've just enrolled your child in a new school. Each day, you drop little Tommy off with a goodbye kiss at the door. Your fridge is proudly adorned with a few scribbly masterpieces, and you've had several brief chats with their teacher at the school gate about how things are going. As the second term draws to a close, the moment of truth arrives—your child's very first school report. With anticipation reminiscent of a scene from *Charlie and the Chocolate Factory*, the envelope makes its way home. Together, you sit down as a family, eager to discover what little Tommy has been up to.

Which one of these reports would you rather receive?

*Tommy has made impressive strides in his academic pursuits this term. He has demonstrated excellent progress in phonics and early literacy skills, confidently identifying letter sounds and blends. In numeracy, Tommy exhibits a strong grasp of fundamental mathematical concepts, proficiently counting and recognising numbers up to 20. His academic achievements include a solid understanding of phonics and early numeracy skills.*

Or:

*Tommy's progress this term shows how he keeps trying and doesn't give up, even when things are tricky. He's making excellent progress in recognising letters and numbers, showing how much he's learning. I'm very proud of him. When he faces problems, he finds clever ways to solve them and always wants to learn more. What's also impressive is how he's always kind to others, helping them when they need it. He's becoming more confident doing things on his own, which is great to see. Overall, Tommy is growing into a smart, caring and independent learner.*

The first report clearly tells you what your child can do academically. But surely there's more to your child than counting and literacy?

The second report demonstrates what kind of person your child is becoming, what values they hold and the essential skills they're developing alongside the academic ones. Inferentially, we know the teacher has had time to observe the child and connected with them enough to understand who they are. It shows the values the school promotes are not just words hanging in the entrance hall; they're part of the classroom and the school's DNA.

While some schools have started observing and reporting on these essential life skills, there is still much progress to be made. The broader educational community has yet to embrace the importance of assessing children holistically—valuing their emotional growth, social skills and character development just as much as their academic achievements.

**Figure 6.** Your little human is developing essential skills along with academic learning

**The true measure of any educational ideology or institution can be seen in the citizens walking the streets in 20 years' time.** Hope sits on the carpet of every kindergarten classroom on the planet; we just need to provide them with an educational experience where they can develop essential skills, while giving parents and teachers time for observation and reflection, so they can see the lasting impact of these skills in their children.

## The role of essential skills

So, how do we make sure our children don't end up on a beach on Goa at 65, trying to figure out what they really want to do? If you ask parents what they want most for their children, the answer is usually: 'I just want them to be happy.' While there are countless paths to happiness, for me, freedom, choice and agency are absolutely key. When we give children these freedoms, empowering them to develop the skills they need to thrive, not just in school but, more importantly, in life, happiness is not too far away.

Essential skills are an ever-evolving, lifelong set of abilities that children develop as they journey towards adulthood. And while many skills are essential, I'd like to focus on the five I believe are crucial for leading the most meaningful and purposeful life:

1. Creativity
2. Determination
3. Compassion
4. Independence
5. Resilience.

These skills can't be taught in the traditional sense. You'll never become a confident public speaker simply by reading books on the subject. Sure, you can learn the strategies but, to master the art, you need to step onto the stage. You need to feel your knees wobble, your heart race and your palms sweat. You have to face the fear, speak and repeat until it becomes second nature. Believe me, I know this firsthand—I nearly ran away from behind the curtain before my own TED Talk!

Essential skills involve emotions, which have to be felt. They can't be graded, ranked or scored, and they can't be taught through a story; they need to be experienced, touched with the hands, and felt in the heart. They are the foundations upon which our children set themselves up as lifelong learners.

While recognising their value is the first step, the real challenge lies in making sure our homes and schools are places where these skills can flourish naturally. The future depends on it.

## 1. Creativity—shaping their stories

*'My contention is that creativity now is as important in education as literacy, and we should treat it with the same status.'*
*—Sir Ken Robinson*

This statement, from Ken Robinson's iconic TED Talk, gets to the heart of what education often overlooks: creativity isn't a luxury, it's a necessity. It's being able to think beyond what's right in front of us, to imagine possibilities and forge new paths.

Yet, creativity has been squeezed out of many classrooms in favour of standardised tests, rote learning and tick-box curricula. But the thing is, creativity isn't just about painting a picture or writing a story. It's about equipping our children with the tools to navigate a complex world. It's about teaching them to dream, problem-solve and see challenges as opportunities rather than obstacles.

When we nurture creativity, we also give children confidence in their capacity to make things happen. Imagine a child who believes they can eventually figure out any problem—whether it's building a rocket or making a new friend. Creativity fosters this belief, planting seeds of resilience and determination that let them think through any problem to better understand how to solve it.

Solving the global challenges we face as a society requires more than knowledge. It requires people who can think differently, innovate and empathise with others. Creativity gives children the tools to become those changemakers.

*'Imagination is more important than knowledge. For knowledge is limited, whereas imagination embraces the entire world.'*
*—Albert Einstein*

When we encourage creativity, we show children their ideas matter. We give them the space to think big, make mistakes and try again. Creativity isn't adding more art into the curriculum on Friday afternoons or painting a beautiful picture; it's the ability to see things from all perspectives.

Without creativity, our education system risks becoming irrelevant because we'll find it impossible to prepare children for a future we can't yet imagine with a curriculum that confines creativity to an art activity. Creativity is so much more than that—it's the spark that fuels our children's ability to think, learn, grow and ultimately shape the world around them.

## 2. Determination—turning creativity into reality

Creativity may help children see the problem and imagine a way forward, but that's only the first step. The real challenge—and opportunity—lies in turning that idea into reality. This is where determination steps in. Determination is the steady, unyielding drive that transforms a spark of inspiration into meaningful action. It teaches children that progress takes time, effort and probably a few missteps along the way.

While creativity lights the path ahead, determination keeps you walking on it. It's about building the resilience to face setbacks, the patience to keep trying when things don't work out and the courage to push through discomfort.

*'In the growth mindset, failure can be a painful experience. But it doesn't define you. It's a problem to be faced, dealt with, and learned from.'*
*—Carol S. Dweck, in* Mindset: The New Psychology of Success

Picture a child learning to swim their first full length of the pool. With every attempt, water splashes in their face and their arms tire, but slowly, stroke by stroke, they gain confidence and strength. When they reach the other side for the first time, their joy isn't just about the achievement—it's about the perseverance that got them there. They've learned challenges are stepping stones to growth, not barriers to success.

Determination flourishes when adults model the perseverance they wish to see and resist stepping in too quickly. We've all seen the difference in a child's reaction when they achieve something on their own compared to when we assist them. It's about designing opportunities where the task feels just out of reach, challenging children to stretch beyond their comfort zone. Whether it's a sports goal, creative project or new skill, these experiences foster the ability to adapt and persist—qualities that will serve them far beyond childhood.

And by not stepping in, but supporting and encouraging, we foster determination in our children, which gives them the mindset to view challenges as opportunities for growth. Our children will have dreams and aspirations—to open their own business, start their own initiative or pursue something deeply meaningful to them. Having a foundation of determination teaches them that, if they put in the effort and show resilience, almost anything is possible. Determination is the bridge between their aspirations and achievements, their hard work and dreams.

## Why creativity and determination?

Creativity and determination complement each other perfectly. They're like cheese and tomato, bread and butter, or Starsky and Hutch—inseparable and essential. Together, they set the stage for success at school, home and far beyond. When a child faces any problem, whether academic, social or emotional, what do we hope they'll do? We want them to consider the issue from multiple perspectives (creativity), envisioning possible solutions and testing their ideas. Even if they stumble at first, we want them to keep trying, refining their approach and persevering until they succeed (determination).

This blend of skills drives innovation and progress in many industries today.

Take Jaguar, for example. In 2024, Jaguar set out to reinvent itself to stand toe-to-toe with trailblazers like Tesla and Build Your Dreams (BYD). Enter the revolutionary Type 00, a car so groundbreaking it turned heads globally. (Seriously, you should look it up!) Professor Gerry McGovern OBE, Jaguar's chief creative officer, summed it up perfectly. He said the Type 00 was born from 'brave, unconstrained creative thinking and unwavering determination.' This wasn't just about redefining Jaguar's design—it was about embracing bold innovation, proving that breaking the mould and thinking outside the box can lead to something extraordinary.

And if we need further evidence of why these skills are so important:

- **Thomas Edison** Known for inventing the electric light bulb, Edison exemplified creative problem-solving and relentless perseverance. He famously said, 'I have gotten a lot of results! I know several thousand things that won't work.'
- **James Dyson** Before he invented the first bagless vacuum cleaner, he had 5127 failed prototypes, demonstrating extraordinary creativity in engineering and unwavering determination.

Once embedded, creativity and determination apply to many aspects of life. They help with solving a mathematical problem like algebra, patching up a broken friendship and dealing with teenage emotional issues. When a child has the opportunity to refine these skills, what effect does it have on their overall development?

When children face a problem, **creativity** allows them to view the issue from multiple angles and come up with innovative solutions. And

**determination** means the child won't give up until they've explored all possibilities.

While STEM (science, technology, engineering and maths) and STEAM (which also includes arts) lessons offer children a chance to refine these skills once a week—or sometimes even less frequently—what if these opportunities were embedded into their everyday lives? What if creativity and determination weren't limited to a single lesson or project, but were woven into the fabric of their school and home experiences?

At home, simple acts can lay the groundwork for nurturing creativity and determination, such as letting children assist in the weekly shopping trip, organise aspects of the family holiday, or even plan and cook meals together.

At school, these skills flourish when children are given meaningful opportunities to take ownership of their learning. Whether it's planning their own free time, organising class excursions or taking on roles to help run the classroom, these activities empower children to learn by doing. They develop confidence, independence and a sense of agency—essential traits that prepare children to face any challenge with resilience and purpose.

## The Nashik temple

In 2022, I was kindly invited to visit an experiential school in Nashik, India. The school principal, Meghaa Ahju, had registered her children into an Upschool course called *Be the Change*.

This online program asks children to choose a UN SDG and find a way to help their community while addressing one of these global challenges. The children have absolute freedom in which SDG to choose and how they will address it. The sky is the limit. If they want to move their school community to the Moon for the sake of humanity, it will be encouraged. They instead decided to plant a forest.

Meghaa invited me because she said amazing things were happening since the school embarked on the course. When I arrived at the school, I was met with a rapturous celebration. The children gave me gifts and shook my hand, but it was like CEOs greeting me for a business meeting. These children weren't like those I'd met in other schools. They greeted me with confidence and, even though I was older and a teacher, we spoke as equals. I loved it. The school was doing more than just teaching them how to solve problems. This new freedom was helping them develop a whole range of skills, such as confidence, organisational skills, communication, persuasion, passion and self-respect.

We all boarded a bus that the children had organised themselves—an achievement in itself—and headed to the shrine where we were going to plant the first tree and inaugurate the forest. We arrived to find a huge crowd of local people holding flowers and garlands for us. As the hot Indian sun baked down and the children dug holes in the ground, I pulled one of the head boys aside and asked him why they chose this specific location.

His beautiful response encapsulated everything we want to see in our children:

*The old people come to worship at this shrine and the sun is so hot, so we want to make sure they can wait in the shade without getting sunburned and we also want some new homes for birds to live in.*

These local changemakers had discovered that a local temple had no shade. Because the climate was warming and the community was growing, the older people who gathered outside the temple were getting sunburned. There were also very few birds and insects around the temple, and the children wanted to change that. So, without any help from the school (the teachers simply guided them without intervening), the thirteen-year-old students decided to solve this problem.

Intrigued by how many saplings they had collected—there were hundreds of them—I asked him how he and his classmates could afford to buy so many.

'We negotiated a sapling loan from a local tree merchant,' he said.

'A sapling loan? What's that?' I asked.

'We tried to raise money in many ways but failed. Since we couldn't afford to buy the trees, we promised the manager that when the trees start to mature, we will take cuttings, repot them in the pots he'll provide and repay him with interest. It's a tree transaction!'

A tree transaction! Whoever would think of that?

As the children rallied with their shovels and spades, with dirty fingernails and beaming smiles, I stood back in the shade and watched. I felt so proud my course could inspire this kind of activity. But I also wished I'd had an education like this. I wished my teachers had told me to choose a problem and work with my friends to try and solve it without limitations.

At that moment, I turned a corner on what is possible when it comes to educating our children. When we put them in an environment where we trust them and give them the agency to make big decisions and solve big problems, they go for it. They can accomplish anything. The children had shown me what educational success looked like and it certainly had nothing to do with grades or points. It was about finding a problem bigger than your own and working hard to solve it.

Now I understood why these children could approach me with such confidence. They had planted a forest, negotiated a sapling loan with a local business and realised their true potential as human beings. Executive functioning isn't just for executives; in the right environment, all children can foster this skill.

## 3. Compassion—perspective is everything

If you've never watched the film *Lion,* I recommend you do so. It changed my life. It's about a young boy in India who goes wandering down the train tracks with his older brother. In the shadow of a passing water tower, he loses sight of his brother, gets onto the wrong train and ends up having to survive on the streets before getting adopted and moving to Tasmania. For 30 years or so, he knows his mum might still be alive. In a moment of determination, he sets off to find her. Spoiler alert—I'm about to reveal the ending. The film's climax is when he finally finds her in a small village after trawling through Google Maps for hundreds of hours, looking for the water tower that was etched in his mind as he sped off on that train all those years ago.

The film is a work of art. The scene that made me cry, along with the rest of the audience, was when his mother finally saw him and realised he was still alive. He walks around the corner in the small Indian village and finds his mum is out for a stroll with her friends. At that moment when they first catch eyes, I could feel the emotion emanating from them. I imagined I was the son, finally finding my mother after all those years away from her, and I could see through the mother's eyes as well: thinking your son is dead, but one day he turns up and falls into your arms.

As I sat in the cinema, my chin started trembling and I fought back the tears stinging my eyes, but it was no use. The flood gates were open. It dawned on me that *so many* mothers lose their children every day, sometimes never to see them again. I knew stories like this existed, but it had never felt so real before.

The tears that fell weren't tears of happiness or sadness. They were tears of compassion. As the neuroscientist Dr Mark Williams said to me in 2024, we have no choice: 'Humans are born as compassionate beings.' We just need to have this quality unlocked.

Compassion is often mistaken for sympathy or empathy, but there are subtle differences. Sympathy involves feeling sadness and pity for someone's misfortune. Empathy means truly understanding and sharing the feelings of another person. Compassion combines deep empathy with a genuine desire to help alleviate that suffering.

And it was this overwhelming compassion I'd felt watching *Lion* that drove me to ask my former school principal, Bill McKeith, if I could complete my final Montessori teaching practicum in Nepal. I wanted to see that part of the world for myself—I had a powerful urge to help. This emotional connection to learning—to feel deeply and respond with a desire to help—is exactly what we need to nurture in our homes, schools and children. This empathy-driven action transforms education into something truly impactful.

Ultimately, we want children to use their newfound creativity to see the world through another's eyes, especially those who are in pain or suffering. We then want them to think of ways to assist the person, animal or insect in question, and use their determination and persistence to keep going until the suffering ends or is alleviated.

The request is simple: if you see something you know is wrong, or a living creature you know needs help, imagine the world through their eyes, consider what they're going through and try to solve the problem—and don't give up until the problem is solved! Look at Greta Thunberg, Malala Yousafzai, Boyan Slat or Jessica Watson—all have overcome adversity, stood up for what's right and inspired the world to see what's possible when you have passion and purpose.

## Nurturing compassion

As we explored in Chapter 1, when we consistently role-model compassion in our interactions, children are more likely to imitate this behaviour. But we can't just act compassionately—actively recognising and discussing acts of compassion reinforce their significance for our children.

When you witness a child assisting somebody who's hurt or taking care of a snail that has perilously wandered onto the footpath, that's the time we jump in and acknowledge it. Express your appreciation for their kindness, highlighting the positive impact it has had. And to mirror that, if a child has developed the emotional intelligence to ask you about your wellbeing, make sure you express gratitude for their concern, even if you don't need their help in that moment. 'Thank you for asking how I'm feeling, I really appreciate it. I'm okay for now but I'll definitely ask you if I need some help later.' These reflections and acknowledgements reinforce the impact and importance of our actions towards others.

Encouraging children to openly express their emotions in front of others allows them to develop a deeper understanding of the world from diverse perspectives. As they hear how others feel and how their behaviour impacts those around them, they begin to see the world through everyone's eyes. And when you know how everyone feels, you're more inclined to offer support to someone experiencing a difficult time.

Whether you're a teacher or a parent, witnessing your children help one another without instruction or reward is always a profoundly beautiful moment and isn't this the kind of quality that builds connections, fosters kindness and helps create a better world?

Kanov and colleagues (2004) define compassion as 'a relational process that involves noticing another person's pain, experiencing an emotional reaction to his or her pain, and acting in some way to help ease or alleviate the pain.' This captures the transformative power of compassion. According to psychologist Paul Gilbert, compassion is 'a sensitivity to suffering in self and others with a commitment to try to alleviate and prevent it.' Together, these perspectives highlight the qualities we hope to nurture in our children, the adults of tomorrow.

The world has never been more in need of people who will lead with empathy, understanding and a desire to make a difference. And there is cause for optimism. School cultures are gradually evolving, placing greater emphasis on compassion, kindness, and the development of character and values. Initiatives like India's National Education Policy (NEP2020), which requires the UN SDGs to be integrated into public school curricula, offer a hopeful glimpse into the future of education.

Imagine if schools worldwide embraced this approach, embedding the UN SDGs—which include quality education, climate action and alleviating poverty—deeply into their learning frameworks. Fostering compassion wouldn't be some add-on program or motivational poster in the corridor, but an intrinsic part of every lesson and activity. Children would grow up with empathy and responsibility at the core of their education, preparing them not only to excel academically but also make a meaningful difference in the world. Wouldn't that be something to celebrate?

## How to foster compassion

Over the years, I've seen how much compassion even the youngest children are capable of when they're encouraged to see the world from a different perspective. Take insects, for example. These tiny creatures, often dismissed as 'creepy crawlies', are the unsung heroes of our ecosystem. Without bees, we'd lose countless crops along with the honey we drizzle on our pancakes. And trees, too—how many times do children break off branches without considering that the tree is a living thing, quietly growing and providing shade, oxygen and homes for other creatures?

Early on, when I was a kindergarten teacher, a group of my students stomped on a trail of ants when walking to the playground. To them, it was harmless fun, but those ants were hard at work, carrying food back to their families. I stopped the stomping, but I had to do more than just tell them it was wrong—I needed to help them truly *see* those living beings.

That week, during circle time, I began telling stories about ants, bees and trees, weaving in their struggles and triumphs. I asked the children to imagine what it might be like to be an ant on a mission or a tree growing its branches, only to lose them to carelessness, then to write up and illustrate these stories. The results were incredible. Not only did the children stop harming insects and trees, but they began treating them with care and respect. They even started naming the insects they encountered and protecting the trees in our playground from harm.

## The importance of compassion

As well as modelling and celebrating compassionate actions and stories, we can engage in conversations that spark children's imaginations: 'What do you think it feels like to be a bumblebee trapped in a jar? Or an ant trying to cross a busy footpath?' Their responses are magical, but their actions can speak louder—small hands rescuing insects, gentle voices reminding others to tread carefully. When caring for all living things becomes part of our daily rituals, we send a powerful message: the world is everyone's home. If we all look out for one another, our home becomes a kinder, better place for everyone. To me, there's no better lesson than that!

## 'Let me show you where you put your bag'

One of my favourite responsibilities as a school principal was inviting potential families for a school tour, which happened every second Thursday. It was a beautiful time in my busy schedule because I got to show new families around the wonderful campus we had created. First, I met them in an upstairs room and explained what they were about to see. Our school was very different from a conventional setting: children had the freedom to work where they liked, engage in passion projects, talk, move, choose materials and even have a snack with their friends when the mood struck them.

After one such tour in mid-2020, one mum hung back, wanting to chat with me further. Her son had some learning difficulties that were causing him to struggle in his current school and she thought ours would be a great place for him to thrive. As she explained their situation, I could completely understand what he must be going through. I asked her to bring him in the next day for a trial, to see if he liked the school.

The next morning as the school opened, there was a new face in the playground. I recognised the mother and her son standing side by side. I could see the anxiety in his body language. His shoulders were hunched, he was looking at the ground and he was clearly feeling nervous.

It's completely natural to be nervous on the first day, so I approached slowly, kneeling on the ground to make eye contact to let him know this was a safe space. In a soft voice, I said we were here to help if he needed. His mum could see that her being there was probably causing more of an issue than aiding, so she silently waved goodbye to me, gave him a kiss on the head and left it to me to get him safely into the classroom.

I reached out to hold his hand. He grabbed it, and I tried to encourage him to join me in walking to the classroom to meet his new friends. But by this time, he was shaking like a leaf, his hand was clammy and it seemed like his feet had grown roots into the ground.

Before I could move on to my next strategy to help him feel comfortable, something miraculous happened. A little head appeared from around the classroom door. It was another boy from the class who had seen through the window that the new boy was feeling nervous.

'Hello there,' he said confidently as he walked over. 'My name is Oliver. I'm your new friend. Come on, let me show you where to put your bag.'

As if by magic, the roots attached to the new boy's feet were released, and off he went into the classroom with his new friend. Astonished, I followed them to the doorway and poked my head around the corner to see how the next few minutes unfolded. To my amazement, another boy popped out of his chair and said, 'Hello, if Oliver is busy, then I can also be your friend.'

I quietly closed the door and left the teacher and her faithful team of compassionate learners to get on with their day. As I sat in my office, I reflected on what had just happened—I knew we were doing something right when students like Oliver at seven years old had the compassion, desire, confidence and ability to act when needed. The new boy graduated from our school in 2023, and I'm very proud of what Oliver did that day—so much so that I based my TED Talk *How Education Can Save the World* on his actions.

## 4. Independence—help me to do it myself

As we've seen, an independent child is absolutely unstoppable. It seems like such a paradox to adults. If our children become independent, they won't need us! And we want them to need us because it gives purpose and meaning to our lives. Isn't it our job to care for them, make their beds, change their clothes and help them brush their teeth? Yes, initially it is, but once we've modelled a behaviour and demonstrated how to navigate a challenge or task, the best thing we can do is get out of their way and let them do it themselves.

Prioritising independence in our children as early as possible opens up the door for many amazing skills to flourish. When a child realises that you're allowing them to carry their own weight in the world, a sense of trust and confidence washes over them. They have a job to do, and you trust them to be able to do it.

*'Independence is the foundation of all human growth.'*
*—Angeline Stoll Lillard, in* Montessori: The Science Behind the Genius

This profound principle highlights that when we encourage our children to be independent, we lay the groundwork for them to develop a myriad of other essential skills. By stepping back, we're allowing them to navigate the world, make decisions and learn from their experiences.

If we can't give children the space to face challenges and solve problems on their own, we risk stifling their growth—emotionally, academically and socially. Unfortunately, this is still the reality in many classrooms because of the unrelenting pressures of ticking boxes: completing textbooks, meeting curriculum outcomes and preparing for standardised tests. These demands leave little room for teachers to help children explore, experiment and develop the critical thinking skills they'll need for life.

While phrases like 'project-based learning', 'child-centred approach' and 'experiential learning' are plastered across almost every school website, in my experience the classrooms often tell a different story. Rows of children facing the front, raising their hands to ask permission for the simplest tasks and ploughing through a predetermined list of exercises. Once again, this isn't the teacher's fault. I've been that teacher, full of aspirations to transform lives but trapped in a system that demands a rigid adherence to timelines, textbooks and tests.

Teaching under these constraints feels more like a mechanical process than a meaningful one—a cycle of ticking off tasks, marking workbooks and preparing endless assessments. It's no wonder that, since the early years of the pandemic, we've witnessed a mass resignation of teachers worldwide. Many educators, feeling overwhelmed and undervalued, have left the profession they once loved. This system not only stifles the creativity and passion of teachers, but also denies children the chance to engage deeply with content, explore at their own pace and develop essential life skills.

## Ad Astra School

One of my favourite examples of the power of independence comes from Dan Lakis, the former vice principal of Ad Astra School, located at Starbase and owned by Elon Musk. While working on a project together in 2023, Dan shared with me the school's approach to thematic learning, where a particular theme or topic is chosen for a set period, and the children are given a challenge aligned with that theme.

In a given timeframe, Dan said, the children were tasked with building a model car, driving it down a ramp and making it travel as far as possible. At Ad Astra, their holistic approach to education meant the teachers embedded the necessary skills, strategies, tools and data the students would need to achieve this task into their lessons, while still using the regular curriculum.

As the children attended these carefully curated lessons, they were acquiring the skills, tools and knowledge they needed to improve their car's performance. The science lessons for that period were on forces and aerodynamics, which could be used on the car. This approach seamlessly tied everything into the curriculum while allowing the children to independently discover a link between what is taught in the classroom and how it can be applied to real-world situations. The children realised that the tools they needed to solve almost all life's problems were within their reach; they just needed to know which ones to take from their toolbox and when.

*'Independent children grow into self-reliant adults who are capable of making sound decisions and handling life's challenges effectively.'*
*—Angeline Stoll Lillard*

During Chapter 6, we'll explore the process of implementing these skills for teachers and parents, but first, let me share another story from when I was the principal of a local Montessori preschool in 2020.

Cultivating independence in children was a key focus, and one of our daily practices and expectations for parents was to encourage their children to carry their own backpacks to and from school.

It was a simple task, but one that carried significant weight literally, according to many parents! The common concern was that the bag was too heavy, or their child was too tired after a long day. But we encouraged families to give it a go anyway. What might seem like a trivial request is actually an opportunity to teach children valuable life lessons. Carrying their own bag helps build resilience, responsibility and confidence. It's not about making life harder for them but about planting the seeds of independence—one small step at a time.

When children carry their own bag, they soon understand if it's too heavy, and if we're the ones who packed it, they'll need to communicate to us that it may be overloaded. First, this lets them express their feelings about something that directly affects them: 'My bag is too heavy because my shoulders are hurting.' But better still, it gives them the opportunity to refine what goes inside. We can say: 'Let me carry it home for you today, but tonight you can help me pack it, and we'll make sure it's not too heavy for you to carry tomorrow.'

When the child is ready, it's also the perfect chance for them to pack their own bag, learning to decide what is and isn't necessary. Do they really need eight cuddly toys for school today? And what about that boulder they picked up on the way home? Don't worry, the ache in their shoulders will soon help them decide.

While it might feel challenging at first to take the extra time to let children pack their own bags—or dare I say it, make their own lunches—the long-term benefits far outweigh the initial effort. Over time, these small, everyday actions lay the foundation for resilience, self-reliance, confidence and capability.

Remember, the work of the adult is the play of the child. While making their lunch, preparing the classroom, refilling the card stock or preparing your briefcase for tomorrow's meetings may be laborious for parents and teachers, children love to do what adults are doing. So, to develop the independence we want to see in them and start the journey early, we first need to make a plan, schedule and time for the modelled learning to take place.

**Figure 7.** Let children pack their own bags

For example:

*It's 6 pm, Sarah, and I'm going to get ready for work tomorrow. Do you want to get your bag and things ready, too, so we can go for a walk in the park together?*

Then, start to model preparing your things. Name them as you pack them, feel the weight of your briefcase and ask yourself some rhetorical questions out loud:

*Is it too heavy?*

*Do I have everything I need?*

*What's happening tomorrow? Let's check the calendar.*

Soon, your child will be doing exactly the same. Your work becomes their play. They'll start checking the calendar, too, asking themselves and you questions, such as, 'Is it a sports day? Will I need suncream? If so, we better pack it.'

And when you're both ready for tomorrow, and your bags are zipped up and on the hook in the corridor, you can reflect on how it feels to be prepared:

*Ahhh, we can finally relax and take a walk now. Doesn't it feel great being prepared?*

You can see how this process of stepping away and allowing the child to do it themselves—first with your guidance and then alone—builds them up to be more self-reliant, confident and independent.

Now, many of you are probably thinking, 'Who is this guy? He's living in a fantasy land. Doesn't he realise that as soon as I arrive home from a busy day at work, I have to fold the clothes, make the beds, send an email, call the bank and still find time for myself?' But my point is this: you only need to do it for a couple of weeks before it becomes routine. Your efforts towards independence today will pay dividends in the long run.

In Montessori schools around the world, you'll find this quote painted on the walls:

*Show me how to do it myself.*

Once we've shown them how to carry out a task, and what the limitations and rules of engagement are, our children finally have the opportunity to develop a whole myriad of skills—independence, confidence, self-reliance, accountability, trust, time management, agency, self-efficacy, decision-making—not to mention taking responsibility for their actions. There is a big difference in a child having to miss playtime because *they* forget to pack their hat than them missing playtime because *you* did. Believe me, I've seen the reactions to both.

Just imagine how many children are raising their hands this very second, asking to go to the toilet—a task we all know how to do from age two. We've shown them a hundred times, but we still refuse to give them that independence because the system doesn't allow for it. I promise you, though, it does work—I've run a school where everything from making your own lunch to organising whole-school excursions was the children's responsibility. The skills the children developed were innumerable.

## 'Going Out'—the story of the shallots

Developing children's independence at school may seem like a tricky undertaking. The curriculum is pre-written, the outcomes are already set, and with the child-protection policies and procedures that govern schools, everything can seem too rigid and doing something different maybe too much trouble or risk. But the truth is, the more choice and freedom the children have—within limits, of course—the more learning will take place.

In 2018, my staff and I initiated a Montessori-inspired, student-led activity at our primary school called 'Going Out'. It involves children going out of school for a set amount of time under adult supervision, but with absolutely no adult intervention or organisation.

Any child could initiate a Going Out activity at any time if they decided that, to pass on their knowledge or deepen their understanding of a given subject, they would need to leave the school premises to access some external resources. This could be going to the local forest for an insect hunt, visiting a museum to take sketches of ancient artefacts, or going shopping for ingredients to cook a meal for the class.

Before the children could officially 'go out', they needed to fill out an application form. This had a checklist of things they needed to complete and present to me and their teacher before the outing could occur. The children had to describe the validity of their journey, explaining why it was necessary and what benefits it would bring to them or the school. They had to document any risks that could occur and mitigate them. They also needed to organise transportation, bus schedules, a route map, timings, send emails to two parents who would be chaperones and get permission from their parents for the outing they'd outlined. You could see the excitement in their faces as they arrived in my office and handed over the documents to me. It was all very official.

In early 2021, four nine-year-old boys decided to utilise the Going Out initiative. They'd recently been studying Indonesia in geography and wanted to cook a traditional Balinese meal for their class, including a starter, main course and dessert. They'd planned the whole trip to the supermarket down to the last second, including bus times and the map route. They had even prepared a menu for the class. They had calculated the cost of the ingredients using the supermarket's website, multiplied it to accommodate for 30 people and gathered the funds to buy all the produce.

The day before they were due to head out, they arrived in my office to have their documents checked. Everything seemed to be in order. All the risks had been mitigated: 'We will only use zebra crossings when crossing the road and we will use the handrails on the bus when leaving the vehicle.'

The day arrived for these four boys to head down to the local supermarket, which was only two kilometres away, to buy the ingredients for their Balinese feast. But there was a problem. One of the parents attending was sick. Intrigued, I put my hand up to step in. I had a lot of work to do for an upcoming government inspection but, according to the boys' paperwork, it was only going to be an hour-long journey.

The children were very excited to be heading out for the morning, and I was excited to see how it went. During a 'Going Out' session, the attending adults aren't allowed to help or intervene unless it becomes absolutely necessary. If problems arise, can the children think creatively, solve them independently and show determination to complete the task no matter what?

Right on schedule, the children arrived at my office with their reusable shopping bags, bus passes and shopping list in hand. But one boy was missing. He'd left his bus pass at home and was standing in the corridor, devastated. He'd tried calling his mum, to no avail. Now, to be honest, I had an extra bus pass in my drawer, but if I solved his problem, what would that teach him about being prepared for school?

I know what you're thinking: *Come on, Gavin, he's worked so hard for this!* And I did sympathise with him, but I knew that if I gave him that card, the lesson he was about to learn by remaining at school would not be learned. So, as harsh as it may seem, we consoled him, told him we would plan another Going Out and left him behind.

I walked behind the children as they led me to the bus stop. We hopped on the bus, the children tapped their cards and off we went. The children spoke politely to the bus driver and rang the bell when it was our stop a few moments later. We'd made it! We were right outside the supermarket and everyone was still alive! The children entered through the automatic doors and started their journey around the supermarket to source the 42 items on the list.

'Item number one, shallots,' one boy said to the others. 'What's a shallot?'

'I think it's meat,' said another.

I put my head in my hands as I reluctantly followed them to the meat section, where they spent the next 30 minutes reading every label trying to find the word 'shallot'. All the while, I stood biting my lip, thinking, *We might still be here at midnight at this rate.* But I let the process play out—this was real learning taking place!

After 30 minutes of fruitless searching for shallots with me trying to send telepathic messages to them via eye signalling, the children thankfully decided to ask a supermarket employee, who helped the children find all the items on the list. *We might just make it back to school for lunch,* I thought!

After the children had paid—by the way, their estimated amount was exactly correct—they carried the bags back to the bus stop. Unfortunately, we'd missed our scheduled bus by 45 minutes due to the hunt for meat-flavoured shallots. And because that was the last bus for the day, we would now have to walk back to school. Uphill all the way.

The children linked arms to carry the bags and, four hours after we'd left school, we were back, one hour after lunch should have been served! What had been predicted to be a one-hour trip had taken four, but that was fine. We were all learning a lot!

After unpacking the goods and apologising to their hungry classmates, the children finally started cooking at 2 pm. By 2.30 pm, the famished students had their meal delivered. Boy, was it tasty. Shallots never tasted so good.

The next day, the boys and I reflected on the experience. We discussed what could have been done better, what we enjoyed and how it made us feel. The boys told me that the child we'd left behind had been the one in charge of the shopping list, and he knew what all the items were. Next time, they said, they would bring a spare bus pass in case anyone forgot theirs.

To some, the day may have seemed like a big waste of everyone's time. But all the children went home with many lessons learned. The hungry pupils learned the value of patience, while the four boys learned that if you're going to go shopping, you need to know what all the ingredients look like. And for the poor boy who had remained at school, I think he was quietly relieved that he'd forgotten his bus pass, knowing we had to walk uphill all the way home, carrying food for 30 children.

Initiatives like these allow our children to develop a real sense of independence while making learning real. They also develop critical thinking skills, build adaptability and learn to solve problems using abstract means. While the trip had its pitfalls, we all learned a lot in those four hours, especially me—if a parent calls in sick when a Going Out is taking place and you have government reporting to do that day, send another staff member instead of going yourself! And if a child forgets their bus pass, just give them a spare one so you don't have to spend 30 minutes watching children look for shallots in the meat freezers of a supermarket.

## The boy on the mound

It was a scorching day in Delhi as I stepped out of the school where I'd spent the day training teachers. I'd been invited to India to run workshops for one of the city's largest school networks, and it had been a fantastic day, full of positive energy and ideas.

As I walked out into the blazing Indian sun, something caught my eye—a boy, maybe thirteen years old, sitting on a mound of soil just outside the school's front door. He was wearing a dusty white shirt and blue trousers that hung loosely on his skinny legs. In his hands, he clutched several pieces of paper and was reciting words in a rhythm, almost like a chant.

I walked over to him. As soon as he saw me, he jumped up, squinted against the sunlight and addressed me as 'sir' with a beaming smile. I asked what he was doing and what was written on the papers he held so tightly.

With a mix of pride and determination, he explained that he had his final exams coming up and wanted to do well. The school had already given him the questions in advance, and those papers held the perfect answers to each one—about seven pages of meticulously handwritten text that he and his father had prepared together.

'I'm memorising them word for word so I can copy them from my brain in the exam and make my mother proud.'

I have never forgotten that moment or the words he said that day.

You see, I have no idea what happened during those exams, or if he managed to memorise all that text. But even if he did achieve 100 per cent in those exams by memorising all that information, the celebrations, certificates and awards that followed would be completely meaningless.

Our children's education must combine social and emotional skills with academics for them to have the best chance in life. Having one without the others is like being a bird with only one wing. You're going to struggle to get off the ground.

A child who is in kindergarten in 2024 will graduate in 2036. Who knows what the world will look like in twelve years from now? With the fast pace of technological development and the rise of AI, for the first time ever, we have no idea what the world will look like in 20 years. Twelve years ago, Tesla started making electric cars; TikTok was a figment of somebody's imagination; and cryptocurrency, digital payments and blockchain were obscure ideas.

This begs the question: if we're so unsure about what the world will look like in the future, how do we know what academic skills our children will need? The answer is, we don't know. With platforms such as ChatGPT, we have seen copywriters being laid off, artists being put out of work, and even editors and computer programmers facing uncertainties. And with so many unknowns due to climate change, overpopulation and wars, which academic skills our children need for a bright future are extremely uncertain. What we don't want is for our children to follow a narrow academic path that leads to a dead end.

If we want to raise a generation of future citizens who know when to change direction and make decisions based on ethics, morals and data, then our education system has to give academics and skills development equal weight. To embed what I call a 'skills-focused curriculum model'. This model allows our children to develop their academic capabilities in mathematics, science, English and the arts, while incorporating a holistic approach to learning and assessment that lets them develop essential skills.

# 5. Resilience—mastering adaptability

*'If you're not prepared to be wrong, you'll never come up with anything original.'*
*—Sir Ken Robinson, in his 2006 TED Talk,* Do Schools Kill Creativity?

Things will go wrong—it's part of life—but how we respond to these mistakes is what matters.

Resilience is a cornerstone skill. It helps children navigate the twists and turns of childhood, and prepares them for adulthood's many hurdles. It's also a quality that employers prize. Simon Sinek, a motivational speaker and bestselling author on leadership in the workplace, emphasises the importance of resilience in teamwork: 'The ability of a group of people to do remarkable things hinges on how well those people pull together as a team.'

Resilience within a team setting, he says, is crucial for achieving great outcomes, because it lets team members handle stress, adapt to changes and work cohesively towards common goals.

Resilience is more than pushing through anything, no matter how tough. For our children to develop resilience, they need a whole toolbox of other skills, values and attitudes. Skills such as optimism (seeing the light at the end of the tunnel), adaptability (changing direction when needed) and emotional regulation (reflecting before reacting). Resilience equips them to bounce back from setbacks, adapt to change with grace and keep moving forward when things get rough.

## Encouraging mistakes—the key to resilience

Parents and teachers can use many strategies to embed resilience in children, such as teaching problem-solving skills, promoting emotional awareness and building a sense of purpose. We'll delve into some of these in Chapters 5 and 6, but we can distil the entire process into one simple mindset shift: as adults, we should be encouraging mistakes.

*'The greatest mistake you can make in life is to be continually fearing you will make one.'*
*—Elbert Hubbard*

**Fear of failure can stifle growth and stop resilience in its tracks.** It may sound paradoxical but, within reason, we want to encourage as many mistakes as possible. I used to say to my students that if they weren't making mistakes, they weren't trying hard enough.

Now, I don't mean we should be telling our children to get everything wrong or behave recklessly. What I mean by encouraging mistakes is that we must create environments where children develop the confidence to try new things, with the understanding that failure is a natural part of the process. When children take on tasks and challenges of their own accord, knowing there's no single 'right' answer, and that the journey of trying and learning is equally as important as the end result, their motivation soars. They keep reinventing and reimagining their learning because they have agency, choice and freedom. Who wouldn't love that? And when they do encounter setbacks, they find ways to overcome them because they know this project is theirs. That's where resilience truly shines.

These journeys are all about exploration and experimentation. The more they experiment, the more they'll fail, and there's no better way to become resilient than by trying, failing and starting over again. Just try building an Ikea wardrobe without looking at the manual.

This doesn't mean abandoning your children and expecting them to figure everything out on their own or dropping them in the city centre and asking them to find their way home—though it's worth noting that in Japan, a reality TV show called *Old Enough!* features very young children running errands alone throughout the city for the first time (monitored carefully, of course!). We, as parents and educators, need to set our children on the right path, ensure they understand the expectations, then get out of their way and let the magic unfold.

## Handing over control—freedom within limits

When I talk about having agency and the freedom to choose, what I really mean is 'freedom within limits'. The secret is to give our children choices from a pre-selected list. Let them pick their sandwich ingredients from a designated shelf in the fridge or choose their outfit from a pre-approved section of the wardrobe. Our children still need guidance and boundaries, but when trust is the foundation, they will flourish.

And you may ask, why bother? What will happen? Well, for starters, you won't have to ask them what they want to be when they grow up. When we create environments where they can experiment with their choices and make mistakes without fear, they'll naturally gravitate towards their passions. A future architect will build models from cardboard, a budding dancer will choreograph routines, and your future novelist or filmmaker will create amazing stories from scratch. The magic is in the discovery—they'll show us their passions and their dreams for the future through the joy of exploration.

**Figure 8.** Freedom within limits—the remote control of choice

Children thrive when given freedom within limits, both at home and school. The skills they need for life will naturally blossom when we give them a sense of control and agency. Just like handing them the TV remote control on family movie night, suddenly they have the keys to determine the future—where they work, which direction they take their projects, how long tasks take, what their finished work will look like, what they do with their work and which materials they want to use. **Remember, a good teacher knows when to teach, but a great one knows when not to.**

## Developing the whole child

Throughout this chapter, we've explored many core skills. But achieving any of these comes down to one simple truth: we need to trust our children. Trust their instincts, trust their curiosity and trust their ability to learn from their mistakes. By giving them the freedom to explore, experiment and fail, we're not just helping them acquire skills, we're nurturing the resilience they'll need to face almost anything.

When children are intrinsically motivated—driven by choice, freedom and agency—without fear of punishment for making mistakes or changing their minds, they develop resilience naturally.

My teacher friend Jack Butler puts it like this:

> *School today is a bit like bowling with the bumpers up. It's fun, sure, but it's not real. We're so busy making sure our children never throw a ball in the gutter that we forget the most important lesson is in the near misses, the wobbly throws that sometimes end in disaster. Those are the moments that teach them how to adjust, how to improve, how to pick themselves up and try again.*

It's time to take the bumpers off. Let them pack their own bags, even if it means a few forgotten lunches or a backpack full of teddy bears. Let them help plan the family holiday, even though the itinerary involves a detour to a dinosaur museum. Let them sit with whoever they wish in class, even though they might be a little chatty. Let them cook the family dinner, despite a few burnt sausages and a messy kitchen, because **in those moments of chaos and imperfection, they're discovering who they are and what they're capable of.**

Once we recognise the real-life potential in our children, everything changes. They're not fragile flowers who need shielding from the wind, they're resilient trees who can stand tall in the strongest gale. They're not helpless, they're resourceful. And they're not just our future, they're the present, brimming with talent and eager to learn.

So, it's time to let go and to take off those bumpers. To stand back and guide our students rather than lead them. The opportunities for growth lie in the moments of experimentation and trial and error. It's time for us to stop underestimating the capabilities of our children and to realise that, by handholding them, we're stifling their innate desire to thrive out in the world, today and tomorrow. While it may be hard at first, your child will never forget the time you let them go shopping with you, help plan the family holiday or make dinner for the whole family. The work of the adult is the play of the child, and what a fun game it is.

It's time to go bowling, people.

## Step 3

# Redefining educational success—what constitutes a 'good education'?

As I stood on the deck of the Aurora Expeditions icebreaker ship *Greg Mortimer*, during my 2023 trip to Antarctica, I watched a pod of orcas swim by. It was a crisp morning, the sun was shining and it was a moment I had long dreamed of. Orcas are remarkable creatures. As a matriarchal species, orca pods are led by mothers, with the young trailing alongside or just behind the adult females. Their intelligence is astonishing—comparable to that of humans. And when you observe them, you soon realise they have so much to teach us, as does much of nature. Each pod of orcas has its own dialect, passed down through generations. As they swim together, they navigate their surroundings using an inbuilt sonar detection system, even in absolute darkness. But what I find truly remarkable about orcas is the way they approach education.

Let's imagine that a pod of orcas see a fur seal stranded on a small iceberg. Now, instead of just grabbing their meal and swimming away, they do something amazing. For these highly intelligent beings, catching a seal on an iceberg is a piece of cake. Orcas have several strategies to catch prey in this scenario, but they have a way of maximising the full potential of the situation that benefits their young ones who are carefully watching.

First, the older whales swim in unison towards the iceberg with the calves trailing just behind. At the perfect moment, the females kick up their tails, causing a giant wave to hit the iceberg and wash the seal from the ice. Then, the females place it back on the iceberg and repeat the same routine, while the young calves watch on and take notes. The mothers are modelling the skills for the younger generation to train them. Eventually, the calves take on the job of washing the exhausted seal off the ice, and when the young can achieve the task themselves, the family celebrates by eating together.

These orcas epitomise what education should look like—it's not about doing the work for the child or picking low-hanging fruit, but about developing their child's skills, putting them into practice and celebrating their victories together.

## What do parents really want?

In my 25 years as a school teacher, I've sat in hundreds of parent-teacher interviews, met with numerous parents after class and, as a school principal, welcomed many parents into my office for long conversations about what would be best for their little angels. What all those conversations had in common was that, no matter what was happening at home, in the classroom or with the children's learning, one invaluable lesson stood out: what parents want most from education is for their children to be happy. Of course, parents also want their children to be smart, feel safe and have friends, but for most, their foremost desire is happiness—and why not? Nothing is more precious than seeing a child truly happy and content in being who they are.

That being said, many of us still enrol our children in schools that boast about achieving the highest grades, having the biggest swimming pools or ranking highest on national league tables—without considering what these schools do to make our children feel content, purposeful and passionate. This raises an important question:

if we genuinely want our children to be happy and thrive in society, should we judge schools solely on their promised academic results? My answer is a resounding 'no'.

I was recently in an Uber on the way to Sydney Airport. As usual, I got talking to the driver. He mentioned he had two children who were ready to go to high school.

'Wow, which school will you send them to?' I asked.

He said the name of the school but also mentioned how expensive it was. 'But I guess you've got to pay the money if you want your children to go to the best school, that's why I drive an Uber at night to pay their school fees.'

'That depends,' I said.

After he stopped he turned around, looked me straight in the eyes and asked, 'What do you mean?'

'It all depends on what the word "best" means to you. I mean, if you're talking about the grades, points, scores, campus facilities and reputation, then yes, maybe it is the best school. But, in my opinion, a successful school journey is not about "what" your child becomes, but "who" they become.

'For me, education is about allowing the child to find their passion and attend a school that embraces the same values and visions for the future that the family holds dear. As the parent, before you enrol your child in any school, you have to decide what the word "best" means to you. And once you've defined it, find a school that meets those ideals, and you'll have made the right decision.'

With that, he shook my hand and said, 'You're right, you've made me think!'

I hopped out, and he drove away, waving and smiling.

## The reality of being number one

As I mentioned earlier, in 2022, the OECD's PISA rankings named Singapore as the number one school system in the world regarding academic attainment. The country has a regular spot in the top five, alongside Taiwan, Macau and Japan, which is an amazing achievement. But does that mean those children are getting the best start in life? Paradoxically, the OECD also releases *The World Happiness Report*, which ranks the world's happiest countries. If academic rankings were linked to happiness levels, surely we'd see the same countries in the top positions on both reports. But that's not the case. Iceland, Sweden, Denmark and Finland all top the happiness rankings. So ... how can that be?

There is a clear mismatch between our children's academic grades and the levels of happiness that follow. I've visited Singapore many times to deliver speeches and workshops on education. Although Singapore's education system is renowned for its academic rigour and high standards, I've heard numerous firsthand accounts that this desire to be the best comes at a cost. Several studies speak to this same cost—alarmingly high levels of anxiety among Singaporean students, primarily attributed to academic pressure—including the 2017 OECD study that found 86 per cent of Singaporean students were worried about getting poor grades, compared to the OECD's global average of 66 per cent (which is still very high). Additionally, 76 per cent reported feeling anxious about tests even when well-prepared.

The study revealed that the pressure stems from various sources, including parental expectations, societal emphasis on academic achievement and the competitive nature of the education system itself, which is not unique to Singapore. Students often internalise these expectations, leading to a fear of failure and a constant need to prove themselves. Now I'm not sure about you, but this doesn't sound like a healthy childhood to me. The consequences of this inappropriate chronic stress can be severe, affecting students' mental and emotional wellbeing, sleep patterns and quality of life. **The focus on academic achievement can also lead to losing interest in learning, because the joy of discovery is often replaced by the anxiety of performance.**

In 2023, the *China Daily*'s article 'Pressure, expectations lead to student depression' reported on a survey by China Education 30 Forum, which found that pressure to get into good schools and parental expectations were major causes of anxiety and depression among teenagers. Granted, China is an extreme case, with many children attending school from 7 am to 7 pm, six days per week, with two hours of mandatory homework each night, but the consequences of this pressure are clear for all to see.

Simply put, if we put too much emphasis on our children getting the top grades, competing against each other and avoiding failure at all costs, they'll inevitably become more anxious. Interestingly, Iceland, Sweden, Denmark and Finland—the top four countries on the 2022 OECD's happiness ranking—all have one thing in common: their citizens have immense *personal freedom, choice* and high *trust* levels within their communities—qualities that all work together to prevent the development of anxiety and depression.

Instead of choosing schools based on glossy brochures, impressive sports facilities, sleek websites or their rankings on league tables, we should ask ourselves the question:

*What does the word 'best' mean in the sentence*
*'I want my child to attend the best school'?*

If we really want to put children's happiness first, then we should choose schools that trust them to make their own decisions, learn from their mistakes, have agency over their learning and engage with the real world. Many schools seem to underestimate children's potential to an almost embarrassing degree. If an eight-year-old Mozart could write Symphony No. 1 in E-flat major (a twelve-minute masterpiece utilising 41 instruments/players), surely our children can complete an independent project, go to the toilet without having to raise their hand and choose where they'd like to sit without being micromanaged by us.

## The history of education

We've heard countless times that education is being reinvented, rewritten or reestablished, but if we can acknowledge the type of education our children are currently receiving, perhaps we can take meaningful action. To understand the origins of education, let's step back in time. Much like a pod of orcas teaching their young how to survive and thrive in the vast blue ocean, humans have been educating their children for millennia. But somewhere along the way, we seem to have lost our direction.

Aboriginal Australians have lived in the Australian landscape for at least 65,000 years and have a profound understanding of what education means. Even today, they continue their traditional practices. Using what they call Dreamtime stories, they sit under the twinkling stars of the Milky Way as elders tell ancient tales of times gone by. These are stories with deep morals, ethics and roots that go back further than we can imagine. Such tales are designed to teach children about life, how to live, and how the Earth and humans can work together to live in peace and harmony.

As early humans spanned the globe, different civilisations developed their own methods of passing down knowledge and skills to the younger generations. These methods included storytelling, practical demonstrations and communal activities that taught survival skills, cultural traditions and social norms. For example, various Native American tribes used intricate storytelling and oral traditions to teach their children about the natural world, spiritual beliefs and community values. Elders would recount tales of animal spirits, creation myths and heroic deeds around the fire, instilling in children a sense of identity and connection to their ancestry. How about that for an outdoor classroom?

Wise teachers on the Indian subcontinent conducted their lessons in forest ashrams, where students lived and learned in close proximity to nature. The *guru–shishya* (*teacher–student*) tradition was based on a holistic approach to education that emphasised not only academic learning, but also moral and spiritual development. Parents would choose a guru based on their morals and ethics, knowing this would have a profound impact on who their child would become. Subjects ranged from philosophy and mathematics to archery and astronomy, with written texts serving as a tool to preserve and deepen the learning experience. The bond between the guru and shishya was deeply personal and transformative. Eventually, after being away from the family for up to fifteen years, the child would return home ready to lead the family forward, spreading their newfound wisdom and knowledge throughout the community.

But to truly understand how education developed, we need to look at ancient Greece and Rome. The Greeks, with philosophers like Socrates, Plato and Aristotle, believed in the power of questioning and critical thinking. Their schools inspired students to think about the bigger questions, like how to live a good and just life. The Romans, on the other hand, were more practical. Their education focused on preparing young people for public life, teaching skills such as rhetoric, law and leadership.

When the Roman Empire fell, much of this classical knowledge risked being lost forever. Instead, it was preserved and advanced by the Islamic world. During this time, the Islamic Empire became the heart of learning, a place where mathematics, science and medicine flourished. Scholars like Al-Khwarizmi, the father of algebra, not only built on earlier knowledge but developed entirely new ideas like algebra. In his own words, he was driven by a 'fondness for science, by which God has distinguished the spirit of man above all other beings.' And through the Islamic world, the Indian invention of the number zero was shared with the West—revolutionising mathematics.

As time moved on, the education of our children began to evolve during the Middle Ages. Monastic schools in Europe became places where knowledge was carefully preserved and passed down through the study of religious texts, philosophy and the sciences. Centuries later, the Renaissance sparked a renewed interest in classical knowledge, and education shifted again. Humanistic education started to take root—a way of learning that wasn't just about facts and figures but about nurturing the whole person: their intellect, emotions, social skills and moral values. This approach laid the groundwork for the universities we know today.

Fast forward to the nineteenth century and the industrial revolution—a time when machines and industry transformed our economies, monetary systems and international trade. This period inadvertently but significantly shaped the modern education system. With the push for mass production and business growth, the world suddenly needed people who could wake up, clock into the factory, work for a salary, clock out, go home and do it all again the next day. This need for a disciplined, efficient and skilled workforce eventually led to compulsory schooling systems that emphasised punctuality, rote learning and obedience ... not too far away from where we are today.

Whatever happened to the Dreamtime lessons under the Milky Way or the stories shared around the campfire? Sadly, for most of the world, that's where the timeline ends.

And here lies the problem. Education hasn't evolved much since the nineteen century. Many schools around the world still have children sitting in rows of predetermined seats, relying on highly skilled professional teachers to deliver a heavily scripted curriculum all geared towards one goal: achieving high grades in standardised tests, so the children can graduate with the hope of landing a job that pays enough to fund that mansion and Maserati they've been told will make them happy.

**So what happened to our children being happy? How did we get it so wrong?**

It may stem from a misunderstanding of the definition of education. The word 'education' has two distinct etymological roots from Latin, each offering a different insight:

1. ***Educare:*** This means 'to bring up' or 'to train'. It suggests nurturing, rearing, and providing guidance and instruction to develop someone's abilities and knowledge.
2. ***Educere:*** This means 'to lead out' or 'to draw out'. It implies a process of drawing out the inherent potential and talents within a person, encouraging self-discovery and development.

From these, it's plain to see that education is only partly about passing tests and following rules. It should be a balance between developing skills and drawing out a child's unique potential. Over time, however, it seems we've leaned too heavily on the training and instruction side of things, forgetting the importance of self-discovery and personal growth.

Perhaps it's time to take education back to its roots—spending a night under the stars with our elders or choosing a school based on its values. No wonder the Green School in Bali is so popular. One step backward could be what we need to take two steps forward.

## Student-centred education

*'When you teach a child something, you take away forever his chance of discovering it for himself.'*
*—Jean Piaget*

By placing the child at the centre of their educational journey, we respect their individual interests and developmental pace, leading to deeper engagement and understanding. This approach can foster independence, critical thinking and a genuine love for learning.

The phrase 'child-centred learning' gets thrown around a lot in education. You'll find it splashed across school websites, glossy brochures and handouts. But what does it really mean? And as educators, how can we bring it to life in our classrooms? And how do we know if we're genuinely following a child-centred approach? As a parent, how can you tell if your child's school truly embraces this philosophy, or if it's just another buzzword?

Traditional, nineteenth-century-style education is the exact opposite of child-centred learning. It's what we now call a teacher-centred approach. Picture it: children sitting in neat rows, the teacher standing at the front of the room—the all-knowing oracle delivering knowledge to passive listeners:

'Good morning, students, I am your teacher. I know everything you need to know, and if you sit where I say, speak when spoken to and listen very carefully to my words, then you might remember everything I say well enough to pass an assessment I have prepared for you at the end of term. Then, hey presto! You're smart, I'm a great teacher and this is a great school!'

I know it may sound like I'm describing something from a bygone era, but sadly, this approach to education persists across the world.

How do I know? I was that teacher, not so long ago. I used to pride myself on how quiet my classroom was during lessons, how much the children listened when I spoke and how well they remembered what I'd said. At the time, I thought I was doing a great job. It wasn't until I started to look into Montessori methodology that I discovered student-centred learning.

Student-centred learning is about valuing everyone in the room equally. It's about creating an environment where ideas, experiences and perspectives flow freely among everyone. The teacher isn't the gatekeeper of all knowledge—they act as an inspirational guide, learning alongside their students and helping them connect the dots.

Every child brings their own unique view of the world, shaped by their beliefs, knowledge and experiences. In a student-centred classroom, the teacher isn't the only one leading the way. It's a shared journey with each child contributing something special and, together, they create a vibrant, collaborative learning community where everyone grows—teacher included. It's not just one teacher; it's 30, all learning from and with each other.

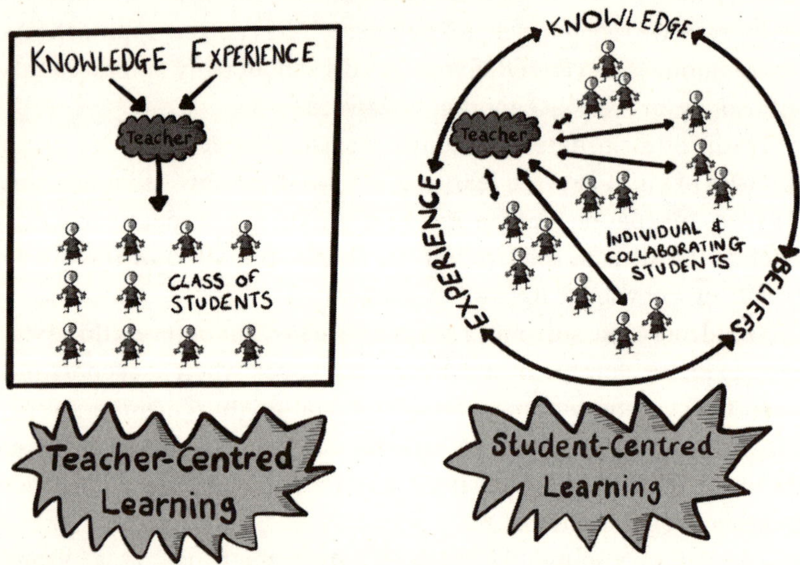


**Figure 9.** Student-centred or teacher-centred learning?

As the guides who craft our children's learning environment, our job is to discover their unique skills, experiences and beliefs. Once we discover these unique traits, we can weave them into the fabric of the learning experience, so every child feels seen, valued and inspired. Because when their skills and passions become part of the lesson, they don't just engage—they thrive. Remember how excited you were about 'show and tell' in preschool? That's just the tip of the iceberg. **When learning becomes personal, it transforms into something deeply meaningful.**

A good teacher profoundly knows their children—their fears, hopes, passions and dreams—and regularly connects the curriculum to what the child is naturally drawn to. This key component ensures students are excited to come to school in the morning because they feel they're becoming their future selves with every learning opportunity.

## The dinosaur boy

According to a 2022 study titled 'Can Holistic Education Solve the World's Problems?', the goal of holistic education is:

> *to cultivate a developing child's physical, emotional, moral, psychological and spiritual attributes. Serving the whole child means providing opportunities that are personalised to a child's skills and feelings. Lessons are conducted in a safe, supportive environment that allows students to utilise their individual strengths.*

When you hear it spelled out like this, it sounds like such a beautiful concept, doesn't it? What a dream—to have lessons personalised to match a child's unique skills and feelings. Who wouldn't want that?

One memory that stands out from my Montessori career is of a boy who joined my class in 2020. I was a teaching principal at the time, covering the first term before a new teacher started. This boy, who was seven years old, had moved internally from kindergarten into my Stage 2 class, a mixed-aged classroom comprising children aged six to nine. He was quiet and a little shy, with his hair combed over his face—a little scared of the transition into a new phase of his learning journey but happy and eager to learn.

As usual, I used all my tricks of the trade to get to know him and make him feel safe in his new classroom. Since he was new, I made regular visits to his table during his 'independent time' to learn more about who he was. The more I got to know him, the more I realised there was something unique about this young man.

He was absolutely obsessed with dinosaurs. He knew every dinosaur by its Latin name, and he knew its habitat, predators and prey. He even carried a miniature magnifying glass in case he discovered any bones on the playground.

By sheer chance, the curriculum I'd planned for that first term said 'dinosaurs' in big, bold letters. So, in true child-centred style, I decided to ask him to help me teach the subject of dinosaurs over the next term. Who better to teach it than him? I only know one type of dinosaur. It's the one with no eyes—the *Doyouthinkhesaurus*. Just joking. I know a few more, but he was clearly the expert.

One day after school, I met him and his mother, and calmly asked if he could help me teach the subject for a few weeks. I told him he was the expert and I could use the help, which was true. After a moment of stunned silence, a grin spread across his face. For the first time since he'd entered my class, his emotions were clearly evident. Without hesitation, he enthusiastically agreed.

The next day, he arrived with an armful of treasures: his models, homemade comics, diagrams, paintings, DVDs and even a tiny flipbook of a dinosaur running along a riverbank he'd made with his dad. His excitement was infectious; I couldn't help but share in it. After a few meetings with him and the rest of the class to introduce our new 'teaching specialist', I assigned him a time slot in the curriculum and a special table where he could give small lessons to targeted groups. During his independent time, he'd set up lessons according to the curriculum we'd agreed upon, using the models and comics he'd prepared at home. The other children came in droves. He even had a waiting list at one point.

Even though he was younger than some of them, the children treated him with respect. I watched as they raised their hands to ask questions and hung on his every word as he shared his knowledge and let them use his homemade teaching aids. The pride he felt in sharing his passion was palpable. By taking the time to find out what he loved then allowing him to use his passion to help others, everybody won—including me. Now, I could drink cups of tea while he took the class! But seriously, seeing the change that a little responsibility, trust and time made in how he felt about himself in the learning environment was like discovering a secret recipe for success. We even made him a badge that read 'Dinosaur Specialist', which he wore proudly for the rest of the year. From that day forward, when anybody wanted to know anything about dinosaurs, they knew there was a living, breathing seven-year-old palaeontologist sitting by the window, always eager to help.

This experience taught me a valuable lesson: that to fully meet the emotional, social, cognitive and physical needs of our children, education must be a collaborative effort.

When we invite children to be active participants in the learning process and take true ownership of their learning, we seamlessly and effortlessly address all their needs. **By meeting them where they are, rather than where we want them to be, children are intrinsically motivated to learn.**

They feel heard, needed and valued by their peers and teachers. They begin to see themselves as vital components of the classroom engine—without them, we'd all move much slower. I mean, what would happen if someone needed crucial information on the *T. rex*? Where would they look? With that, they start to develop responsibility. They take ownership of who they are and the role they play.

And while all this holistic development is unfolding, the other social and cognitive benefits are impossible to miss—children learning from one another, sharing ideas freely, without the pressure or fear of judgement from results or rankings. And just like that, we edge closer to the idea of sitting by the fire again, sharing stories. But this time, it's not the elders distributing the wisdom—the youngest members of society are the ones leading the way. No matter how young they are, children have their own rich inner lives. They're bursting with knowledge, experiences, passions and beliefs, and to overlook these treasures would be nothing short of a crime.

When we take the time and effort to place children at the centre of learning, something magical happens. We create a wonderful exchange of ideas, beliefs and experiences where every voice is heard. We cultivate an inclusive environment where leadership skills blossom naturally and our classrooms and homes become places where children feel valued. This empowers them with the confidence to try and the resilience to bounce back when things don't go as planned—they know they have our support and that of the children around them. Education becomes a shared experience with the responsibility carried by everyone.

**The classrooms of today should reflect the society our children are stepping into.** The world is a vastly different place today than it was 150 years ago, and our education system should be, too.

## The holistic approach—a new era

The term 'holistic education' has been around for a while. This educational philosophy aims to develop all aspects of a person's being: intellectual, emotional, social, physical, artistic, creative and spiritual. It recognises that each child is unique and emphasises the interconnectedness of life and all living things. By integrating different learning styles and methods alongside it, the holistic approach seeks to create well-rounded individuals who can think critically, act compassionately and engage meaningfully with the world. Sounds wonderful to me! This approach not only benefits children by allowing them to learn in the way that suits them best, nurturing their innate curiosity and potential, but it also values experiential learning, self-reflection and observation. This lets teachers use their unique skills and passions as inspirations and catalysts for the wonder of learning.

At university, I became obsessed with this approach. In my second year, I had a teaching mentor who often expressed her sadness that, as she put it, 'the magic has been taken away from teaching.' The curriculum told her to say one thing, but she wanted to say something else. It was a constant tug of war. She still wanted to teach the curriculum, but her new and novel ideas were frowned upon by her principal at the time. As we sat around her desk at lunchtimes, her advice to me was always the same: 'Follow your heart.'

After I graduated from university, she gave me a collection of essays by Ron Miller and told me they might help me in my future teaching career. The essays, called *Caring for New Life*, stress the importance of nurturing not just a child's academic brainpower, but their emotions, social skills and even their spiritual side. Sound familiar? That's right—Indigenous Australians were giving these lessons under the Milky Way 65,000 years ago.

Today, a revolution is upon us. More and more people are realising that success in life isn't just about acing tests, being top of the class and making money—it's about having a well-rounded set of skills and values that enable us to engage positively with the world. It's about finding our passion, living with purpose and developing our character as humans. Perhaps the holistic approach Miller talks about is that step into the *past* that will help us all move into the *future*.

Right now, you might be asking yourself, how can we implement this approach in our homes and schools without having to knock down the whole system and start again? Don't worry—the later part of this book is dedicated to practical strategies we can all adopt to implement a holistic approach to learning.

Study after study shows us that when schools focus on developing the whole child, students tend to perform better academically and exhibit improved emotional wellbeing. A 2019 study by Linda Darling-Hammond, a prominent education researcher and professor at Stanford University, and her colleagues, found that holistic approaches to education lead to higher academic achievement and better emotional health. Similarly, Metin Kaya and Cahit Erdem's 2021 meta-analysis highlights the importance of student wellbeing—a core principle of holistic approaches—in influencing academic success. Their findings suggest that when educational practices prioritise well-being, students thrive both emotionally and academically. This aligns with the essence of holistic education.

This is because a holistic approach recognises that learning extends beyond the classroom and encompasses all aspects of a child's life. So, by fostering a supportive and engaging environment that nurtures creativity, critical thinking, independence and emotional intelligence, schools empower students to engage with learning everywhere they go.

A holistic approach to education shapes children's character, builds their confidence and equips them with the skills they'll need to thrive in the 21st-century world. Skills like empathy, communication, time management, adaptability and compassion are in high demand in our future-focused world. These are precisely the skills a holistic education aims to cultivate, preparing students not only for academic success but also a fulfilling and adaptable career in a rapidly changing world.

## Ranking our children: A lesson learned in India

I've never really understood the point of ranking children and comparing them against each other. I guess it stems from when, in Year 6, Mrs Williams read out my 26 per cent maths score in front of the whole class, causing me to cry. As if getting 26 per cent wasn't bad enough, I was now the person who cried in front of everyone as well. Whether it's naming and shaming the children who get low scores, or celebrating those with top grades, none of it makes sense to me.

I can vividly remember those end-of-year assemblies where top-scoring students were awkwardly paraded on stage, certificates in hand, for their exceptional ability to memorise and regurgitate facts on tests. I've always found the concept of 'best child in school' or 'top of the class' unfair. What about all the unique, ungraded and ungradable skills other children possess? Like the child who always cares for others, the one who looks after nature or the one who shows determination no matter what? Take my childhood friend Sean, for example; at nine years old, he could perform magic tricks in front of the entire playground, confidently entertaining so many people. These incredible skills were never recognised because they didn't fit the academic mould or translate into points on a score chart.

Though I've never been on stage for being top of the class, I want to be clear that my words don't come from a place of resentment or jealousy. I've just always wondered why we're compared on some things but not on others. What about participation awards? Children know those awards don't carry the same weight. If we're determined to hand out awards, then couldn't everyone get a certificate for the progress they made in any area? Wouldn't that be better? I'm often baffled when I hear people say their child came top of the class or aced a test, because I can't help but think about how the others feel—the forgotten ones who didn't make the list or get a certificate.

I've always been captivated by watching people—the fleeting expressions that dance across faces, the subtle shifts in body language and those quiet moments of connection that words can't capture. During award ceremonies and assemblies, both in childhood and as an educator, I've been drawn to the subtle social cues that take place as the awards are distributed. In doing so, I began to notice recurring patterns.

First, the award recipients often wore a look of embarrassment. Being labelled the 'best' can be isolating, despite the supposedly positive intent. And who wants to be isolated? Second, there's the immense pressure to maintain that top position, leading to incredible stress.

*'Once you become a champion, you're*
*expected to stay at the top.'*
*—Serena Willams*

**Figure 10.** The school awards ceremony

I once heard a grandfather utter the words, 'Well done, Tommy. Now let's see if you can keep it up' as the family left the ceremony after the boy had achieved first place in mathematics. Although everyone was smiling as they left the hall to head home, the unspoken question lingers in the back of the child's mind:

*What happens if I fall behind next year?*
*How will it feel to be second best after being crowned the top of the school?*

The truth is, ranking and comparing children is a lose–lose scenario. The 'top' child feels burdened by pressure and stigma, while the rest are deemed 'not good enough' to warrant recognition. We end up with one so-called winner and countless perceived failures. What's the alternative? How can we celebrate our children's achievements without pitting them against each other?

The answer is something that I call 'the collective step forward'.

In 2019, I worked with a school in India to help shift parental expectations towards a more child-centred approach. The school's executive team had reached out for help, knowing the kind of work I had been doing and my approach to teaching and learning. After much thought and deliberation, I decided that if we wanted to change the way the school operated, we first needed to get the parents on board with the school's new vision and direction.

The existing school community was one where if the children didn't achieve 100 per cent in their exams or in-house tests, the families would be up in arms. Their expectations were that their children should achieve 100 per cent because this was supposed to be a good school. However, expecting *every* child to achieve 100 per cent is not only a flawed assessment system but also extremely unrealistic. But I had to find a way to tell them.

On a hot Indian morning in a huge hall with no air conditioning, nearly 1000 parents gathered for a talk on 'Innovations in Education'. A real buzz was in the air. After the introductions, it was time for the full-day workshop to begin.

As part of my plan, I asked them to complete a warm-up activity. It was a simple task. They were presented with a slide on the overhead projector listing 20 best practices for perfect parenting, including reading with your child daily, listening to understand rather than reply, allowing your child to help with house chores, not using phones during meal times, going to bed at the same time every day, and telling your child you love them unconditionally. Before the seminar commenced, I gave the parents ten minutes to talk and self-reflect on how they met each of the perfect parenting targets. Each item was to be scored out of five, based on how well they felt they embodied that practice.

As the parents worked, a buzz of conversation filled the room, with much deliberation and comparison of scores. I remember one father remarking, 'I'm definitely a five for reading every day', only for his wife to retort, 'Don't be ridiculous, you're never home!' It was fascinating to watch. Once they finished, I asked them to calculate their total out of 100. Yes, that's right, I was going to rank them, and I was going to do it publicly. I believed it was the only way to demonstrate how it felt to be compared. Then, with slight apprehension, I asked those scoring 0–40 to move to the left side of the hall, those scoring 70–100 to the right and those in the middle to remain seated.

Once everyone had moved into position, I declared those on the right to be the 'best' parents in the community, calling them the crème de la crème and asking the rest of the hall to applaud them, which they did, reluctantly. I then turned to those on the left, labelling them the 'worst', prompting one father to become quite upset with me. The middle group was simply ignored. It was a sombre moment. The organisers caught my eye, and I could see they were starting to get worried: *What on Earth is this guy up to?*

Gazing at those parents, I saw humiliation on the left, embarrassment on the right and resentment in the middle. Although I've never done this activity again for fear of getting beaten up by a disgruntled parent in the 0–40 bracket, it was a powerful demonstration of how rankings and comparisons lead to no winners. Not even the 'best' parents felt good about it.

I asked everyone to return to their seats. They did this slowly and without speaking. Feeling the resentment in the room, I told them that this is exactly how their children feel each time they get graded and compared against each other.

Then I said I wanted to show them something. I asked them to pull out their perfect parenting score chart and identify one low-scoring item they could improve upon that very night. Perhaps it was reading a bedtime story or expressing unconditional love to their child. Maybe it was taking a few minutes to listen to what their child had to say or letting their child help them take out the rubbish. Slowly, the conversations started again as the parents began to understand what I was about to do.

As a species, I said, we're not at the top of the food chain because we have the biggest brains or are the fastest or smartest. We're at the top because we know how to work together. If every parent in that room returned the next day having made one small improvement in the way they parent their children, the entire community would have taken a collaborative step forward. Instead of ranking our children from top to bottom, the focus should be on meeting the children where they are, discovering what makes them excited and uncovering where they might be struggling. As communities, we should work hard to ensure everyone—both children and parents—takes one step forward every day they attend school. The goal is to progress together as a family—as a community—not to clamber over each other to reach the so-called 'top'!

As the penny dropped, the parents started to chat more, making plans about which parenting actions they would tackle next. It was an amazing moment—an exercise that helped shift the parents' mindset on what 'good education' meant. **Rather than children competing against each other, the goal was now to identify each child's strengths and weaknesses so the community could progress as a whole.** It was about working together, not against each other. As we broke for morning tea, I apologised to the parents for the public humiliation. The executive team looked over at me and the principal gave me a covert thumbs-up, which was reassuring.

The problem doesn't lie with the parents, teachers or leadership team, but with the age-old competitive nature of how schools use grades and scores to climb higher on league tables and governmental lists so they can gather more enrolments by showcasing their academic abilities. And just because we've always done it this way doesn't mean it's right.

Harvey Goldstein and George Leckie from the University of Bristol have studied the use and impact of school league tables extensively. Their 2008 research highlights that ranking systems often fail to provide parents with meaningful information about a school's quality or a child's individual progress. Instead, they tend to focus on narrow measures of academic achievement, fostering unhealthy competition and potentially neglecting other important aspects of a child's development and schooling.

Goldstein and Leckie argue that league tables can be misleading and detrimental to the educational environment, echoing my experience in the Indian school community. That school had so much more to offer than the grades they produced. It had a low turnover of staff, meaning the team culture team was solid and cohesive. Their values were part of the school's DNA, and they genuinely cared about the wellbeing of the children in their care. None of this can be graded or counted, but to any parent considering a potential new school for their child, it's extremely important.

Ranking and comparing our children simply doesn't work. It creates unnecessary stress, fosters unhealthy competition and nobody wins, apart from the companies that sell the badges and trophies or print the certificates. **The only meaningful comparison we should be making is against who our children were yesterday.** As long as everyone is making progress, even in different directions and on different parts of the educational continuum, the community thrives and the children grow. That's the essence of a holistic, child-centred approach to education. Now, doesn't that sound beautiful?

## Preparing our children for tomorrow—designing a future school

*'The only thing that is constant is change.'*
*—Heraclitus, Greek philosopher*

You might think education is changing rapidly—after all, with the rise of AI, things feel like they're moving faster than ever. But here's the reality: much like coding, STEM, robotics or even the iPad before it, AI is just another tool. And while it's certainly a powerful tool that can enhance the journey of raising wonderfully creative, kind and smart humans, it won't solve the underlying issue.

The problem is that, regardless of what new innovations enter the educational arena, the educational cogs of change move painfully slowly. The bureaucratic hierarchy is often out of sync with what's actually needed to inspire or prepare children for the world. Decisions are made away from classrooms, with little input from teachers—the very people who know what works and what doesn't. So, by the time innovations, research or strategies filter through the endless layers of bureaucracy to reach the classroom, the world has already moved on—and our children are left playing catch-up.

**The secret to preparing our children for tomorrow is to trust our teachers.** They are on the frontlines at school, day in and day out. They're holding the litmus paper and reading the results. They understand each child's unique likes, dislikes and talents, and can make fractions and long division seem fun and meaningful. But we fail to involve them in any kind of reform, and this is our greatest mistake.

For me, future schools are places where teachers are trusted to do the job they've trained for. Where our children are allowed to be human, to develop values and skills so they can work in our ever-changing technological world ethically and reasonably. Even though technology is moving the world forward, it doesn't mean our schools should be filled with it. Yes, our children need exposure to this tech, but future schools aren't littered with iPads and laptops. Instead of schools purchasing a laptop for every student, sitting children in rows and teaching from our desks using Google Classroom for laborious impersonalised chores, they should individualise and humanise the educational journey for everyone, regardless of the outcome.

The World Economic Forum's *The Future of Jobs Report 2020* highlights that educational success is no longer about memorising facts and figures. It is about critical thinking, problem-solving, creativity, emotional intelligence and adaptability. These skills will make our children excel in the future job market, giving them the ability to apply for their dream jobs based on their experiences and values, not on their scores or marks.

*Not everything that can be counted counts, and*
*not everything that counts can be counted.*
*—William Bruce Cameron, sociologist*

While grades and points give us tangible things to grab hold of and talk about with our friends or report in the school newsletter, they hold no real value in the long run. **The true value of education lies not in *what* your child is, but in *who* they are becoming.** Education is not just about preparing children for the workforce, it's about empowering them to become well-rounded, adaptable individuals who have the confidence to follow their dreams, make ethical decisions and choices, and tackle whatever life throws their way.

In Australia, primary school-aged children sit for standardised tests in Grades 3 and 5. They're tested on their writing, numeracy, spelling, grammar and reading comprehension. Over several days, the children are expected to sit in silence for about 40 minutes as they tackle these tests. Understandably, like many schools worldwide, some schools run mock tests to prepare children for the big day.

Now, let's be clear, as our children progress through life, they'll need to meet deadlines and work under pressure. So as far as I'm concerned, the problem isn't the test itself; what causes so much harm is the rationale behind the test and what we do with the results.

You can judge a lot about a school's values by looking at how they prepare their children for these tests. In extreme cases, schools run Saturday classes for up to six months beforehand, drilling the children to ensure they're well-prepared and can get a good grade on the day. Six months! Imagine all the self-discovery and character growth that could have happened instead. Others barely mention the tests until a few days prior, downplaying their importance. But I'm guessing that most schools sit somewhere in between these two extremes.

For me, I've witnessed the effects of both strategies firsthand. While intense preparation might yield better results on the day, in my opinion, the pressure on the children and the loss of their precious Saturdays and other developmental opportunities is too high a cost. And for the teachers running those Saturday classes? Teachers should be with their families, recharging their emotional batteries to be inspirational all over again on Monday morning.

As for the children, even though they are prepared, the continuous focus on one thing for a prolonged period often ends in tears and anxiety on the day. Imagine all that preparation, then hearing the teacher announce there are only fifteen minutes left and you still have 20 maths questions to answer. I've been that teacher—I've seen the fear in the children's eyes and I can tell you, it's not good!

## The standardised test—an ancient Chinese tale

To many of us, the standardised test may seem like a modern invention, but this form of assessment can be traced back to ancient China. The imperial examinations, known as the *keju* system, was developed during the Sui Dynasty (581–618 AD).

This game-changing system was designed to select government officials based on merit rather than social status or connections. It covered subjects including Confucian classics, literature and administrative skills, giving hope to even the poorest citizens. Imagine the impact: a fair, objective way of choosing leaders that promoted education and scholarly achievement throughout the empire. Mind you, the *keju* system was only open to men so it was only fair if you were a male.

Many families made sure their children started preparing for the exam from almost the day they were born. Children dedicated years to mastering the required texts and attitude to pass the exam. When the time came, students were isolated in cubicles within massive halls holding thousands at a time, spending several days writing essays, poetry and responses to questions. The candidates would even sleep and eat inside their cubicles to ensure there was no cheating. This intense, high-pressure environment led to incredible stress—some candidates even fell ill or died during the examination process. The exams were then graded anonymously. The ancient Chinese believed this was the fairest way to elevate those who deserved it.

When the results were announced, successful candidates were celebrated and their lives transformed overnight. The most prestigious achievement was the *jinshi* degree, which opened doors to influential government roles. This system didn't just change individual lives, it reshaped society, embedding the values of education and merit-based advancement deeply into the culture. The remnants of this process are still evident in today's classrooms.

As you can probably imagine, I prefer a more relaxed approach. Yes, I do think familiarising children with the test's setting and procedure can help lower anxiety. But despite our best efforts to downplay the importance of tests and create a relaxing environment, the pressure on the children still mounts. Sometimes it ends in tears or deep regret when a child can't finish the test or gets stuck on a single question and can't move forward.

It's heartbreaking to witness this. Knowing the strict nature of these assessments, we're forced to suppress what comes naturally—to assist, guide or, depending on the school's policy, even comfort the child during such a challenging moment. And it stays with you long after the test papers have been collected.

But there is an alternative! Through targeted conversations and offering children different ways to demonstrate their value to the community and themselves, they begin to understand test results aren't the only things that reflect their knowledge or ability. While the results provide a point or grade on a linear scale, they don't prove anything to the world about a child's value or impact. And that, to me, is our ultimate goal.

## A change is upon us

In 2021, something interesting happened that gave me a glimmer of hope. Seven graduates were heading off to their respective high schools after finishing their primary school years with me. In my previous schools, the high school principals would call or email and ask for their NAPLAN (Australian Standardised Test) results before accepting them. But on this occasion, the phone didn't ring. I'd heard from the parents that the children had been accepted into their new schools, but none of the principals had contacted my office to ask for their results.

Curious, I called one of the schools and asked why they hadn't called. His answer was humbling.

'Well,' he said, 'the young lady walked into my office, shook my hand, looked me in the eye, and started telling me all about her goals to make the world a better place through the books she had published and the charity work she had started with her Year 6 friends. So I obviously accepted her. I want children like that in my school.'

With that, I could see a shift happening. Our children were finally being recognised for the wonderful individuals they had become and the work they were doing to build a better world. **The human skills and values our children discover as they embark on a holistic approach to learning are written all over their faces, in every step they take and every memory they forge.**

Once we start to recognise children's unique qualities, passions and characters, we uncover not just 'what' they are but 'who' they have become. My hope is that more schools will look beyond scores and grades towards the human values and attitudes our children hold so dearly. These qualities can't be measured in a 40-minute test; they have to be lived and experienced. The authors of *The Future of Jobs Report 2020* aren't the only ones who see the value of these skills—they are slowly being recognised by our schools. As the phone lay silent in my office, it was as if the whole world was waking up to a new reality.

## The importance of choice in lifelong learning

Imagine you're hungry at home. Opening the Uber eats or Deliveroo app on your phone, you only see one button: 'Food.' No menus or choice of cuisines, just one button. Once clicked, the driver decides what you'll eat that night, not you. You're craving a Hawaiian pizza, but the delivery guy decides that, tonight, you're eating an extra spicy prawn pad thai. You'd be more than a little upset, wouldn't you? And rightly so!

We all value the freedom to choose. When those freedoms are restricted, we feel it and we feel it hard! Remember the Covid pandemic lockdowns, when we couldn't leave our houses or see our family and had to wear masks all day long? Those were difficult times. Yet, when it comes to our children's education, we often forget this basic human right.

## Freedom to roam in Iceland

Iceland is one of the happiest nations on Earth. Why? The OECD attributes it to many factors, but mainly the community's high levels of trust and people's freedoms. In Iceland, a concept called *almannaréttur* means the freedom to roam. It's a cornerstone of Icelandic culture, allowing people to explore their beautiful land freely and revel in the great outdoors, no matter who owns the land. Many people also let their children sleep outside in the fresh air at night, leaving their doors unlocked without fear of intrusion. The nation's farmers even let their livestock run free; they believe animals are happier when they have freedom to roam the land, too, and they're probably right. Once winter comes, the country's farmers come together to gather the livestock and sort out who owns what. How liberating!

Why am I telling you this? Because freedom and trust work in the same way for our children. When we allow our children to choose, and trust in their abilities, we unlock the doors to a lifelong adventure of learning. Quite the opposite to sitting in chairs all day, listening to a teacher's instructions and being told when they can go to the toilet and what work to produce.

The key to fostering lifelong learners is to give children as much choice as possible, both at school and home. Lifelong learning is about viewing problems as intriguing puzzles, knowledge as a treasure to be uncovered, and the future not as something to be feared, but an exciting landscape to explore.

The big mistake we make is thinking we have to wait until adulthood to embark on this lifelong learning journey. But why we can't begin earlier? Well, the journey can begin the moment children develop the ability to start exploring the world around them. To achieve this, two things need to happen:

1. **Teachers and parents need to shift their roles.** Instead of being the keepers of all knowledge, we need to step back and become the spark that ignites curiosity. This means taking children to where knowledge is lurking, asking thought-provoking questions and opening doors to new avenues of exploration.
2. **Let children take the lead.** Once children have developed the intrinsic motivation to learn, we step back and let them take the lead. We need to trust them and get out of their way. Of course, if they seek help or guidance, we'll be there. **But we must let go of our need to be needed and trust that our children can navigate the journey without us.**

Have you ever seen that sparkle in a child's eye when they see or hear something for the first time? That's what wonder looks like! As adults, with the pressures of everyday life, we can easily lose it—and that's a shame. To me, the world we live in is a fascinating place and a lifelong learner's dream.

Our world has rich history dating back billions of years with an astonishing array of flora and fauna to spark even the most sceptical mind. There are more than 10,000 known species of birds and more than 80 per cent of the world's oceans remain unexplored. We've recently discovered that trees can communicate and share nutrients using fungal networks. Better still, we're standing on a floating rock orbiting the centre of the Milky Way galaxy at about 800,000 kilometres per hour. No wonder children get that look in their eye when they see or hear something new. It's amazing. And if we want our children to grow up with that sparkle of curiosity for the unknown, the secret is to find that awe in our own lives. To look into the unknown with a lens of intrigue.

Imagine you're at home one day with your daughter Amara, and a bird lands on your balcony outside with its beautiful chirping sound. Instead of shooing it away or ignoring it completely because the news is on, we need to seize every moment like this. So, you quietly sneak over to the balcony door, careful not to disturb the bird, and get down low. Pointing at the creature, you whisper:

*Hey Amara, come here and look at this. Did you know birds are actually dinosaurs? They can fly because their bones are hollow, not like ours. Our bones are so heavy, it's no wonder we can't fly! Come look closer ... What kind of bird do you think this is?*

Amara, seeing your excitement, comes over. Once her interest is piqued, the key is to see if she has any knowledge to share. Maybe she knows something you don't? After she's had a chance to speak and you've listened carefully, the next step is to pose even more engaging questions.

*I wonder why seagulls have that funny little tube on their beak?*

*Is there anything you'd like to know about this bird?*

Once Amara comes up with her own research question, the next step is to empower her to find the answer and share it, thus becoming the inspiration herself. This can happen in the classroom or at home—the location is less important than the process. The goal is for your child to delight in uncovering new information and solving problems. Even better, they can then use their newfound knowledge to make the world a better place, educating those around them and sharing their discoveries in whatever way they choose.

Later that day, Amara emerges from her room with a beautifully drawn picture of a seagull.

*'Guess what?' she says. 'Seagulls are also called tubenoses because of that valve on their beak. It helps them remove salt from seawater so they don't get thirsty when they're far away from land! And the bird with the biggest wingspan in the world is a tubenose, too. It's called a wandering albatross and it can fly while asleep!'*

Just like that, their lifelong learning journey has begun.

Fostering this kind of exploration cultivates essential skills like independence, a growth mindset and a sense of wonder. In the long run, our children rely on us less for answers and become more confident in their own ability to seek out knowledge. They discover learning isn't just about storing information to pass a test or impress a teacher, it's an exciting adventure of exploration and discovery. You'll know if you've succeeded once your own role shifts from gatekeeper to guide.

One of my favourite books is *Adult Education and Lifelong Learning: Theory and Practice* by Peter Jarvis. In this book, Jarvis emphasises the importance of self-directed learning in fostering lifelong learners. He argues that true learning isn't just about absorbing information but actively seeking it out, questioning and reflecting upon it.

You can follow this six-step approach to nurture your children's lifelong learning:

- **Step1: Show intrigue** Look for wonders all around you and share your curiosity.
- **Step 2: Inspire** Highlight things that inspire you to spark their interest. Share what you know and what you'd love to know.
- **Step 3: Question** Engage them with open-ended questions and see if they have any of their own insights to share.
- **Step 4: Release** Encourage them to explore and find the answers on their own. You do the same.
- **Step 5: Reflect** Come together to discuss and share what you've both discovered.
- **Step 6: Repeat** Continue the cycle, fostering a love of learning.

**Figure 11.** How to nurture your child's learning

# Hope in our classrooms

There is much debate about what our classrooms should look like and what materials they should have: Computers? Class libraries? Shared or individual stationery? But the real question is, what values does your classroom have? What moral code does your school live by? Fostering future leaders with the right attitudes, character traits and values to make the world a better place starts with the values we promote in our schools and homes.

Dr Neil Hawkes, the founder of Values-Based Education, a dear friend of mine and a global voice in values-based education, recently shared:

*By embedding an ethical understanding rooted in universal human values in many schools, I have witnessed children not only understanding but also embodying care, trust, honesty and compassion in their daily lives. This transformation, I believe, is the cornerstone for building a more harmonious and sustainable world.*

Every day, we buckle our children into the car on the way to school, with the morning news playing on the radio. And what do they hear? War, murder, rape, child abuse, deforestation, climate change, attempted assassinations and then ... maybe a little sport. While we might think they're not listening, they are. Even if they're not paying close attention, a picture of the world is slowly seeping into their beautiful brains that is scary, but also inaccurate. Most people are lovely, and most places are safe. Why?

As Dr Mark Williams, author of *The Connected Species*, explains:

*We as humans evolved to collaborate, connect, empathise, and take care of each other. It is in our genes. We thrive off endorphins that are released when we help each other.*

But in the mainstream media, the world is shown as a bleak, dangerous and competitive place where it's every person for themselves. No wonder anxiety levels are on the rise.

So how can we mitigate this? Well, for a start, we can turn off the news and pop on some uplifting music instead, but we can also transform our homes and classrooms into miniature versions of an ideal world. First, we need to identify what's causing the problems in our world today. Maybe it's the marginalisation of minority groups, a lack of understanding of other cultures and religions, the disregard for the natural world, or the prevalence of unhealthy food over whole foods. Whatever we see as the problem, the cure is sitting on the carpet of a classroom wearing a big smile and a backpack filled with books, pencils and scrunched-up homework. That's right—our children.

The next step is to ensure the issues we see in the world don't exist in our classrooms or homes. Whatever we see as wrong or unjust in the world, we can actively correct within our classrooms. **We make decisions together, we never harm a living creature intentionally, we care for each other, we are inclusive and we never waste anything if it can be reused.** And the results of our hard work? They'll become evident in the values and moral code of every child who leaves your class and becomes an active citizen of positive change in society. You may not see the fruits of your labour today or even tomorrow, but someday, somebody will, and that's what matters.

When I first started building schools in Nepal, I met a man called Anand Devkota. He's one of the kindest, most caring people I've ever met and, over the years, he's been my partner on almost every school project, and he's become like a brother.

In Nepalese culture, it's normal for brothers and close friends of the same gender to walk hand in hand. So, after spending just a few days with Anand back in 2017, we were heading to the market in Kathmandu when he reached for my hand. I've got to admit, the first time I felt his palm in mine, I was a bit taken aback. But over time, it's become completely natural. Now, when we walk through the streets hand in hand, laughing and chatting, I don't even think about it.

But when other tourists see us, it's a different story. A two-metre tall white guy and a shorter Nepalese man holding hands in the middle of Kathmandu? Their faces are priceless—usually a mix of confusion, curiosity and sometimes judgement. I can only imagine what's running through their minds. And I'll admit, it feels awkward at times. I've often wanted to stop and explain, to tell them what's really going on, but I never do.

While there are many reasons for stigma, misunderstanding or judgement of others, part of the issue stems from how our schools—and the schooling system—handle anyone who looks, acts or learns differently. Take how children are grouped at tables in many schools with names like 'tomatoes', 'bananas', or 'strawberries'. These names may seem harmless, but they're often a thinly veiled attempt to disguise the children's perceived ability levels in a particular subject, allowing for covert differentiated tasks to take place.

And while we might think the children are oblivious to this, they're not. It doesn't take long for them to figure out that one table always has the teacher nearby, while others are left to work independently, with tasks that clearly vary in difficulty.

Wouldn't it make more sense to group children of varying abilities together, so they can learn from one another? Sure, it might be harder to organise the worksheets they'll use or decide on the right textbook, but the focus shifts from segregation by ability levels towards collaboration and shared growth.

In some schools, certain children are even removed from the classroom altogether. Barbara turns up at the start of maths and whisks away her 'special group' to the 'special room' for 'special work'. Why? Because they're either in the 'bottom group' needing extra support, or they're in the 'gifted and talented' group needing a push. The world's obsession with 'gifted and talented' makes me quite ill, by the way. We're all gifted and talented in our own unique ways, if only someone would take the time to notice.

What message does this send to our children? To me, it suggests that if you're different in any way, then you'll need to go somewhere else to learn. You're either too bright or too slow, and you should be in another table or room where we'll try our best to help you while the rest of the 'normal' children do 'normal' work. The result? Our children don't get to see and celebrate the incredible diversity that makes their classroom society so rich and vibrant. They become unaccustomed to those who act or behave differently and, just like the tourists on the streets of Kathmandu, they become confused or even judgemental when they encounter such differences in the real world.

To build a better, more inclusive world outside, we must first create the ideal world inside our classrooms and homes—a world where all children are treated equally. We understand that we're all unique, learning in different ways and at different speeds, and that's okay. It's what makes the human species so wonderful. And if you do need help, well, we all need help sometimes, but it should happen in the classroom because this is your home. A home where everyone's voice is equal, uniqueness is celebrated and everyone gets a chance to speak, be heard and be seen.

If our ultimate goal is to raise children who are happy, confident and prepared for tomorrow's world, then we must start at home and school. **The closer these places resemble the kind of world we want to see outside, the better that future world will inevitably become.** Our task is to identify the issues we want to change and then create learning environments and homes with cultures that actively promote and celebrate the exact opposite. It's one simple way we can all work towards a better tomorrow.

## The boy in the sequined shoes

As many educators around the world know, before organising any class-based or whole school initiative, it's important to ask ourselves a series of questions. Questions like:

*How will everyone feel about this?*

*Will anyone feel left out or isolated?*

*What message does this send to the community?*

As a teacher, I've encountered a diverse mix of learners—from preschoolers to adults, including refugees, autistic children, trauma survivors and individuals from various religious backgrounds. I've worked across different schooling systems in various countries and in multilingual classrooms, with each offering its own unique challenges and insights. But I've always believed that acceptance and inclusivity are the pillars of a successful schooling system.

After becoming a school leader, my staff and I always worked hard to make sure our classrooms fostered inclusion, acceptance and empathy. The team I was lucky enough to work alongside was an astounding set of individuals. If a child needed help, for any reason, they received it right there in the room where they belonged—it was their classroom, after all. We had no school uniforms, allowing everyone to dress as they pleased and express their individuality, and everyone was called by their first name—even me, the principal. Although, I did have to draw the line when one child called me 'Big G' in front of the Department of Education's annual inspector!

Over time, our small school on top of a hill on the outskirts of Sydney developed a reputation as a melting pot for young changemakers. We were always collecting materials for Nepal or raising money for local organisations. One year, we decided to participate in a local event: the Manly Fun Run. The whole school community—including students, parents, teachers and even some grandparents—gathered on a sunny Sunday morning to run six kilometres together along the Sydney coastline and raise money for yet another school in the Himalayas. But there was a twist: we all decided to dress up as grannies! I'm not sure why, but we did. We wore hats, pearl necklaces and all sorts of flowery dresses. Everyone was out of their comfort zone and it felt fantastic.

When the race was over and everyone had caught their breath and found their parents, we gathered at the finish line to take a group photo and celebrate our amazing achievement. A nine-year-old student tapped me on the hip and asked if he could whisper something in my ear. I bent down and listened. He pointed to his feet without speaking. I looked down. He was wearing a pair of sparkly granny shoes that looked like something from the film *Saturday Night Fever*. Goodness knows how he'd run six kilometres in them.

After 30 seconds of silence, he tentatively said, 'Gavin, would it be okay if I wear these shoes to school on Monday?'

Nobody had ever asked me what they could wear to school before. I was a little taken aback, but the boy clearly needed my approval. Without hesitation, I said, 'Of course, yes! They're beautiful.'

With a big smile on his face, he ran to his mum to tell her. She gave me the thumbs-up.

Monday morning soon arrived. My calves were hurting, but the children all showed up to school fit as fiddles, full of energy and excitement from the day before. Then the boy with the sequined shoes arrived. As I greeted him at the door, I looked down at his feet.

There they were, those beautifully sequined shoes. As usual, I shook his hand, looked him in the eye, told him that I loved his shoes and said good morning. As he entered the building, I made sure to look over my shoulder to watch as he walked down the corridor towards his classroom, creating a kind of disco ball effect on the walls as the sunlight caught the sequins on his shoes.

Some other children were milling in the corridor, unpacking their bags and reminiscing about the previous day. As he entered, I paid particular attention to the other children's reactions as they noticed the shoes he was wearing. To my joy, I heard no negative comments or mocking. Instead, I heard one girl say in passing, 'I like your shoes' as she put her bag away, and another boy say, 'Wow, cool shoes!'

If I had worn those shoes to school as a child, I would've been eaten alive, but it was this moment, among others, that reinforced my belief that the values we model and promote in our schools and homes determine the kind of people our children will become.

## Collective vision: The key to educational success

If you're a parent reading this book, you might be wondering what to do if these ideals we're talking about simply aren't an option for you. Maybe there are no schools like this in your area, or if there are, they're either full or too expensive. Well, here's something important to understand. **When it comes to the path of future education, parents hold a lot of power.** What most parents in any given community want from this thing we call school is ultimately what the school will deliver—you just need to voice your opinions.

Schools depend on enrolments. The more students schools have, the more sustainable they are, and often that means more government funding. In Australia, school funding is directly tied to enrolment numbers, which means your voice matters. The school board and principal know this, so the last thing they want is an unhappy parent community. What can you do? As my grandfather used to say, 'If you don't ask, you don't get!'

First, decide what you want from your children's educational journey. If it's high grades, certificates and award charts, you're probably reading the wrong book. But if you're after child-centred learning; ownership over the curriculum; and freedom, choice and agency, then that's what you need to ask for. And guess what? If you have enough support from the community, the school will pivot to meet your needs, and if enough schools shift, then that's educational reform. Yahoo!

However, before we ask ourselves what we want, remember that other voices within the school community also need to be heard. What do teachers need from this journey? When teachers are satisfied with the school's vision and their professional path, children benefit the most. And what about the children? Has anyone asked them what they would like? Probably not!

Here are some ideas that might give you some perspective:

- **Students:** They want to be inspired, supported in their choices and empowered to make a difference.
- **Teachers:** They want to make a difference, be trusted and bring their passions into the classroom.
- **Parents:** They want to be included in the learning journey—to be heard, informed and feel connected with all aspects of the community.

Parents, students and teachers are the pillars of our educational system. By giving them a voice in defining what successful education looks like, we create a solid and meaningful foundation. This ensures everyone is equally invested in the school's direction and vision.

When schools around the world actively include these three key stakeholders, they can begin to offer bespoke, unique educational journeys that reflect the needs of their communities. And if the foundations are strong, and everyone's needs are met, then educating the children becomes a wonderful byproduct of this cohesive, collaborative approach.

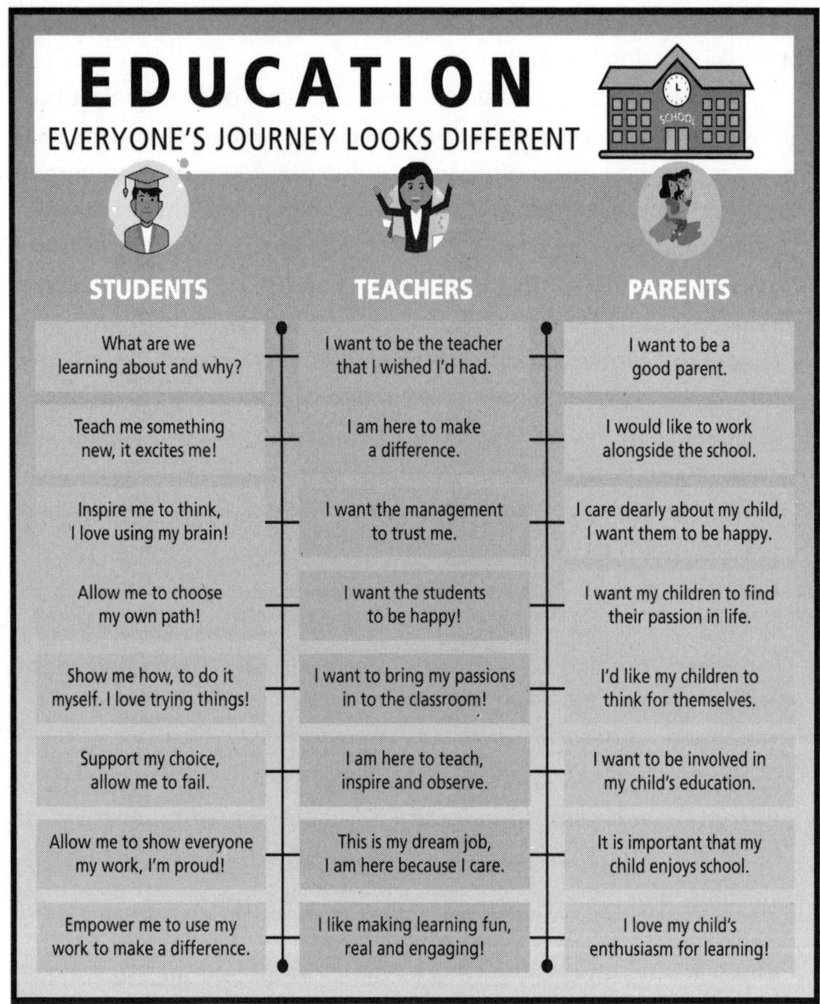


**Figure 12.** Everybody's education journey looks different

## Making the world a better place—purposeful learning

Have you ever thought about why teachers spend hours at home long after our families have gone to bed, preparing lessons about the wonders of ocean animals, the incredible ways trees create their own energy using sunlight or how Confucius solved a conflict high in the Chinese mountains in the late 5th century BCE?

It's because we want our students to understand how the world works. We want them to learn from our past mistakes, avoid or correct them in the future, and use this newfound knowledge to start their changemaker journey. And while it's common practice for teachers to explain 'why' we learn a particular subject, there's a crucial step we could all incorporate into our teaching that would vastly improve both children's educational experience and their influence on the world—I like to call it the 'emotional circle of learning'.

When I was a school principal, one of the most significant initiatives my team and I embraced was to adopt a 'yes' attitude towards children's ideas (for more, see Chapter 6). One fundamental rule was that when children came to us with an idea or proposal, no matter how outlandish or seemingly unattainable, we'd always ask one question before approving the project:

*How will this project make the world a better place?*

Because if we let our students come up with their own world-improving ideas, empowering them to conceive, pursue and hopefully achieve these dreams—with our guidance—they begin to feel the full emotional spectrum of the learning journey, thus completing the full 'circle' of learning.

Children can achieve incredible things when we give them freedom, trust their judgement, believe in them and support them through the process. It doesn't matter whether they decide to make flashcards of sea creatures to send to under-resourced schools overseas, rejuvenate a local waterway with the help of the local council, or create a poster on the history of bicycles to cheer up their grandma. These activities, big or small, are all on the spectrum of positive change and nudge the world in the right direction. **They let the child experience the emotional response of working towards something bigger than themselves.** Once the 'circle of learning' is embedded into common classroom practice, children realise their work and actions matter and can actually make a difference. This emotional response is not only tangible, but is also highly addictive (in a good way).

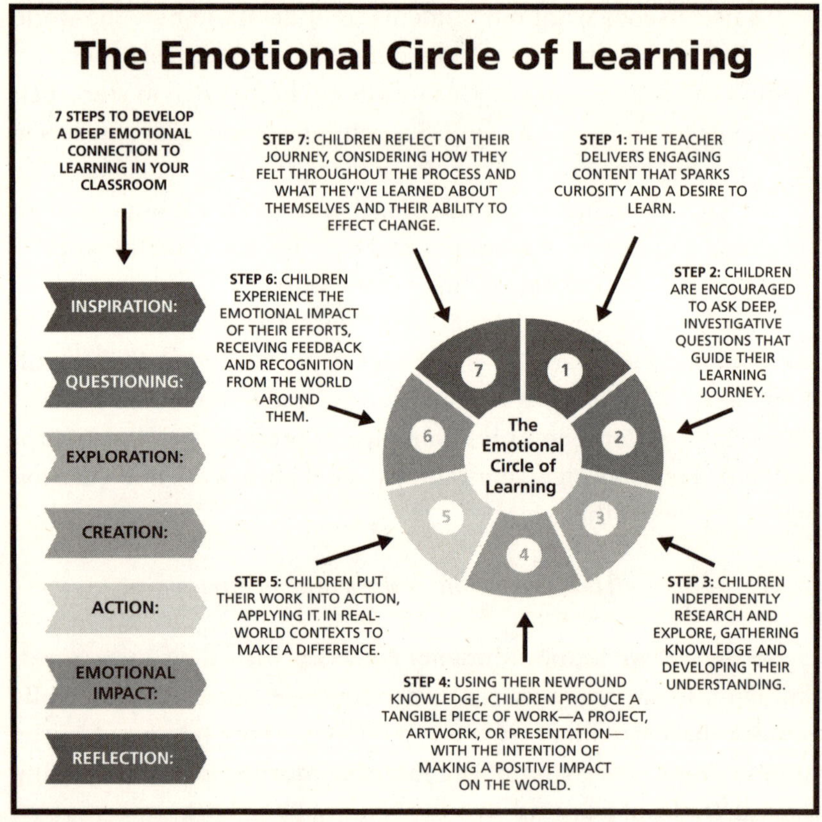


**Figure 13.** The emotional circle of learning

Educational reform isn't about rewriting the curriculum or making huge bureaucratic changes. It's about making small adaptations to our expectations of children and schools to see if each child can be a voice of change. Simple adaptations like the one just described cost no money, require no policy changes and need only a shift in mindset. We don't have to wait for policy makers to debate and consult on the matter. We have the power to make these changes today. Once implemented, they add a wonderful layer of emotional engagement to every child's learning journey, while allowing teachers to follow their dreams of making the world a better place.

## Write a book to change the world

In my quest to validate my existence and use my voice to make the world a better place, in 2013 I decided to start writing children's books. I'd read many of them on the carpets of kindergarten classrooms, and they seemed pretty easy to write. A few words here and there, not-so-complicated language, and messages of kindness and love. What could be easier? Well, more fool me! Writing a children's book is a lot harder than it looks. Distilling a complicated message and story to just a few words, and conveying that to kindergarten children without them falling asleep or looking out the window, is almost impossible. Still, I didn't let that stop me.

I had just one objective: to bring messages of hope, love and empathy into as many classrooms as possible. My first book tells the story of Sergio, a penguin who discovers that kindness is the greatest gift of all. After being bullied and left out at school for being poor, he finds someone who needs help, helps them and, in the end, he gets the girl penguin—wow, how Hollywood! The intention behind writing this book was partly as a therapeutic way for me to tell my own story, but it was also for those who have felt the same way growing up.

Over subsequent years, I wrote more books, including the life story of Sir Kenny Dalglish, the famous Liverpool football manager. I started to get pretty good at it—well, at least I thought so. Then, in 2020, the world came to a halt due to the Covid-19 pandemic. We suddenly lost the one thing we all need most: connection to each other and our shared stories.

The stories of hope we'd known since the Indigenous Australians started whispering under the Milky Way were now different. The stories were no longer of mythical creatures from the sky or heroes from a time gone by; they were stories of death, case numbers and hospitalisations. I found it so depressing that I stopped watching the news altogether. Instead, I decided to bring some good news to the world. So, every day at 7 pm, I went online and read a story to the children of the world.

At first, it was hardly the world—on the first night, only my niece was in the livestream—but it felt good and meaningful. Soon enough, like anything we persevere at, people started to show up. I had hundreds, then thousands, tuning in each night from all over the world. Children in Pakistan joined from their homes, schools in India tuned in with hundreds of kids listening, all seeking a glimmer of hope and connection during a time of isolation and fear. The community became so close that if I dared to be a few minutes late, my social media channels would be flooded with questions and worries about where I was.

Then, all the pieces of everything I'd done with writing storybooks and building a framework about purposeful learning merged in a beautiful way. Like most schools, everyone was working and learning from home. Although my school was closed at the time, one of my students' parents reached out to me. They explained she was struggling to engage with online learning and needed an extra incentive to keep her spirits up while being away from her friends and teachers.

Together, we hatched a plan. We decided that I would meet with her every Saturday morning and she would, alongside me, write, illustrate and publish her own children's book. I met with her online (with her parents present in the background) and informed her of the plan and she happily agreed. Each week, we met on Zoom and I guided her through the process of choosing characters, crafting a storyline and, using the Canva design platform, designing the front cover and page illustrations. During a time when most people were isolated at home, those weekly meetings became a wonderful source of connection for both of us.

After ten weeks of hard work, determination and consistent perseverance, her 30-page book—about a shark who joins a new school and feels left out, only to be welcomed by a big whale, thus realising that being kind is far better than being angry—was finished. It had a front cover, a blurb and even a barcode on the back. It was a work of art with a wonderful message inside and she had done it all on her own.

Once I saw the finished copy, I immediately ordered it for the school. By the time the printed version arrived, the lockdown was over and all the children were back in the classroom. Because of the lockdown and delays in post and deliveries, by the time the book arrived, we'd almost forgotten all about it. But once I received the parcel, I quickly took the book down to her classroom and announced its arrival.

The children eagerly gathered around the girl, their excitement contagious. The finished book was spectacular—the front cover depicted a shark swimming through the ocean. When she turned the first page to reveal her illustrations, the class lit up with a burst of energy. 'I want to write a book, too!' they exclaimed, grabbing paper and starting to plan.

To my amazement, and proving that true inspiration comes from the children themselves, about two months later the entire class had written their own books filled with messages of hope, love, determination and friendship. Each time a new book arrived on the doorstep, the excitement was palpable. Some children even started their own book club, meeting up to write comics, stories and news articles. And the excitement didn't stop there. Older children began visiting younger classrooms to guide them on how to write and publish their own books. It became a whole school initiative—even parents were getting involved!

On that day, when this young girl proved the unthinkable was possible, she did more than just ignite a classroom full of curiosity for learning, she inspired a global initiative that would change the lives of tens of thousands of children around the world.

In 2022, after leaving my position as school principal and starting Upschool.co, one of our first and most popular courses we created was *Write a Book to Change the World*. In this course, children choose their message to the world; dream up their characters; and write, illustrate and publish their own children's book. Once complete, children can upload it to our digital library for the world to read.

Over the last two years, the course has inevitably evolved. Now, when children publish their books, we ask them a question: 'If someone buys a copy of your book, where would you like some of the profits to go?' And we give them twelve charities to choose from.

When someone buys a child's book, two things happen: their story's message goes out into the world to make it a better place, and some real and tangible changes occur. Depending on the charity they choose, trees are planted in the Daintree Rainforest in Queensland, children in Indonesia have their eyesight restored, or girls in Uganda are sent to school instead of being sold into marriage.

No matter where they are in the world, every child gets to feel what it means to complete 'the circle of learning'. Instead of writing the story to impress their teacher, then sitting it on a shelf with ticks, points and grades, the story they've poured so much heart, soul and effort into literally changes the world.

So far, thousands of children from around the world have published their books in the Upschool library. Their stories are beautiful, filled with messages of hope, personal tales of triumph over adversity and guiding lights that give us a glimmer of what children are capable of when we trust them and set their imagination free. I've spent countless nights at my desk reading these stories, tears streaming down my face. To me, they paint a picture of a hopeful tomorrow. A tomorrow where our children can use their words, values and experiences to engage in educational projects and activities that make them feel that, with each word they write, every number they crunch and every problem they solve, they can make the world a little brighter for everyone.

And while there are so many ways we can improve the education we offer our children, to me, **a successful education system cultivates knowledge, love, empathy, compassion, understanding and perspective.** It allows the community to work on projects together while empowering our children through trust and independence. It asks the fundamental question of everyone:

*How will what we're doing make the world a better place?*

Our children don't need to be compared to each other. They need to feel they are part of a group of individuals who turn up each day to work on their passion and develop the character of the person they want to eventually become.

My colleague, Dr Julie Maakrun, senior lecturer at Notre Dame University, Sydney, put it beautifully when we met recently:

*Children cannot afford to be passengers on someone else's education bus. As educators, we have the responsibility to provide children with an education that will inspire and empower them to be well-informed, active citizens who are true agents of global social change. This must be our legacy for them.*

If we want to set a new precedent for educational success, we must not let the weight of tradition and the lure of conformity stifle the spark of innovation and flame of passion within every child. We know better than that.

For me, the question that deserves our unwavering attention, deepest reflection and most courageous action is this:

*What kind of citizens are we shaping our children to become?*

Step 4

# The neuroscience of learning—how children learn

## The astonishing human brain

As I sit down to write this chapter, I'm in a small, dark room in my apartment, facing a blank wall with hardly any stimulation around me. Just the soft sounds of Tibetan flutes playing quietly from my speakers, a 1970s lamp casting a cosy glow behind me and my cat snoozing peacefully on the carpet by my side. Why aren't I in a café, sipping soy lattes on a busy street in Sydney, where I live? Or in a rustic old house in the countryside, gazing out over endless fields? Surely that's the writer's dream, right? While it may sound idyllic, I'd get absolutely nothing done and this book you're holding wouldn't exist. Every little thing would pull my attention—cars driving, planes overhead, every person strolling down the street—it would all set my mind racing. My brain would wander off, thinking about what everyone else is doing, where they're heading and everything in between.

You see, when I have to get serious work done, I need a space with almost no distractions. That's just how I function. But others can sit on the busiest streets and crank out the same amount of work or even more. That's because our brains are wired differently, think differently, cope with stress differently and, as we'll explore in this chapter, learn differently.

Several years ago, a teacher came to me concerned about one of her students. This child couldn't get any work done. He spent the entire day sitting in his chair, staring off into space, not listening to instructions or engaging with the lesson at all. What could the issue be?

*Was he too tired?*

*Was the lesson not engaging enough, or maybe the wrong medium?*

*Was something going on at home?*

We tried everything we could think of, but nothing seemed to work. After speaking with his parents and putting the child on a long waitlist to see a specialist, we started asking ourselves more open-ended questions:

*Is the learning environment conducive to his style of learning?*

*Can we rearrange the classroom setup to give him more options for how he'd like to work?*

Once we did this, the problem became perfectly clear.

After speaking with a Montessori teacher friend, we experimented by allowing the children to choose where they wanted to sit in the classroom. We arranged the tables in various ways—some in groups, others in pairs, some facing each other and others as single-seated tables facing a wall with no distractions. The next morning, during circle time, we informed the children they could sit wherever they liked for the rest of the week. As expected, they were thrilled, hugging each other and eagerly saying things like 'Can I sit with you?' and 'Let's work by the window over there.' What was remarkable was that the child in question stood up and walked straight to the single table facing a blank wall, away from all stimuli.

Once the teacher gave the expectations and instructions for the session, this child got straight to work. He produced more in that one day than he had in the previous three weeks combined. Months later, when the specialist's results came back, we discovered this child had a sensory processing disorder, meaning his brain became overwhelmed in overly stimulating environments. And guess what? His original seat was right in the middle of the classroom, surrounded by colourful displays, hanging labels, windows with a view of the outside hustle and 20 other children—no wonder he couldn't focus with all that going on!

In earlier chapters, we discussed the importance of keen observation—not only of children's abilities but also of signs that something might be amiss. Early intervention is key to helping our children learn and engage in a way that suits them best, and while the guidance of an educational child psychologist would be ideal in such situations, it's not always feasible. In some countries, these specialists are either non-existent, rare or prohibitively expensive. Waitlists for evaluation can also be extremely long.

In Australia and the UK, children often face lengthy wait times to see a psychologist. The UK's Royal College of Psychiatrists highlights that some children may wait up to two years to be assessed by child and adolescent mental health services, with significant regional disparities creating a 'postcode lottery'. Similarly, the Australian Psychological Society notes that wait times can exceed twelve months, particularly in rural areas where access to services is more limited.

Given these lengthy wait times—even in developed countries—it becomes even more important that we, as educators and caregivers, deepen our understanding of how children learn. By doing so, we can create daily routines and nurturing environments that support their development while they await professional assistance, rather than unintentionally adding to their difficulties. Note that our role isn't to diagnose the children in our care—we aren't equipped or authorised to do that. The more we understand about how children learn, however, the better positioned we are to provide the right support while waiting for the system to catch up.

## Learning before birth

Weighing in at 1.5 kg, the human brain is one of the most complex and powerful biological structures we know. Containing nearly 86 billion neurons, it orchestrates and manages every thought, emotion and action, weaving the intricate tapestry of our lives. Despite accounting for about two per cent of our body weight, the brain consumes approximately 20 per cent of its energy. But what truly astonishes is the brain's boundless capacity to learn, adapt and evolve—a journey that begins before birth and continues throughout our entire lives.

In the womb, the brain is already a bustling hive of activity. Charlene Krueger PhD, an associate professor at the University of Florida's College of Nursing, led a study published in 2014 that revealed how, by the third trimester, a foetus can discern and respond to external sounds, and develop a strong connection to the mother's voice. Proving that this early education lays the foundation for a lifetime of learning. It turns out that all that reading aloud we do during pregnancy is worthwhile—thanks, Mum!

When it comes to learning, there's no better place to start than with the organ that lies behind our eyes and between our ears: the brain.

# Practice makes perfect

During my Montessori training, a key principle my trainer emphasised was that repetition leads to mastery. Day after day, in a classroom in Melbourne's south, she made us practise using the Montessori materials hundreds of times until we were nearly in tears. At the time, I didn't understand why I had to keep repeating those same tasks. But today, it's second nature—you could drop me into any Montessori classroom in the world and I'd know exactly how to use every single material without a second thought—and for that I'm very grateful.

When we do something repeatedly and eventually achieve mastery, it might feel like we're not even thinking about it, but that's not entirely true. What's actually happening is that our brain is working so quickly it feels automatic.

In our lives, we'll master many things—some by choice, others influenced by our environment and still more through learned behaviour. For instance, speaking is a skill that's been around for about 150,000 years and it's one of the most complex abilities we develop. Let's break down what actually happens when we speak:

1. First, your brain's auditory cortex kicks into gear to comprehend what the other person has just said. This involves decoding sounds into words, understanding their meaning and considering the context. Did they raise their eyebrows while they said it? Was there an inflection in the last word? This information travels to the prefrontal cortex, where your brain rapidly assesses the situation—weighing social cues, emotions and memories—and formulates a reply that fits the conversation.
2. Next, your brain's Broca area, which is responsible for speech production, organises your chosen vocabulary in the correct order. It ensures your grammar, syntax and vocabulary align so your message is clear and coherent.
3. After this, the motor cortex takes over, sending precise signals to the muscles in your tongue, windpipe, lips and face. These muscles must coordinate perfectly to produce the correct sounds, intonation, facial expressions and emphasis. Simultaneously, the brain manages your breathing so your voice has the right volume and pace.

All this unfolds in the blink of an eye, creating the illusion of effortlessness. The complexity of such a seemingly simple task showcases the brain's extraordinary capabilities. However, without an awareness of this complexity, we risk underestimating how challenging it is for children to master these skills. Worse still, we might unknowingly work against the learning process, hindering the very development we aim to nurture.

**Figure 14.** What goes on when we speak?

## The brain map

I like to think of the brain as a map, with roads representing the well-worn neural pathways that govern essential functions like talking, walking, reading, tying your shoe shoelaces, brushing your teeth and writing your name. These pathways are like major highways: frequently used, easy to find, strong and efficient.

But what about things we've only done or seen once or twice? These less-travelled neural routes are like small lanes or hidden paths. They might be tucked away and rarely used, but they're still there, ready to be activated when needed.

Imagine a child who, in the right environment, decides to take up a new hobby or becomes fascinated by plants. This curiosity awakens a quiet side street in their brain, beginning the process of turning that little lane into a highway. It's an exciting moment that could be life-changing, but it only arises when children have the freedom to choose their journey. What they practise repeatedly becomes what they excel at and eventually master—possibly shaping their future profession.

*'Choose a job you love and you'll never work a day in your life.'*
*—Anonymous*

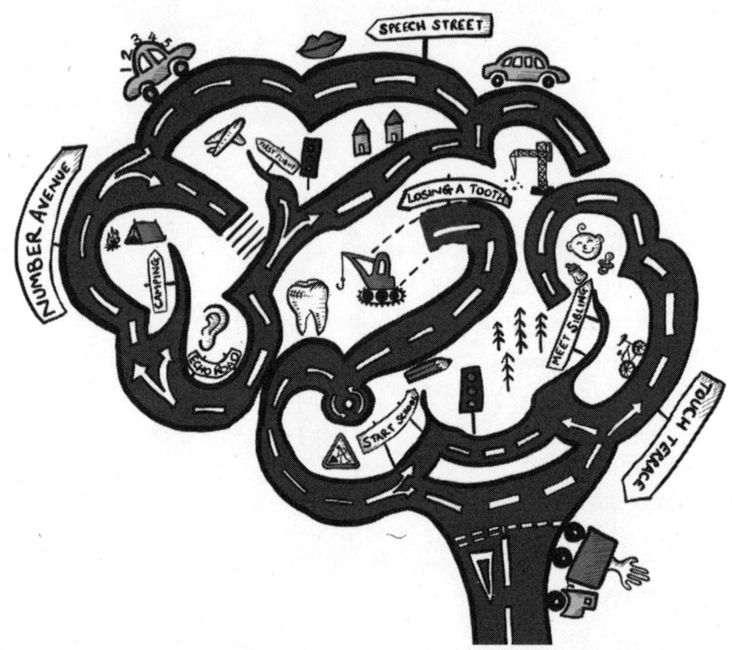


**Figure 15.** The brain map

This saying resonates for a reason. But without the choice to develop new neural pathways and cultivate a love of learning, we risk stifling our children's potential to discover what they want to master, because the skills we develop in childhood can shape who we become and influence the professions we choose—so shouldn't it be the child's choice to decide what they want to learn?

We've talked a lot about choice, freedom, agency and dedication. But how much dedication is necessary before our children achieve mastery?

In *Outliers: The Story of Success* (2008), Malcolm Gladwell writes about the famous '10,000 hours rule'. This is based on research by psychologist Dr K. Anders Ericsson, which suggests it takes 10,000 hours of practice to achieve mastery. However, what often gets lost in translation is that Ericsson's research focuses on *deliberate* practice—practice with the intent of improving, not just clocking hours. It's purposeful effort, rather than mere repetition, that leads to true expertise.

While children may excel when they're given freedom to explore their interests, it's not just endless repetition that will get them there—it's the quality and intent behind their work that propels them forward. Therefore, when a child is free to choose how they express their work with the purpose of following their dreams and the intent of changing the world, they can find their chosen field long before anyone asks them what they want to be when they're older.

Imagine your child loving the creative aspects of visual art, dance or design with no other intention than the enjoyment of the craft, all the while refining a skill that could become their profession. Sounds ideal, right?

## 100 ways to represent your learning

What if we allowed children to design their entire learning experience around what excites them, and let them choose which skills to master? By giving them the freedom to explore their own interests, we have the ability to create an educational environment that sparks strong emotions, enhances memory and deepens their understanding of any subject. They have the choice to express what matters to them through the work they produce. When done right, we'll never need to ask them what they want to be when they grow up—they've already shown us through the work they do.

I can only remember two moments from my primary school days. The first was when a girl in my class was crying because her cat had died. I vividly recall feeling her pain as I watched her sitting in the cloakroom, tears streaming down her face, while the teacher tried to console her. The other memory is of my teacher Mr Bun, who had a very red face and a giant orange moustache. One day, he told us he had a headache and gave us the freedom to do whatever we wanted for the whole day. My friend Sean and I decided to build a full-sized, three-dimensional Ferrari out of cardboard, which we then painted and carried home, pretending to drive it as we did so.

Why do I remember these two moments? Because they were charged with strong emotions—one filled with deep sadness, the other with absolute glee. Now, I ask you to do the same:

*What were the most memorable moments of your primary school experience?*

I suspect they were also tied to strong emotions.

To make learning meaningful, we must redefine what we mean by 'work' when it comes to how children demonstrate their understanding. Too often in classrooms, we dictate how children should express their learning by using predetermined resources. By handing out textbooks, worksheets, rubrics or set tasks, we choose the 'work' for them, ensuring they meet specific benchmarks. While this approach offers structure and consistency, it also limits creativity and individual expression.

Now imagine if, as often as possible, we allowed students to demonstrate their understanding through child-centred methods. Instead of guiding every step, what if we gave them the space to explore creative outlets like dance, art or other media? Just imagine the engagement levels after saying something like this:

*Okay, class, thanks for listening to my introduction on pollination and the importance of bees. You now have 45 minutes to work with whomever you like, using any of the resources in the classroom. You can represent your learning in any way you choose, but at 10 am, we'll meet on the carpet, where you'll showcase your work and teach us something new about pollination and bees. Good luck!*

Believe me, it works, even with adults. Why? Because this approach empowers children to showcase their learning in ways that reflect their unique talents and interests. Our brains focus on new and engaging experiences rather than on what's already familiar. It's like when you drive home each day. Unless something unusual happens along the way, your brain tunes out, shifting its attention elsewhere, and you forget the whole trip.

When we dictate how children should prove their learning, it's like going to a restaurant with only one item on the menu—you know exactly what you're getting, right down to the flavours. It's predictable and, unless something unexpected happens, it won't leave a lasting impression. But what about a restaurant with ten meal options from ten different countries, many of which you've never tasted before. That's 100 new flavours to explore. How exciting! Suddenly, your brain is fully engaged, eager to experience something new and different.

And so, if we want to bring that excitement into our classrooms, our education system needs to offer children choices—a menu of ways they can demonstrate their journey towards mastery. Before long, they'll find something that sparks their enthusiasm for school each day. Perhaps, after a lesson on beetles, a child will be inspired to start a school podcast about amazing insects. Maybe another will design a line of T-shirts featuring snails, with fun facts printed on the back. Or perhaps a group of students will launch a science club where they investigate ancient insects and create engaging videos for the school newsletter.

When they're given the chance to choose, they'll venture into new educational territories, discovering ways to express their learning. **The real magic happens when school becomes more than just a place to acquire knowledge—it becomes a space where kids can explore their passions and catch a glimpse of who they might become in the future.**

The table on the following page highlights some of the many ways children can show us their work. So, next time you're planning a project at home or school, consider offering them this list or one like it.

## The ever-changing brain

Children's brains are in constant motion—absorbing, adapting and growing. The brain isn't a static organ, it's an extraordinary structure capable of reshaping itself with every piece of information and emotion. This continuous process is called neuroplasticity. This allows the brain to constantly evolve, much like a living sculpture, adjusting to every new challenge and opportunity.

This adaptability is what helps children acquire new skills, recover from setbacks and respond to life's twists and turns. It's at its peak during childhood, when the brain is absorbing knowledge at an

| Visual Representations | Performative Methods | Technological Approaches | Written Work | Craft-Based Projects | Group Activities | Interactive and Experiential Learning | Sharing Your Knowledge | Technology Integration | Artistic Expression |
|---|---|---|---|---|---|---|---|---|---|
| Draw a Picture | Act in a Short Play | Record a Podcast | Write a Story | Make a Model | Class Discussion | Go on a Nature Walk | Teach Another Class | Online Quiz | Colouring |
| Make a Poster | Perform a Puppet Show | Write a Blog Post | Keep a Diary | Paper Crafts | Tell a Group Story | Work in the School Garden | Show Younger Children | Digital Photo Album | Painting |
| Create a Comic | Pretend to be Someone | Make a Short Video | Write a Poem | Create a Collage | Interview a Friend | Go on a Treasure Hunt | Make a Video Lesson | Digital Story | Clay Modelling |
| Map a Story | Sing a Song | Show a Presentation | Write a Letter | Make a Mask | Team Quiz | Organise a Field Trip | Create a Teaching Poster | Simple Coding | Dance Performance |
| Photo Collage | Drama Games | Build a Slideshow | Write a Recipe | Finger Puppets | Circle Time | Class Market Day | Give a Demonstration | Educational Games | Music Performance |
| Illustrated Chart | Play Charades | Design a Digital Poster | Book Review | Bead Jewellery | Class Survey | Observe the Weather | Host a Mini-Lesson | Class Blog | Chalk Drawing |
| Mind Map | Tell a Story | Voice Recording | Write Facts | Friendship Bracelets | Story Circle | Science Experiment | Explain Your Work to Parents | Animated Story | Origami |
| Photo Story | Music Performance | Virtual Tour | Write Jokes | Cardboard Creations | Class Debate | Pet Care Day | Share in Assembly | Online Drawing | Puppet Making |
| Picture Book | Perform Magic | Make a Simple Webpage | Riddles | Build a Kite | Roleplay Games | Storytelling Circle | Run a Learning Station | Simple Robotics | Stamping Art |
| Make a Flipbook | Dance Routine | Create a Timeline | Greeting Card | Recycling Project | Group Craft | Make a Mini Museum | Create a Class Display | Tablet Photo Story | Mosaic Art |

**Figure 16.** 100 alternative ways your students can demonstrate their learning

astonishing rate. According to Dr Patricia Kuhl, a leading expert in early language and brain development, by age twelve, children have already absorbed up to 80 per cent of their lifetime learning. Sounds unbelievable, right? But even so, it underscores the critical importance of these early years in shaping future success.

To give you an idea of the brain's incredible capacity, Dr Paul Reber from Northwestern University, Illinois, USA, estimates that the human brain can store around 2.5 petabytes of data—that's like holding 300 years' worth of continuous 4K video! This amazing organ works tirelessly, managing everything from keeping our hearts beating to processing thoughts at lightning speed, all while efficiently organising our memories and experiences.

A study from Queen's University in Canada found that the average person has between 6000 and 7000 thoughts each day. Each thought gives the brain a chance to process new information, which can subtly or significantly shape development. For children who are encountering experiences for the first time, this constant mental activity can be draining. Unlike adults, who've already processed much of what life throws at us, children are in a continuous state of learning and adaptation. This relentless cognitive workload, combined with the brain's storage capacity, shows how extraordinary the human brain is—and why children often feel mentally exhausted by the end of the day and seem able to fall asleep in the most ridiculous of situations.

*'People will forget what you said, people will forget what you did, but people will never forget how you made them feel.'*
*—Maya Angelou*

If we want children to truly learn, we must make them feel the learning experience deeply. The lesson we're about to embark on needs to be a journey filled with emotions and wonder. Ultimately, our goal is to convince the brain that this information we are providing is worth keeping.

When children encounter new information, the brain stores it in the short-term memory while deciding what to do with it. *Is it worth keeping or not?* If they revisit it, engage with it emotionally or

## Synaptic pruning

Even with all its storage, the brain doesn't hang onto everything it encounters. Through a process called synaptic pruning, which mainly happens during sleep, the brain clears out information it deems unnecessary. This process, most active during childhood and adolescence, helps streamline brain function by clearing out weaker neural connections and strengthening those that matter most. It's a bit like an old computer cleaning up disc space and organising the things it wants to keep. If you've ever felt foggy after a bad night's sleep, now you know why—your brain is literally a mess! Synaptic pruning not only optimises the brain's storage but also enhances its processing power, ensuring children wake up refreshed and ready to learn and adapt as the day unfolds.

The brain's primary role is to keep us alive for as long as possible and learning is a crucial part of that. Things the brain considers important—like new skills, emotions and sensory experiences—are stored because they impact how we'll react the next time we face a similar situation. It's why, in Montessori classrooms, we let children drink from glass cups instead of plastic ones. Yes, they might drop it once and cause a big crash, but because of their emotional response to that accident, they'll learn quickly: *when I hold a glass, I need to be careful, or it will shatter.* The brain moves this important lesson into the long-term memory, the hippocampus, making sure it sticks.

connect it to something they already know, the hippocampus—the brain's memory centre—determines it's worth keeping. This process, called consolidation, moves information from the short- to long-term memory, where it can remain for years or a lifetime. The more senses involved in learning (seeing, hearing, touching, etc.), the stronger the memory becomes because the brain creates multiple pathways to that information, making it easier to recall later.

Think of it like the famous Arc de Triomphe in Paris. It's surrounded by a roundabout with twelve lanes and twelve exits, each leading from a different part of the city. No matter where you are in Paris, it's easy to make your way to this famous archway. Essentially, the more pathways to reach the information, the easier it is to retrieve later. And when emotions are involved, that memory becomes deeply ingrained in the brain, never to be erased.

## The seven levels of learning

Imagine we want our children to learn as much as they possibly can about rabbits. To grasp how different learning experiences impact the brain, let's break it down into seven distinct levels of learning. I call this the 'seven levels of learning'.

| Level | Learning activity | Neural response |
|---|---|---|
| **1. Reading words** *Decoding written words* | A child reads a paragraph of text about rabbits. | Engages the visual cortex as the brain processes and decodes text. It's mostly passive, recognising patterns and symbols (words), with limited deeper cognitive processing. |
| **2. Listening and reading** *Combining visual and auditory input* | A child listens to a teacher talk about rabbits then reads some text. | Both visual and auditory cortices are engaged, leading to dual coding. The brain processes information through both channels, strengthening neural connections and enhancing memory retention. |
| **3. Discussing ideas** *Engaging in discussion* | A child reads about rabbits then discusses the information with a classmate or teacher. | Involves the visual, auditory and language centres (Broca's and Wernicke's areas). Activates the prefrontal cortex, enhancing critical thinking, reasoning and retention. |

| Level | Learning activity | Neural response |
|---|---|---|
| **4. Hands-on learning** *Incorporating touch* | A child reads about rabbits, discusses them, then touches a rabbit's fur or holds a real rabbit. | Engages the somatosensory cortex for tactile information. This multi-sensory experience strengthens neural pathways and improves memory formation. |
| **5. Learning by doing** *Active participation* | A child reads about rabbits, discusses them, and participates in feeding or caring for a rabbit. | Engages the motor cortex, responsible for planning and executing movements. Active participation with multi-sensory input reinforces procedural memory and builds interconnected neural networks. |
| **6. Teaching others** *Sharing knowledge* | A child learns about rabbits then teaches others about them. | Activates the prefrontal cortex (for planning and organising thoughts), hippocampus (for memory retrieval) and mirror neurone system (for empathy and understanding). Teaching solidifies learning through retrieval and reframing. |
| **7. Reflecting on learning** *Thinking about the experience* | A child reflects on their learning about rabbits by writing or talking about how it made them feel. | Engages the prefrontal cortex for reflective thinking and metacognition. Reflection consolidates learning by integrating new knowledge with existing mental frameworks, reinforcing neural connections and promoting long-term retention. |

Everything our children see, hear and experience shapes who they are and who they will become. The brain meticulously maps out these experiences, so it's essential to understand not only how children learn, but also the environment in which they learn, the materials they use and the stimuli they encounter. We must be mindful of what we expose our children to, because these experiences will ultimately affect their development.

When learning is made meaningful and emotionally engaging—by offering choice, freedom, agency and (most importantly) opportunities for reflection—the brain retains this information, deepening the connections between learning pathways. One critical element often missing from our lesson plans and curriculum documents is reflective thinking. **Reflective thinking lets children integrate new knowledge with their existing understanding, transforming simple lessons into lasting wisdom.**

It's like the difference between reading that a rabbit's fur is soft and actually feeling the softness with your own hands—one is abstract knowledge, while the other is a physical experience. And while it may not be possible for every subject, the more we can strive to create deeper connections to the learning experience through touch, choice, emotions and reflection, the more enjoyable, consolidated and enduring the learning journey will be.

## The role of failure in learning

Okay, it might seem counterintuitive to suggest we should encourage failure in our schools and homes, but when you consider the science of learning, it makes sense. If we want our children to develop deep, enduring knowledge, we need to foster emotional connections and sensory experiences to their learning experiences. But how can we do this? Well, there's no more powerful emotion than the sting of failure, especially when it's tied to something we care about.

I'm not talking about the failure that occurs during a standardised test when the teacher reads out your grades in front of the whole class or sends you to a special class for children falling behind. I've made my stance on that abundantly clear. I'm referring to the failure that arises when pursuing a passion, dream or personal project. One that ignites a desire for improvement and a determination to succeed.

This type of failure is a catalyst for growth. It forces us to confront our limitations, learn from our mistakes and develop resilience. It's like the first time you take your driving test. You know it's going to be hard, with a person watching and observing your every move, but because you chose this path and you can smell the freedom of the open road, you keep trying until you finally succeed.

## Walt Disney—a failure?

Before Walt Disney created Mickey Mouse and Disneyland, he faced failures that could have easily derailed his dreams. Early in his career, Disney was fired from his job at a newspaper because, astonishingly, his editor believed he 'lacked imagination'. Imagine being told you don't have what it takes to dream big! Many would have given up, changed careers or tried something new, but Disney was different. He didn't let this crush his spirit—he kept pushing forward, believing in his vision.

He set up his first animation company, Laugh-O-Gram Studios. He saw it as a chance to prove himself to the naysayers, but once again, he stumbled. Poor business decisions and a lack of financial management skills led the company into bankruptcy. It seemed like Disney was destined to put his creative spirit on the shelf.

But from these mistakes, he learned valuable lessons. He learned to stick to his guns, follow his passion and never give up on his dreams. These lessons eventually allowed him to create and grow the Disney company into the global powerhouse it is today. If it weren't for him failing initially, lacking the imagination and financial literacy to make it work at first, then maybe there wouldn't be any movies about Snow White, Donald Duck or Aladdin.

Now, wouldn't that be a shame?

## Don't get involved—unless absolutely necessary

When we see a child struggling with something, it's only natural to want to help them succeed. It's hard to resist stepping in—I still struggle with it myself. But the truth is, by helping too much, we're actually hindering their long-term development.

The thing is: for children to refine their skills and transfer those experiences into long-term memories, they need to repeat the activity or form an emotional connection to it. This process, known as synaptic strengthening, turns short-term experiences into lasting knowledge and eventually wisdom. When children experience frustration then push through with perseverance and determination until they finally succeed, that's when what we call 'deep learning' occurs.

You could argue that by helping, we're modelling the activity for them, and that's certainly the first step. But after you've shown them once or twice, it's time to step back. Once the child can attempt the activity independently, we must resist the urge to intervene (unless they're in danger). Instead, sit back and watch as they develop life skills like resilience, problem-solving and independence.

Our children are heading into a fast-paced, dopamine-driven world of instant gratification from likes, tweets and comments. So there's never been a more critical time for children to learn that good things take time and effort. Helping too much will only slow down the process. Letting them struggle, persevere and ultimately triumph on their own is one of the greatest gifts we can give them.

## The soggy Colosseum

When I was a newly qualified Stage 3 Montessori teacher, I found myself in charge of a class of students aged nine to twelve. With a new mindset focused on open-ended projects and child-centred learning, my goal was to try and step back as much as possible.

One young boy was very enthusiastic about my lesson on the ancient Romans. As his follow-up, he decided to continue his learning by building a scale model of the Colosseum using papier-mâché (newspaper, water and glue). Once complete, he planned to use it as a teaching tool for another class to showcase some of the amazing, yet blood-curdling, activities that took place there. I thought it was a brilliant idea.

After completing his research on paper, he approached me for guidance on how to start his one-metre-wide construction. He'd decided to 'go big or go home'. I loved his ambition! I guided him on how to build the skeleton from craft sticks and glue, then cover the scaffold with the papier-mâché mixture. As many of you probably know, papier-mâché requires a pretty accurate mix of glue and water. Too much glue, and the mixture is too heavy; too little glue, and the whole thing flakes away.

His eyes were filled with excitement and he was eager to get started. I urged him to take his time and walked him through the laminated instructions I'd prepared, which I could tell he had no intention of reading. A bit like me when I get something from Ikea—the first thing I do is throw the instructions in the bin, only to end up with twelve screws left over at the end and a wonky wardrobe.

As the class worked away independently, I observed him carefully. Over the following week, he used his free time to create the craft-stick skeleton structure. It was absolutely amazing—a bit like scaffolding on a building. In anticipation of the project being completed in time for the school newsletter, he'd invited the kindergarten class to come up the next day at 11 am to learn about the Romans, and arranged for his friends to take photos. It was all coming together.

And so, it was time for him to cover his scaffold with papier-mâché. As he started mixing the two components, I watched eagerly to see if he would use my laminated card to measure it out. As I had predicted, he didn't even look at it once. Maybe he had memorised it? Who was I kidding? I watched in horror as he poured three jugs of PVA glue into a bowl with only half a cup of water, when the instructions clearly stated equal parts of glue and water.

Oblivious, he stood by his construction, whistling and happily dipping the strips of newspaper into the bucket, carefully layering them all over the wooden frame. Now, I know what you're thinking. Surely, I intervened? And yes, my natural instinct was to rush over and say, 'Hey, have you read the instructions? You've got way too much glue in that bucket. The paper is going to be so heavy it could collapse the entire structure overnight.' But I knew that, if I stepped in, he would (like me) always have a wonky wardrobe from Ikea or listen to people when they gave him advice. So, as I sat with a small group, teaching them about three-dimensional shapes, I watched from afar as he unknowingly set himself up for disaster the next morning.

As the day came to an end and the children cleaned up the room, the boy was eager to show me his model. I congratulated him on his effort. But as our eyes met, there was a look in his eyes and a quiver in his lips. He knew something wasn't quite right. The paper was already starting to drag itself south, like a soggy omelette that had been thrown at a wall.

To ease the uncomfortable silence, I said, 'It's time to go home. Let's leave it to dry, and we can paint it first thing in the morning before your lesson at 11 am.' That seemed to ease his discomfort. He shook my hand, said goodbye and ran off to meet his mum. I turned back to look at his model, where the internal structure was already beginning to buckle.

The next morning, when I arrived at school, he was already at the door, eager to see his creation that he'd worked so hard on. Together, we opened the classroom door. Like a bolt of lightning, he shot into the room to his model. As he approached it, he froze. Overnight, his Colosseum had collapsed into a soggy mess—structure and all. His beloved model of this great monument was now a pile of mush. He stood there, shoulders slumped, staring at the wreckage. Bursting into tears, he said, 'I think I used too much glue.'

I nodded, put my hand on his shoulder and gently asked if he had any idea of what could have happened. His look said it all. He knew where he'd gone wrong. Before we could start to unpack the issue, he dragged the bin over to the table, pushed the structure into the rubbish, wiped his eyes, fetched some more craft sticks and started building it again from scratch. Throughout the day, our eyes met many times, but we didn't say a word. I could see he was determined to fix his mistake, so I left him alone.

This time, he followed the instructions carefully. He postponed his lesson until Friday and worked harder than anyone I'd ever seen in my life to get the model built. When Friday came, the glee on his face as he presented his structure and taught his lesson to the younger children was so infectious, it almost made me cry. The giant, radiant smile on his face is why I remember this story so well.

You see, determination, resilience and grit aren't something we can teach—they have to be cultivated in environments that allow for freedom, experimentation and deep learning. In these environments, failure is inevitable. But when we fail, we learn a lot more than we ever could if everything had been carefully prepared to avoid failure. **The lessons we gain from failure, though challenging and requiring patience, shape us for long-term success.** These moments of struggle become the building blocks for growth and resilience, paving the way to long-lasting achievement.

## Failure builds resilience

When children experience failure, their brain's prefrontal cortex—responsible for decision-making and problem-solving—springs into action as they figure out what went wrong and how to tackle the challenge. This process sharpens their critical thinking skills and builds resilience. Carol Dweck, a renowned psychologist and author of *Mindset: The New Psychology of Success*, explains that 'In a growth mindset, challenges are exciting rather than threatening. So rather than thinking, "Oh, I'm going to reveal my weaknesses," you say, "Wow, here's a chance to grow."'

However, not all children handle failure the same way. Some children develop a deep fear of failure, because they equate their mistakes with a lack of ability or worth. This fear can be rooted in various factors: high expectations from parents or teachers, past negative experiences such as public humiliation or societal pressure, or seeing their abilities as static and unchangeable due to comments like:

*Maths has never been his strong point.*

*She's just not good at sports.*

When children fear failure, they may avoid taking risks, give up too easily or become overly anxious when confronted with challenges. This fear can stifle their growth, keeping them from learning the valuable lessons that come from making mistakes. Our children's lives are going to be littered with hurdles, so they need permission to fail so they can learn how to navigate them. **If we try to shield children from failure out of concern for the sadness or disappointment they may feel, we're actually depriving them of some of the most fundamental skills they'll need in life.** And none of us wants that for our children.

Our brains have a built-in error detection system, primarily through the anterior cingulate cortex (ACC). The ACC kicks in when we make mistakes and signals that we need to make adjustments and this is vital for learning from failure, so we can adapt our behaviour and strategies the next time we encounter a similar situation. Hence the saying: 'We learn from our mistakes'. The hippocampus, where long-term memories are stored, also plays a significant role so we can apply the lessons learned later on.

Moser and colleagues (2011) found that people with a growth mindset (who believe they can improve their abilities) showed more brain activity when they made a mistake and this increased brain activity, especially in the ACC, helps them learn and do better next time.

In simpler terms, when children are in an environment where making mistakes is okay and simply part of the learning journey, they develop resilience and a growth mindset. When they make an error, their brains work harder to learn from it. They start to see failure not as a setback but as an opportunity to learn and improve. This perspective helps them build perseverance to overcome obstacles, leading to deep satisfaction, and more meaningful and lasting success.

## What the hand touches, the brain remembers

In her work, Maria Montessori highlighted the importance of sensory experiences, particularly those involving touch, for intellectual growth. She believed the hands serve as a direct link to the mind, letting children learn by observing and actively engaging with their environment. Her famous quote 'What the hand does, the mind remembers' reflects the deep connection between tactile experiences and cognitive development. This is why, when you walk into any Montessori classroom, you see hundreds of tactile materials that children can engage with any time they choose.

Each of our fingertips is packed with thousands of sensory receptors called mechanoreceptors, which act like little feelers to explore the world around us. Every time we touch something, our fingertips send rich, detailed information to the brain, giving us a deeper, more vivid picture of the world.

When we use multiple senses—like touching, seeing and hearing—our brain builds stronger connections to the knowledge we're taking in. The more senses we engage, the more deeply that learning sticks with us, turning it into something that lasts. Unfortunately, more often than not, the only things children in many schools around the world touch each day are pencils and paper.

As a child I had—and still have today—a strong urge to touch everything. I'll often find myself touching walls in the city to see if they're hot, feeling the materials of clothes that I have no intention of buying in shopping malls, and I dislike certain foods because of how they feel in my mouth. As a primary school student, however, I remember being told to stop touching things and was eventually ordered to sit on my hands in class. My teacher was frustrated with what she called my 'fidgeting', but I couldn't help it. The smoothness of the desk, the texture of my pencil case, the zipper moving back and forth—I was simply exploring the world through touch, like many children do.

Of course, it's important to note that children can't just go around touching everything—they need to understand boundaries, respect personal space and consider other people's belongings. But because our brains are wired to want to understand the world through every sense we have, the more we can let our children touch while they learn, the better. And if Montessori materials and wooden toys seem financially out of reach, don't despair—nature provides all the teaching materials we need right outside our doorsteps, for free.

## The snail lesson

I gauge the success of my lessons by many standards, but one of them is this: if a parent meets me at the door the next day and says, 'Ahmed came home and wouldn't stop talking about [insert the subject I was teaching]', I know I've done something right. The question is, how can we inspire the kind of excitement that compels children to go home and retell it to the whole family without forcing it?

Several years ago, I decided to kick off a ten-week program of teaching on animals and insects by introducing my favourite mollusc—the snail—to my Year 1 class. My goal wasn't just to make the lesson memorable and exciting, but to inspire the children to want to learn more and share what they'd discovered with others.

Now, I could have reeled off a bunch of fascinating facts about snails to spark their interest. Snails are pretty incredible. They have more teeth than any other animal on Earth—about 17,000 microscopic teeth lining their radulae, which they use to scrape food. Their shells are made of calcium carbonate and can support 100 times their own weight, providing excellent protection. Snails can also sleep for up to three years during extreme conditions and snail fossils date back more than 500 million years. Pretty inspiring stuff, I'm sure you'd agree.

But I knew it was going to take more than a few exciting facts. I needed a real snail, some emotion needed to be involved, and the children needed to touch something.

Before the lesson, I placed a snail I'd collected from the garden on a table at the front of the class. This is a living creature, I explained, and we needed to be gentle with it because its snail family was probably waiting for it to come back home. The snail is hiding in its shell at the moment because you've just walked in, talking and chatting after recess. Because snails sense ground vibrations as signals of potential predators, it might take a while for it to feel safe enough to come out again. Keep an eye on it, I encouraged. Your quiet attention and soft voices will help the snail feel less threatened.

Just like that, silence swept the room.

With the snail on a leaf in front of me, I began my lesson. I had visuals, diagrams and a short video, but halfway through my presentation, I noticed every single eye in the class was on the snail, waiting to see if it would emerge. Right on cue, one of its antennae peeked out to an audience of wide-open mouths, all pointing but not talking.

Within a few moments, the snail was out on the leaf on my table, my introduction was over, and the children could ask questions about snails as they decided which aspects of a snail's life they wanted to explore and research for the remainder of the lesson. Before they went off to continue their projects independently in groups, pairs or alone, I informed them that they could come up to the table at any point during the next 45 minutes and gently touch the snail's shell if they wished.

As the children worked on their various projects, I watched with careful trepidation as students approached the table to gently stroke its shell and look at it through a magnifying glass. Each time, the snail retreated inside only to come out again. The excitement in each group was palpable. Children returned to their tables to inform others of how it felt. It was amazing to see how something so simple as a snail could cause such an outburst of excitement and joy. At the end of the day, as the children prepared to go home, I carefully returned the snail to the garden.

The next day, as I welcomed the children to school, the impact of this lesson was clear. Some children came to school with drawings of snails, one child brought his snail teddy bear to keep him company and almost every parent asked me a question about snails. The circle of learning was complete: the children had been so inspired that everyone had relayed the information and experience at home. All thanks to that tiny little mollusc in the garden, and a bit of careful consideration and planning, the knowledge and experience were securely locked away in their hippocampi to be used another day.

In 1949, Maria Montessori famously said, 'The hand is the instrument of the mind'. This idea is supported by Gallace and Spence in their 2014 book, *In Touch with the Future*, where they aptly state:

*The sense of touch can provide crucial sensory information that strengthens the learning experience and facilitates deeper understanding and memory consolidation.*

Tactile learning doesn't need to be complicated. It needs to be meaningful, resourceful and delivered with passion. When we approach teaching in this way, learning is deep and lasting. It's shaped by the emotions children feel as they engage with the lesson—like when they saw the snail emerge or gently touched its shell—and by the knowledge they then share with their parents and each other.

No textbook, video or worksheet could ever replicate the kind of learning that tiny creature brought into our classroom that day.

## Homunculus—the boy with huge hands

When children engage in activities that involve simultaneous touching, reading and listening, their brains begin working on multiple levels. Sensory receptors in their skin, the mechanoreceptors, activate as they touch objects, sending signals to the somatosensory cortex, which processes tactile information. Their visual and auditory cortices are also engaged as they read and listen.

Now, when these different senses are engaged at the same time, neural pathways in the brain strengthen and multiply. The brain is creating connections between these sensory inputs, a bit like the strands of silk in a spider's web.

**The more these neural pathways are activated together, the stronger they become, making it easier for children to recall the information later.** This is why activities that combine touch, reading and listening are so effective in the classroom—they engage the whole brain, leading to what many people refer to as deep or immersive learning.

When parents or teachers ask me about tactile materials or incorporating a multi-sensory approach into teaching, I often turn to the homunculus, or 'the little man' as it's often called, to illustrate why this approach is so important. Created in the 1930s by Canadian neurosurgeon Dr Wilder Penfield and his colleague Edwin Boldrey,

**Figure 17.** The homunculus model

the homunculus reveals that the brain doesn't distribute its resources equally across the body. Instead, it dedicates more space and processing power to the hands, lips and tongue, which are heavily involved in touch, movement and communication.

So by limiting children's use of these parts during learning, we're asking children to learn in ways that don't align with how their brains can process information most effectively. Statements like 'Don't touch', 'Stop talking', 'Be quiet' and 'Stop fidgeting' are really just ways of saying, 'Please don't learn in the way that maximises your potential for retention and understanding.' Our children learn through touch, movement and communication, so any opportunity for learning that restricts these actions is working against the child's natural instincts.

Simply put, if we want our children to learn effectively, we must create learning experiences that not only allow but encourage them to touch, talk and move at every opportunity, actively promoting these as essential aspects of any learning framework.

## How much learning can our brains handle?

The human brain is an incredible machine. With about 86 billion neurones, it's a complicated yet extremely efficient organ. However, even with its amazing processing power, it does have its limitations. These are key to us understanding exactly what role we should play in the process called education. To understand this better, let's talk about something called cognitive load theory, an idea developed in the late 1980s by John Sweller, an educational psychologist from Australia.

The term 'cognitive load' refers to how much information our brains can handle at one time. Think of your brain as a computer. Just like when you have 30 tabs open in three different browsers and your PC suddenly freezes, causing you to see the dreaded message: 'Word has stopped responding', our children's brains can also become overloaded. Whether it's learning a new topic, solving a complex problem, remembering everything they need for their day at school or simply paying attention in class, the brain can only handle so much at once. More importantly, we need to recognise what we can do to prevent the brain from reaching capacity.

As well as the brain's processing power, it's about how we adults present the information to our children. To be as efficient as possible, the brain prefers learning in a certain way; therefore, once we understand how cognitive load theory impacts our children's learning, we can tailor our delivery and expectations to match the brain's processing power, so we don't overwhelm them.

According to Sweller, we need to be aware of three types of cognitive load:

### 1. Intrinsic load (How difficult is the task?)

This refers to the difficulty of the material or task a child is working on. Easy tasks require less cognitive effort than more difficult ones. For example, when a Year 3 child is learning basic addition, the intrinsic load is low because the concepts are simple. But if that same child is suddenly asked to tackle complex algebraic equations, the intrinsic load shoots up because the material is more challenging and demands more brainpower.

## 2. Extraneous load (How is it presented?)

This type is related to how the material is presented to the child. Imagine trying to work at a cluttered desk with phones ringing and people constantly interrupting you—that's what extraneous load feels like in the brain.

If a teacher explains something in a confusing or overly complicated way without clear instructions, the child's brain has to work extra hard to filter out the noise, reorganise the instructions, then try to focus on what's important and what the expectations are. We should always aim to reduce this load. If a child isn't grasping the lesson or utters the phrase 'I don't understand', it's probably because the instructions weren't clear enough.

## 3. Germane load (Connecting the learning)

This is like putting together a puzzle where all the pieces fit to create a full picture. It's the mental effort children use to connect what they've learned and form a complete understanding. For example, when teaching the water cycle, you might first explain how evaporation forms clouds. Next, you introduce how gravity pulls water from the clouds, causing rainfall. Then you talk about how the rain flows into rivers and lakes, eventually reaching the ocean. Finally, you explain how the sun evaporates water from the ocean, completing the cycle. The brain connects these dots, understanding the whole process, thus promoting deeper learning and mastery.

## Designing effective learning experiences

To ensure children have the most effective learning experience at home or school, we should begin by asking ourselves three critical questions:

1. **Is this task designed to build upon the child's existing knowledge while steadily edging them forward?**
   Learning is a journey and every new concept should connect to what children already know, pushing them just enough to grow without overwhelming them.
2. **Are my instructions and expectations communicated clearly and in order of priority?**
   Clear, concise and well-organised instructions help children focus on the task at hand, minimising confusion and maximising their ability to succeed.
3. **Does this lesson allow children to draw connections between different subjects and previous learning experiences?**
   True learning happens when children can see the links between various ideas, letting them integrate knowledge across subjects and deepen their understanding of the world.

When developing new learning journeys or curricula for my students, I always start by considering these three key questions, which remind me that it's not just about *what* children are learning but *how* they're learning it.

When instructions are clear, sequential and organised, the brain can process them more efficiently. By ensuring our lessons are appropriately challenging, well-structured and connected to the children's existing knowledge, we help their brains connect the dots across various subjects and experiences. Once adopted, this approach transforms learning from a mere memorisation task into a journey towards lifelong knowledge and wisdom built on extremely robust foundations.

## The importance of boredom

Several years ago, a teacher came to see me about a little boy who was falling asleep in class and struggling to concentrate. Naturally, I called the boy to my office for a friendly chat. When he arrived, he looked absolutely exhausted—feet dragging on the floor, rubbing his eyes and yawning. My approach is always to have a relaxed conversation rather than direct questioning to get a sense of what's happening in the child's life. I tend to ask the same question: 'What did you get up to last night?' Children love talking about their lives and it's fascinating to get that 'fly on the wall' account of what happens when they leave school. It can tell us so much and usually holds lots of hidden clues about why certain traits are surfacing.

After school, he said, he went to a birthday party for a friend from another school, then had a flute lesson followed by dinner, reading with his father, doing his chores and finally heading to bed. It all sounded pretty hectic to me, especially after a full day of school. I asked him about his plans for that night. Rubbing his eyes again, he rattled off a schedule that included cricket club, a playdate, dinner and so on. He had absolutely no downtime. His weekdays were jam-packed with tennis classes, football matches and breakdance clubs, and his weekends were just as full. Not a single moment was left for him to rest, relax or, more importantly, be bored.

When I was young—and I'm sure many of you had a similar experience—we didn't have many extracurricular activities. For one, we couldn't afford it, but it also wasn't really a thing. Nowadays, it seems that something's on every day of the week. I'm not sure when it all started and, of course, activities like martial arts, horse riding or rock climbing can't be learned in the classroom, but it's equally important that children have opportunities where absolutely nothing is planned.

When I was about eleven years old, my brothers and I all got chickenpox. We were stuck in our room for about ten days, covered in calamine lotion, with our mother telling us not to pick the scabs or we'd be scarred for life. During that time, we were bored out of our minds—no television or radio, just some paper and pens. So, we decided to make our own game. It was a sort of homemade version of Dungeons and Dragons. Being the older brother, I made up some characters, drew them on cards and created another set of cards with magical spells, potions and various scenarios. The game revolved around me telling a story with my brothers flipping over cards to see what spells they could use and how the story would unfold.

It turned out to be one of the most memorable weeks of my life. Not just because we were itchy and covered in lotion, but because we had so much fun. The ten days flew by. We would even wake up in the middle of the night to play. When we got better and our scabs had healed, we started inviting other kids from the neighbourhood to play. Before long, we had fifteen kids in our room playing this fantastic game every day after school.

But here's the thing: if we hadn't been so bored and detached from all the usual forms of entertainment, the game would never have existed. The same goes for children today. If we fill up their classroom schedules too much or enrol them in every after-school club on Earth, they'll never have time to be bored and thus tap into that creative part of their brain. Like the little boy in my office, they end up exhausted and unable to learn.

Boredom often gets a bad rap—it's seen as something to be avoided, a sign that we're not keeping our kids engaged enough. **But boredom is a powerful tool for cognitive development.** When bored, the child's brain has the space it needs to wander, explore and engage in a process known as default mode network (DMN) activity.

The DMN is a network of interacting brain regions that become active when we're not focused on the outside world. It's when the brain starts to daydream, reflect and solve problems. Have you ever been sitting in a café or car and it feels like you've been asleep, but you never closed your eyes? You've just entered the DMN. This mental downtime lets us process our experiences, connect ideas and develop creativity. It's during these moments of nothingness that some of the most profound thinking can happen.

In a study titled 'Does Being Bored Make Us More Creative?', participants were given the monotonous task of copying numbers from a phonebook—a deliberately tedious activity designed to induce boredom. Afterwards, participants were given creative exercises, such as coming up with as many uses as possible for a pair of plastic cups. The researchers found that the participants who had experienced the boredom-inducing task came up with significantly more creative ideas than those who hadn't undergone the same level of boredom. This finding led the researchers to conclude that 'boredom is not necessarily something to be avoided; it can serve as a "mental incubator" for creative ideas' (Mann & Cadman, 2014).

You see, the brain isn't idle when we're bored. It's busy making connections and strengthening neural pathways, laying the groundwork for creativity, problem-solving and critical thinking. This is where we start to join the dots (or 'germane load' in cognitive load theory). When a child isn't actively engaged with external stimuli, their brain has the opportunity to reflect, process and integrate information in a way that fosters deeper understanding.

A study by Mason et al. (2007), titled 'Wandering Minds', explored the role of the DMN in cognitive functioning. The researchers used MRI scanners to observe what happens during moments of absolute boredom. They found that the DMN becomes highly active, leading them to conclude that 'the DMN appears to play a vital role in the incubation of ideas, allowing individuals to connect disparate thoughts and form novel solutions.'

However, we often fall into the trap of thinking that if our children aren't busy or continuously on task, then we're somehow failing them. But we couldn't be more wrong. Filling every moment with structured activities or constant entertainment can rob our children of the opportunity to engage in essential brain work. By leaving space in their classroom schedules and evenings—what I like to call 'the educational void'—we give their brain the chance to exercise the DMN. Without these moments of downtime, children may miss out on developing critical thinking skills, learning to entertain themselves, or having the mental space to let their minds wander and explore new ideas.

When our children drift away into their minds, we allow for those 'ah-ha' moments or lightbulb ideas to emerge. And it's during these moments that they conjure up amazing ideas. Then, when they seem to awaken and return to the real world, they have the choice of whether to turn those daydreams into reality or not.

Today, it seems parents face a certain level of societal pressure to enrol their children in as many after-school clubs as possible and for every moment of the classroom timetable to be filled with teaching and learning. But when we actively include the educational void as part of our weekly or daily timetable, we're supporting our children's long-term cognitive and emotional development. **It's not just okay for our children to be bored—it's absolutely essential for their growth.**

## It's okay to say 'I don't know'

I was lucky to travel to Antarctica in 2023 with the famous Australian astrophysicist and TV and radio star, Dr Karl Kruszelnicki. We were there to film a course for Upschool on the solar system and beyond, and Dr Karl was the perfect person for the job. First, he's an encyclopaedia of knowledge on all things science, especially the solar system. Second, he has a wonderful personality that I knew children would connect with. And third, Dr Karl isn't afraid to say, 'I don't know.'

As a Montessori teacher, I see immense value in those three words. They might just be some of the most important words in our vocabulary as adults. When we say 'I don't know' to our children, a few things happen. First, they realise it's okay to not know everything. They see us as human, not oracles with the world's knowledge stored between our ears. Second, it opens the door for them to explore, research and maybe even teach us something, which builds trust, responsibility and a lovely balance between child and adult.

It's not our job to know everything—it's also impossible. Just thinking about the sheer amount of information out there is mind-boggling. According to a blog written in 2010 by Google Books software engineer Leonid Taycher, about 130 million books have been published since the beginning of time. Add in all the wars, civilisations and every organism that has ever lived, and there's no way we can even know one per cent of it. Yet, when children ask us something we don't know, we sometimes feel the need to make up an answer or give a half-baked one.

So, what should we do in this situation? Well, if you want to avoid giving your children wrong information and help them develop skills like research, independence and confidence, take the Dr Karl approach. Just say:

*I don't know, but I'd love to find out.*
*Maybe you can teach me?*

When we make up answers to questions we're unsure about, we risk causing problems later on. If incorrect information enters a child's brain and isn't corrected, they can store it as a long-term memory. The brain tends to hold on to information that's repeated or reinforced, and research shows that this could lead to something called the 'continued influence effect', where even after information is corrected, its impact can still persist in our thinking.

Studies by Wilkes and Leatherbarrow (1988) show that, even when false information is retracted, people still rely on the original information to make decisions. This happens because our brains form mental models, and when we hear something new, especially if it fills in a gap in our understanding, it sticks with us. When that information is later retracted or corrected, our brain struggles to let go of it.

The continued influence effect is closely related to the difficulties our brain has in managing negation and forgetting. Research by Groves (2016) and others suggests that when we negate or try to forget something, the brain must work harder to process the negation because it first has to imagine the scenario before reversing it. This can lead to confusion when recalling the memory later. In other words, the brain holds on to the original information, making it difficult to fully erase or overwrite it with the correct version.

For example, if you told your child that spiders spin webs because they love art and symmetry, they might share that story with friends or family, unknowingly reinforcing the false information. Later, in a science class, when they learn that spiders actually build webs to catch prey, they will first feel embarrassed for having shared the incorrect information, but later, when asked about webs and spiders, the original idea of spiders loving art can interfere with retrieving the correct explanation.

I experienced this firsthand. When I was in Year 5, someone told me eggs were unborn chickens and it was disgusting to eat them. From that moment onwards, I avoided eggs, convinced they were baby chicks. Even after I learned the truth at age fourteen, I still cringed whenever someone offered me eggs. To this day, at 46 years old, I pause before eating an egg, remembering that old, false belief—despite knowing it isn't true.

This is why advertisers and media outlets repeat the same misleading messages over and over. Even when we discover the truth, the original false narrative can still influence our decisions. This is because the brain's memory system is designed to recall familiar information, and the more something is repeated, the more 'true' it feels—even if it's wrong.

So, next time a child asks you a question and you don't know the answer, resist the urge to make something up. Instead, say, 'I don't know, but I'd love to find out. Can you help me with that?' You'll not only avoid spreading incorrect information but also spark curiosity and give the child the chance to learn and teach. That way, both of you end up with the right answer, and you avoid having false ideas lodged in their memory, potentially messing with future decisions and critical thinking.

## Putting it all together—the ideal learning scenario

When I decided to include a neuroscience chapter in this book, I must admit I was a little scared. What if the methods I'm promoting go against what the human brain wants? What if I get it all wrong? But we need to ask ourselves: are we guiding them in the best possible way?

Well, the answer is nuanced. Classrooms worldwide are home to about 1.5 billion children, each with unique brains—some touched by trauma, others neurodiverse and all wired slightly differently. There is no 'one size fits all'. By understanding how the average brain is wired to learn, we can craft learning environments, curricula and expectations that help our children foster profound, lifelong understanding.

## 1. The responsibility for this transformation lies with us.

If a child doesn't grasp a concept, it's our responsibility to adjust our approach. If they're confused, we need to clarify and adapt. Our children's brains are designed to filter and retain what they find meaningful for their futures, while discarding the irrelevant. Our task is to weave relevance into every lesson, connecting what we teach to their lives and world in a meaningful way. When we build upon what a child already knows and gently guide them towards new horizons, we honour the brain's natural learning process. Engaging the senses—sight, sound, touch—enriches this process, embedding the learning more deeply. And having emotional resonance ensures this learning endures, making it part of who they are.

## 2. Don't spoon-feed children with knowledge—that's not our role.

A good teacher knows when to teach, but a great teacher knows when to step back, allowing the child to explore, take risks and discover. In these moments of freedom, learning becomes deeply personal and the risks they take make it emotional and meaningful. Our role is to create learning environments rich with opportunities for choice and agency, where children feel empowered to chart their own course.

## 3. Ensure lessons are not just informative, but transformative.

The human brain allocates space only to what it deems valuable. Our duty is to ensure that the lessons we deliver aren't just informative but transformative—stimulating, meaningful and open to the unique interpretations of each child. In doing so, we lay the groundwork for lifelong learning, where they can think critically, feel deeply and engage fully with the world.

## 4. Create a convergence of emotions, choices and personal connections.

The ideal learning scenario transcends mere content delivery; it's about creating an experience where emotions, choice and personal connections converge. This is how we cultivate not just learners but thinkers and doers—individuals equipped to navigate the complexities of life, driven by curiosity, resilience and a deep-seated love of learning.

*

Now we can begin to grasp what a well-rounded education system should look like, what it must deliver, the standards it sets for both the preparation of teaching and learning, and the expectations placed upon the children who partake in it.

Our brains have been evolving for more than 2.5 million years, constantly adapting and refining how we learn. It has a natural rhythm and preference for how it absorbs and processes information. The question is:

*Do we, as adults, fully comprehend and honour these evolutionary instincts in our teaching methods?*

*Are we aligning our educational practices with how the brain is naturally inclined to learn?*

Stories have stood the test of time as powerful forces for learning because they resonate deeply—they connect the known with the unknown and have the ability to evoke deep emotions.

As you may have noticed, I've woven heartfelt stories throughout this book—stories that I hope make you smile or perhaps shed a tear of joy. Why have I done this? Because if I can evoke an emotional response as you read these words and turn these pages, then perhaps tonight your brain will move this information into your hippocampus for long-term use. Maybe you'll take what you've read here and apply it in your classroom or home. I'm tapping into how most brains like to learn—through stories, emotions and personal connections—and hopefully it's working.

We've barely scratched the surface of what the brain is capable of—its capacity for learning is extraordinary. From synaptic pruning to the DMN, our understanding of how children's brains learn is continuously evolving. But by aligning our classrooms, curricula and expectations with the brain's processes—through choice, sensory engagement, emotional connection and reflection—children might have the opportunity to dive into deep learning**. A child's journey towards mastery isn't about perfection but about finding out who they are by fostering creativity and embracing the freedom to fail.**

We owe it to the next generation to create an education system that respects and nurtures their cognitive, emotional and physical development. When we do, we set the stage for a future full of curious, resilient and lifelong learners.

For me, it's more than a goal: it's our duty.

# Step 5

# Learning with purpose—making learning real

In the previous chapter, we explored how making learning real—by evoking an emotional response—helps children hold on to it. For me, there's no better way to achieve this than by connecting what we teach in the classroom and at home to what's happening in society. The more we act as a bridge between education and the real world, the more impactful the learning becomes for everyone involved.

From the start of my teaching career, I've believed that education should help children engage with the world in meaningful ways. Partly because I wanted school to be something children could enjoy rather than endure, and also because I wanted to guide children towards becoming a force for good in the world. For anyone reading this, I'm sure we can all recall moments in our own educational journeys, whether at home or in school, when the learning felt real and resonated with us.

Back in my high school years, my friends and I wanted to play football in the sports hall after hours. Our sports teacher told us we could use it after school for an hour—but only if we agreed to teach the younger children how to play during lunchtime once a week. As future England players (or so we thought), we were ready to do anything to follow our dreams, so we agreed. In an interesting twist, we ended up enjoying teaching the younger children more than playing ourselves.

We even started running our own mini junior team, refereeing games in our spare time.

Moments like these made me realise how easily teachers can link almost any school-based activity to the real world, transforming almost any lesson into powerful learning experiences that teach valuable skills and can reshape our lives in profound ways.

## Learning from the heart

They say 'good' teachers teach from the heart, but children should learn from the heart, too. Children are a powerful force, and their collective voice and energy is something we can't ignore. They are the leaders and changemakers of tomorrow, responsible for the climate, the forests and the future of humanity.

Education is more than filling their minds with knowledge; it helps them realise the incredible power they already have—a power we often underestimate. Our role isn't to control or suppress that power but to guide it, helping them see how they can use it to impact the world around them positively. That same unstoppable drive, when nurtured and given purpose, can become a force for good—children are capable of transforming the world from the ground up.

*'Moral virtue comes about as a result of habit and practice.'*
*—Aristotle*

To me, education should be a continuous process of cultivating good habits and values that are intertwined with meaningful activities that work towards shaping a better world—it can't just be about passing exams or being top of the class. To truly instil habits of goodness into the core of our children's characters, the learning journey has to matter deeply to them. They need to feel personally connected to what they're doing and see the impact of their efforts. We know that when learning evokes emotions, deeper understanding takes place. So, the question is:

*How do we get our children emotionally invested in activities at home and school so these habits of virtue become a part of who our children eventually become?*

## The Evergreen Editorial

In 2017, I was working at a small school on the outskirts of Sydney. The children had the opportunity to work on what the school called 'passion projects'—tasks they could choose to complete in their own time once they'd finished their other work. One Year 6 girl came to me and a colleague for help with her idea. She wanted to write and publish her own newspaper and sell it to parents to raise money for charity. As soon as she started talking, I could tell this was going to be something I would remember forever. Once she'd finished her pitch, I was gobsmacked—her plan was even better than I imagined.

The next day, she started by putting up posters around the school, inviting other children to apply for jobs as journalists for her newspaper, which she'd named *The Evergreen Editorial*. 'Journalists Required' read the headline! The posters included the newspaper's logo, which she had designed with a friend of hers, and they were everywhere—even in the toilets. She'd painted a big red post-box for the school's reception area, asking children to submit written applications if they were interested in applying for a job. Seven positions were available: head of sport, travel, current affairs, local news, international news and designer, and the girl herself would be the editor-in-chief. The post-box was soon overflowing with applications. Children from kindergarten to Year 6 were all applying for roles; the entire school was now writing with purpose.

The girl read through the letters and set up interviews in the playground, complete with a table and a schedule for those who were shortlisted. She thoughtfully apologised to applicants who didn't make the cut, letting them know they might have another chance as the newspaper grew. During the interviews, I overheard her asking a boy in Year 6: 'So, you've applied for the travel reporter job—what experience do you have?' He replied that his father owned a travel agency and he'd been to many places.

I know what you're thinking: *Who is this girl?* She got the whole school writing, using persuasive language, speaking and listening with not a teacher in sight. Well, that's the power of determination when children are on a mission. The interviews continued all day. Once all the jobs were filled, she gave the journalists deadlines and clear guidelines on how much they should write, the kinds of images they should provide, and off they went to gather their news. Her designer (a ten-year-old girl) pulled everything together into a template, added the logo and *The Evergreen Editorial* was ready to go—or so I thought.

When the editor-in-chief showed me the newspaper, it looked amazing—almost like a real newspaper but on A4 paper. However, there was a problem: that morning, she'd planned to print 200 copies of the newspaper, in full colour, using the school photocopier! My colleague quickly explained that doing so wouldn't be environmentally friendly, so the girls departed for the day, feeling rather disheartened.

The next morning, the girls arrived clutching their newspaper while directing our attention to an empty section on the back page. Curious, I asked them about it. In response, the editor asked if she could use the school phone. Her plan was to call a local printer who only used recycled materials and offer them advertising space on the back page in exchange for printing the newspaper for free. I'm not sure where this idea came from, but it was pure genius!

I gave the printer a heads-up that she was about to call, then watched in awe as she confidently dialled the number and made the deal. The printer agreed and we sent them the files. A week later, 1000 copies of *The Evergreen Editorial* arrived at the school, printed in full colour with the company's ad on the back.

On the day of the newspaper's launch, she sold every single copy to parents in the community, raising thousands of dollars for a local food bank. The food bank, in turn, contacted the local community newspaper, where the girl was featured on the front cover, holding her giant cheque with a smile of pride as big as the Sydney Harbour Bridge.

Initially, the girl's goal was to create a newspaper because she wanted to become a journalist, but this project became so much more. It inspired the entire school to write with purpose. It showed her peers what's possible when you follow your passions and made the world just a little bit better—all because one girl had the freedom to think, the confidence to choose and the time to work on something that truly mattered to her.

Much of what we do today to promote this kind of learning is influenced by one of my heroes, John Dewey. In his 1938 theory of experiential learning, Dewey emphasised that children learn best through hands-on experiences and active participation. He believed education should be deeply connected to real-world experiences, stating:

> *Education is not preparation for life; education is life itself.*

Learning shouldn't just be about memorising facts for exams, but about engaging with the world in ways that spark curiosity and a desire for continuous learning.

Dewey also argued, 'the most important attitude that can be formed is that of the desire to go on learning', reinforcing the idea that, when children are emotionally and actively involved in their learning, they become more motivated and invested. They not only retain information but also develop a genuine passion for learning that extends far beyond the classroom.

Teachers may ask: 'Where is the time to fit in these passion projects?' The secret lies in trusting teachers to make cross-curricular links between topics and cover several areas in a single lesson. Instead of viewing subjects as separate entities, teachers can weave them together, turning a history lesson into an opportunity for writing, maths or science. Passion projects don't need to be an add-on, they can be integrated into the existing curriculum. Many teachers want this freedom, but the system forces them into a corner, where ticking the curriculum checklist becomes the priority over inspiring deep learning.

When children are inspired by a topic, they naturally want to explore it further, and this is where 'passion projects' step in. These self-directed projects are where real, lasting learning happens as children take what they've learned and apply it in meaningful, creative ways. Teachers long to nurture this, and with the right trust and flexibility, they can.

But for this to work, we need to encourage teachers to make lessons real and meaningful. By allowing teachers to bring their own perspective into the lessons they teach, they can link real-world experiences to the topics they're covering. This empowers teachers to connect their students' learning with the world outside the classroom, ensuring lessons aren't just relevant, but engaging. When teachers are trusted to interpret the curriculum in a way that reflects their unique style of teaching and understanding of how their students learn best, their learning becomes more dynamic and impactful.

## Why are we learning this?

Much of what's in our curricula is outdated and the children know it. We know it, too, yet we still teach it. Why? Because it's on the end-of-term exam and if you don't know it, you can't answer the questions and your life will fall apart, leaving you with nothing. Obviously, that's not true—but many of us carry this fear, which we must work to dispel. First, because our children pick up on our anxiety around scores and rankings, and they end up feeling that pressure, too. And second, it simply isn't true.

Many of the world's most successful and influential people struggled in traditional education systems, yet they went on to achieve incredible things:

- **Albert Einstein** struggled in school and was even considered 'slow' by some of his teachers.

- **Oprah Winfrey** grew up in poverty and faced numerous hardships throughout her childhood, including being told she was 'too emotional' for television. She went on to become one of the most influential media figures in history.
- **Malala Yousafzai** was denied an education simply for being a girl. After surviving an attack for standing up for her right to learn, she became the youngest ever Nobel Prize laureate and a global voice for education.
- **Steve Jobs** dropped out of college after just one semester because he felt disconnected from the rigid structure of formal education.

And the list goes on.

It almost seems laughable—how could such incredible talent go unrecognised? But our system isn't designed to spot each child's unique genius. It's designed to churn out students who can all pass the same mediocre, non-specific, mundane test. For many children, education doesn't feel real at all; it's just something you endure until you're old enough to enter the 'real world'. But it doesn't have to be that way.

You see, making learning feel real is one thing, but making it relevant is even harder. Some topics we teach have absolutely no use in the real world and unless you're going into a niche, specific field, you'll never use them again. I remember a child asking me during a lesson on long division:

*Why is it important for me to learn this method?*

Having no real answer, I made up something on the spot about winning the lottery, not having a calculator and needing to divide the winnings among your family members. The child looked at me like, 'You've got no idea,' and he was right. Despite learning these things myself, I've never used them. So why was I teaching long division, Roman numerals or adding fractions with different denominators? They have almost no relevance or practical application in today's world.

After having many of these conversations with children, I've realised that certain subjects in our curriculum have no real-world use. Sure, you develop skills through learning things like long division—understanding place value, working with decimals, multiplication facts—but the method itself? It's highly unlikely you'll ever use it again. So, we need to ask ourselves: for these outdated yet mandated topics, how can we make learning feel as real as possible? How can we ignite the passion and investment that Dewey and so many others talk about?

The truth is, our curricula are long overdue for a refresh. I'm not suggesting we toss things out of the classroom altogether, but we need to understand why we're teaching them. We should be asking:

*Does this still matter?*

The one thing we can rely on in education is change, yet the world seems to evolve much faster than our curricula do. With the rise of mental health concerns in young people and the ever-growing influence of fake news and social media, wouldn't it make more sense to replace long division with media literacy, or swap Roman numerals for lessons on wellbeing and mindfulness? These skills and tools will serve children in the world they're growing up in.

As educators, parents or policymakers, we need the foresight to equip children for the future, rather than reacting so slowly that new ideas are already outdated by the time they're introduced. We must question what's truly relevant. If a topic doesn't have a clear real-world application, we need to either find that link or teach something else that will genuinely benefit children and the world they will inherit. If we can't make it relevant, we shouldn't be teaching it—because children will see through it and the opportunity for meaningful learning is lost.

## Using knowledge to make a difference

As teachers or parents, our children often present their work to us for our thoughts. 'Do you like my work?' they might ask. And while it's easy to say, 'Yes, wow, it's brilliant,' this response can mean children end up doing the work to please us, seeking our approval and validation for their efforts.

A simple way to bring a sense of purpose into the work our children do is to shift from congratulating or praising them to asking:

*What will you do with it to make the world a better place?*

At first, you'll see their minds begin to wander as they imagine all the possibilities for applying what they've learned, but eventually it becomes the prerequisite for starting any task. Asking this question helps close the circle of learning, giving their work real meaning and purpose.

**Figure 18**. What will you do with it?

Most of the work children produce ends up in textbooks or workbooks, on classroom walls, in a box under the stairs, or pinned onto the fridge at home. And while that's all fine, we're missing a huge opportunity for children to use their work to make a real impact. Instead of letting it sit on a shelf gathering dust with a big red tick and a 'Well done, Stephanie' next to it, we should be asking:

*What would you like to do with your work?*

*Is there someone out there who could benefit from what you're about to create?*

Of course, not all the work our children do needs to be for others—that would be impossible. I mean, how can adding fractions be used to make the world better? Well, I'm sure we could think of a few ways, but the goal is to shift our focus. We want to help children see school and education as more than just a process they go through. We want to create classrooms and homes where the focus is on the value they can bring to the world through their work.

*'Knowledge, if it does not determine action, is dead to us.'*
*—Plotinus, Greek philosopher from the third century*

Plotinus believed that knowledge must lead to action—it should transform the way we engage with the world. This is especially powerful when thinking about education. Knowledge is only valuable when it's applied and used to make a difference.

Our biggest mistake is that we often measure success by the future jobs and money that come from the grades children earn—the opportunities they'll have or the people they'll work alongside. But what if we shifted the focus? What if children saw school as a place where they can use their work to make the world a better place, not just for themselves but for others? In my opinion, when we make that shift, the skills that lead to future opportunities (like good jobs and financial success) become by-products of the bigger mission—adding value and making a difference.

This is the kind of mindset we want to instil in our children: that their work, no matter how small it may seem, has the potential to make a difference. When children see their work in this light, education becomes more than just a stepping stone to a future job—it's a journey filled with purpose, impact and a genuine connection to the world.

When children have a sense of purpose, they become more engaged, creative and resilient. Challenges become opportunities

## Focusing on impact, not profit

When you work for the greater good, the world often works for you. Just ask Yvon Chouinard, the founder of Patagonia. He made headlines by giving away his entire company—not to his family or shareholders, but to help combat climate change. His decision wasn't about amassing personal wealth or leaving a financial legacy. It was driven by a deep desire to make a real, lasting impact on the planet.

After Yvon transferred ownership of the company to a trust and non-profit organisation, all future profits—estimated to be about $100 million a year—will be used to tackle environmental crises.

This decision sent shockwaves around the world. Yvon didn't just talk about making a difference; he acted on it, and his story resonated deeply with people everywhere. Patagonia's brand, already a symbol of ethical business, became even more popular, with more people drawn to its mission. It's a perfect example of how working for the greater good not only benefits the world but can lead to unexpected success. When you focus on impact rather than profit, the rewards—both tangible and intangible—can be far greater than you ever imagined.

rather than things to shy away from. Learning isn't just about getting good grades or securing a future job, it's about using what they learn to contribute in meaningful ways. Children get to develop their intellect, empathy, compassion and sense of responsibility. And those are precisely the qualities we need in the leaders and changemakers of tomorrow—individuals who can build a better world while also achieving personal success.

When we ask children, 'What are you going to do with your new knowledge?', we encourage them to think differently about their work. Suddenly, their learning isn't just for the sake of passing tests, it's for making an impact. They realise that, for their work to matter, it needs to meet a certain standard. It's no longer just about pleasing the teacher, it's about achieving something real.

**The moment when a child sees the impact they've made is incredibly powerful.** It becomes a source of motivation far stronger than any external reward. They become proud, not just of what they've done, but of who they are becoming. It fuels a cycle of growth where they strive to improve, do better and keep making a difference. This is how we nurture lifelong learners—children who are passionate about learning because they see its value beyond the classroom walls. Learning has a new purpose.

The greatest reward for our children is in the transformation of their character, minds and hearts. Learning is less about the reward they get than who they become. The next time a child shows you their project or their writing and asks for your opinion, instead of saying, 'I love your work', try saying, 'I love who you are becoming.'

## Learning with purpose

The issue with making learning real is that our children dream big—they want to go all out. For us, that can seem a little scary. We don't want them to fail. We're afraid they'll be upset, or maybe we'll feel embarrassed by their failure. And we overlook that failure is one of the best ways to learn. Because of these fears, we aim for the low-hanging fruit—something we know will lead to success for the children. But if we're going to make learning real, we should go big and share the success—or failure—together.

In every curriculum globally, under literacy outcomes, you'll find something like: 'The children will learn to write persuasive letters.' To write a persuasive letter, children need many skills— they need to know how to structure a sentence, use emotive language, organise paragraphs, spell correctly and use powerful vocabulary. So we teach these skills and then, to avoid failure while making the learning seem real, we ask them to write to the school principal asking for things like more recess, chocolate in the canteen or banning school uniforms. The children get excited because they think their efforts might actually change something—imagine ten more minutes on the playground or chocolate in the canteen!

In my early days as a teacher, I did exactly this. The children were enthusiastic and poured their hearts into those letters. They believed they could make a difference—change something about their daily lives. But then, reality hit. The principal, understandably, was too busy to read through them all and the changes they asked for didn't happen. The children were left wondering, 'What's the point? I put in all that effort and nothing changed. They didn't even read it.'

That experience taught me a hard but valuable lesson: by setting up this failure, I'd accidentally reduced their hope they could influence the world. It wasn't fair to them. I realised that if I wanted them to write with purpose, it had to be for something real—something where they could see a result, even if it was small. And if they failed? Well, at least we'd fail trying something meaningful, and they'd learn something valuable from the journey.

Now, imagine that same letter-writing lesson, but this time, the children choose a UN SDG that matters to them—maybe it's 'Quality Education' or 'Reduced Inequalities'. What if we asked them to write to anyone in the world who could help make the changes they'd like to see happen? It could be the prime minister, the local mayor, the head of a local business or even the president of the European Union. And what if we joined them in their mission by writing our own letters? Our joint objective: to be heard, get a response and seek help from those in power.

Why? Because when we empower them to go big then walk alongside them, they see that we're in the same situation as they are. Even though we're adults, making big changes is still hard and it's not without setbacks or failures. Maybe none of us will get a response—what will we do then? We'll reflect, we'll learn and we'll try again. And if we do get a response, even better, because that's when real learning takes place.

By taking these steps together, we give children something powerful—hope. We show them that if they have a pen and paper, anything is possible. Everyone is accessible and every problem, no matter how big, can be tackled if enough people care and work together to solve it. Writing is no longer just an exercise in language skills, it's a tool for change.

And now imagine the impact when the child receives a reply. It doesn't even have to be a promise of change—just the acknowledgement that their voice was heard is enough to light a spark. This kind of experience plants a seed that grows into a belief that they have the power to make things happen, no matter how small. This is what real, purpose-driven learning looks like—taking a skill and using it in a way that feels meaningful. We're not only teaching them to be good students, we're teaching them to be active, engaged citizens who understand they have a voice and their voice matters.

**Figure 19.** Persuasive letters with a purpose

## Each one teach one

As part of my work with Upschool, I've started running a good news channel on YouTube, where children from around the world submit good news from their community and I help them share it with the world. I dress up as a news presenter, wear fake glasses and a blazer, and cut the clips together to create a heartwarming show where only good news is aired. It's been one of the most humbling experiences of my life.

During the filming of Episode 2, I received an incredible story from Manav Rachna School in Delhi. As part of the school's project-based learning initiative, the older children decided to create their own after-school classes, inviting the cleaners, chefs and gardeners to attend English lessons they taught themselves.

The initiative, which the students coined 'Each One Teach One', involved the children passing on the knowledge they'd just gained in class, designing English lessons for adults (the school's cleaners, chefs and gardeners) and teaching them in small, bespoke classrooms once the regular school day was over. As they shared how much the initiative had impacted their lives, the adults were almost in tears. One man said he could now read the newspaper and keep up with current affairs, all thanks to the children. For the children who started this initiative, this experience will stay with them for a long time and will help them develop a whole plethora of life skills.

The term 'project-based learning' has become common in education after John W. Thomas, an educational researcher, published research in 2000 highlighting the profound impact of hands-on, meaningful tasks on student motivation and knowledge retention. When students are engaged in real-world, practical projects, he found they can connect what they're learning to their own experiences, making education more engaging and deeply relevant. As Thomas puts it:

> *Students working on projects have a deeper understanding of content and demonstrate increased motivation to learn.*

Thomas's research revealed that giving students more control over their learning and involving them in projects that genuinely mattered improved their motivation, long-term knowledge retention and problem-solving skills.

This research underscores that when we give our children real reasons to learn, their engagement deepens. When their work has a positive impact on others—whether it's teaching adults how to read or sharing good news online—children see the power of their knowledge firsthand. They understand that learning isn't just about passing tests or getting good grades, it's about making a difference. By nurturing this understanding, we raise children who are not only academically capable but also empathetic and proactive global citizens. Education becomes a mechanism for positive global change and I'm sure I speak for many of us in the education sector when I say this is why we enter the teaching profession in the first place.

## The power of 'big work'

I'm sure you'll agree when I say that the phrase 'project-based learning' can sound quite vague. It might seem like children are doing random projects on any subject they wish. But of course, it's far more complex than that. To me, no one understands this better than Montessori educators, who call it 'Big Work'.

Big Work refers to giving children the chance to engage in meaningful, complex tasks or projects that spark their interest, allowing them to dive deeply into their learning. The beauty of Big Work is its flexibility. The children have the autonomy to decide what their project will be, how they'll approach it and how long it will take to complete. There's no limit to the project's time or scope, which is why this kind of work lets them go far beyond the traditional boundaries of classroom learning.

*'The greatest sign of success for a teacher is to be able to say, "The children are now working as if I did not exist."'*
*—Dr Maria Montessori*

Big Work encapsulates this philosophy—children are so engaged and absorbed in their work, they don't need constant supervision or direction. Instead, they take the reins of their learning, driven by their own curiosity and passion.

In practice, Big Work could be anything from building a model of an ancient civilisation, writing and illustrating a book, designing a community project, or conducting a scientific experiment. What's important is that the work is meaningful to the child, taps into their intrinsic motivation and provides an avenue for deep, sustained engagement.

Now, some teachers might be thinking, 'This sounds wonderful in theory, but how can I fit this into an already packed curriculum?' So, let's explore how you can adopt it in your classrooms.

Imagine a child in your class becomes fascinated by a lesson on ancient Greece. They dive deep into researching the Greek gods and become obsessed. As an observing adult, you notice the spark in their eyes and begin cultivating this curiosity, nurturing it like seeds of inquiry. Their passion drives them to take their learning further. After careful consideration, they decide to create a booklet detailing every Greek god—from Apollo to Zeus—with full-page illustrations and descriptions of their powers.

But what comes next? When children engage in Big Work, the key is to let the child decide how it looks and how it comes together. Our role is to guide, not direct. And don't forget to ask them, 'What are you going to do with your work to make the world a better place?' This powerful question prompts them to think about the impact of their efforts. Because this thing they're about to create is meant to make the world better, it's important to see it through to completion.

From this point on, there's no need for homework, extension activities or extra work for 'fast finishers'. In every single moment of free time from now until the Big Work is complete, the child will always have something to do—something they're intrinsically motivated to work on. And when one child is deeply engaged in their passion project, the enthusiasm is contagious—it motivates their classmates to take on similar projects.

When you have 30 children in a classroom, all working on individual passion projects, there's an eruption of activity, all driven by choice and the collective desire to make the world a better place. Now, fast forward a few months. Each child has several passion projects they're working on—some individually, some in pairs or groups—all progressing at different paces and driven by unique motivations. The classroom has now become much more like the real world, filled with purposeful work and collaboration.

The beauty of this approach is that mainstream subjects are still being taught through direct instruction, but they now serve a different purpose. These foundational skills feed directly into the children's Big Work. Whether it's learning maths to solve a problem in their project or honing their writing skills to communicate their ideas effectively, everything they learn contributes to their ultimate mission.

## Implementing 'Big Work Week'

As I've toured the world training teachers on these activities, some teachers have been hesitant to implement this approach in their classrooms. Often, they fear that too many things happening at once will make the environment feel chaotic or unmanageable. So if you're a teacher who feels this way, but is still excited by Big Work, here's what to do.

At the start of your next term, sit the children down and explain that, this term, you're going to try something extremely exciting. It's important to show your enthusiasm. Go over all the topics you'll be covering—fractions, dinosaurs, persuasive writing—the lot. Then ask them which subjects they're excited about and why. This will reveal their educational 'hooks'.

Once they've seen the full scope of the term's curriculum, let them know that you won't be teaching in Week 10. Instead, it will be 'Big Work Week'. During this week, they'll get to create a project of their choice and they'll have the entire week to work on it. And the best part is that it can be anything: a model, dance, performance, piece of art. All the school's resources will be available for them to use, but anything not available in the classroom will need to be sourced from home. Anything is possible and acceptable. The only requirements are that, when they present their project, they must explain why they chose the topic, why they selected that medium, what they plan to do with their work to make the world a better place and use their project to teach the class about their chosen subject.

Watch what happens when you say this. Each child takes control of their learning and, from that moment, they're already thinking about what they're going to do and who they'll work with. Throughout the term, as you teach various subjects and reflect on them, you'll see children picking topics, forming teams, gathering resources and coming to you for advice on their Big Work projects. Encourage them to think big and reach for the stars, and approach every idea they have with enthusiasm. Your job is to guide, not to dictate.

It's like a performer spinning plates at the circus. Your role is to ensure they start thinking about their Big Work project. Once they've decided and their plate is carefully balanced on the stick, your job is to keep those plates spinning—providing encouragement and support—until the final week, when they finally get to put everything together.

When Big Work Week finally arrives, the children will show up buzzing with excitement, carrying all sorts of materials. Some will have already started working on their projects at home during their free time, which should be celebrated. But if you're a parent reading this book and your child comes home with this new initiative, keep your hands off the work—it's not yours, it's theirs.

Since you're not teaching during Big Work Week, the children will have a full four days to dedicate to their projects, preparing for their big presentation on Friday. What will you do during this time? Well, how about taking the week off—maybe heading to Spain for some lovely food and sunshine? Only joking! You'll be busy observing.

You'll finally have the rare opportunity to observe them in action. Big Work involves life skills that can't be seen in the traditional 'sit down, hands up' classroom setting. You'll witness everything—from negotiating and borrowing resources to managing group dynamics—all while the children develop the skills they'll need for the future.

**Figure 20.** Big Work Week—life skills in action

And the beauty of it all? You don't have to lift a finger. Just be present, stay positive and be available if they need advice.

On Friday, after the children have cleaned the paint from their hair, peeled glue from their fingers and brushed the glitter from the floor, each group will be ready to present their projects. You might see papermâché dinosaurs, booklets about the Caribbean islands or even plays about Socrates. Each project will reflect something new—a fresh idea, a future job prospect, a boost in confidence and endless creativity. And the most exciting aspect is that everyone will be learning from one another, inspired by their peers' incredible creations.

You celebrate the effort each group has made: the courage to try something new, the determination to complete the task, the confidence to share it with others. There are no grades, no points, no competition and certainly no negative comments on the work they've produced. Everyone tried their best and that's what matters.

For a group that may not have produced as much as they could, it really doesn't matter. They know they could have done better—there's no need for you to spell it out. Barry J. Zimmerman, an educational psychologist who studies how students learn best, talks about how important it is for learners to take control of their own process through self-monitoring and reflection:

> *Self-reflection fosters deeper learning and helps students become more self-regulated learners by understanding their strengths and areas for improvement.*

So, you might encourage them to reflect on their work, and they might just say, 'I think I could've done more.' And your response? 'Well done for reflecting on that. There's always next term.' They know how they feel about it and they'll fix it themselves. It's all part of the process.

And the best part? You get to do it all again next term.

## If it looks perfect, it probably isn't

To make learning purposeful, we need to let go of that little bit of ego we might attach to our children's work—as if what *they* produce somehow represents how good *we* are. Honestly, I've been dumbfounded by educational systems that reward teachers for producing 'perfect' results—high grades, flawless exams and neatly packaged outcomes. Because the reality is that striving for perfection often strips away the fundamentals of learning.

It's only natural that we adults worry if our children's work isn't spotless. We think it reflects on us as teachers or parents. If our child's homework doesn't look polished, or if their handwriting is messy with spelling errors, we worry about being judged. Children make mistakes—beautiful, glorious mistakes—and it's in those moments of error that real discovery happens. That's where the magic lies, and we should embrace it, not hide it away.

At a school I visited recently, the principal gave me a tour. She was really proud of what she was showing me and, honestly, from the outside, it looked fantastic. The children were sitting quietly but seemed genuinely engaged, the teachers were animated and enthusiastic, and the place had a positive buzz.

But then I noticed the display boards in the hallway. The student work was beautifully presented, but every piece looked exactly the same. Apart from the handwriting and some colour differences, you couldn't tell them apart. It all looked perfect but, in reality, it was far from that. The children weren't taking risks or pushing their creativity; they were producing what they thought the teacher wanted and there lies the problem. True learning is supposed to be messy, full of trial and error, and overflowing with originality. While it might sound counterintuitive, when the work isn't perfect, it usually means we're doing something right.

You see, what was displayed on those boards reflected what I call 'goal-driven learning'. Every child had the same goal: to produce the same outcome. The focus was on achieving a uniform result as evidence of their learning.

But I believe there's a stark alternative, which gives children the chance to make learning their own. One that lets them push boundaries and venture into unknown areas of untapped potential. That alternative is 'growth-driven learning'.

Let's explore how these two approaches differ.

## Goal-driven learning

Let's imagine a Year 3 class has spent the term learning about ocean creatures. To wrap it up, the teacher decides the children will create an octopus-themed art project. Sounds fun, right?

When the children return from recess, they find neatly pre-cut pink card on their desks: eight strips for tentacles, two googly eyes and some glue. The teacher gives step-by-step instructions on how to put together the octopus. The kids follow along enthusiastically, sticking on the tentacles, adding the eyes and drawing a mouth with a black sharpie as the teacher does the same at the front of the class. By the end, every child has an octopus that resembles the teacher's version.

The results are neat, consistent and perfect for the class newsletter. As each child arrives home, parents will probably say, 'Wow,

**Figure 21.** Goal-driven learning

what a fantastic artist you are!' The teacher might even receive praise for great teaching, and thus the cycle of goal-driven learning continues.

But what did the children actually learn? No child had a chance to think critically, make their own choices or express themselves. They were just following steps, doing the same thing as everyone else. They followed a recipe for guaranteed success.

> *'Human communities depend upon a diversity of talent, not a singular conception of ability.'*
> *—Sir Ken Robinson*

This scenario has no room for diversity, no opportunity to explore unique ideas or talents. The children were nudged towards conformity, leaving creativity and critical thinking behind. It certainly would look fantastic in the school newsletter but beware if you ever see this. Where there is uniformity, creativity is non-existent.

## Growth-driven learning

Imagine the same Year 3 class, still learning about ocean creatures, but this time the teacher takes a different approach:

*We've been learning about ocean life. Today, I want you to create your own unique sea creature using any materials you like. Think about its habitat, its features and what makes it special.*

The classroom buzzes with excitement. Some children dive straight into the art supplies—grabbing pipe cleaners, paper plates and buttons—while others prefer to sketch out their ideas first. There's no specific template or rules—just freedom to explore, experiment and let their imaginations run wild.

A child makes a shark-like creature with a cereal box for its body and colourful feathers for fins. Another makes an octopus with straws for tentacles and bottle caps for eyes. One constructs a deep-sea fish covered in shiny tinfoil scales and glitter-covered yarn tentacles. Every creation reflects each child's ideas and personality.

There's laughter, conversation and the occasional bit of frustration as the children troubleshoot and adapt their ideas—but the room is alive with learning. The teacher moves around the classroom, asking questions like:

*Why did you choose this material?*

*What does your sea creature eat?*

These help the children think more deeply about their designs and connect their creativity to the knowledge they've gained about ocean life.

By the end, the classroom has transformed into a vibrant sea of original creations. Some are whimsical, others rooted in realism, but all are the product of the children's creativity. There's pride and ownership in the air because this task wasn't just about following instructions, it was about bringing their own ideas to life.

**Figure 22.** Growth-driven learning

When these quirky creatures go home, the parents' reactions aren't predictable. Instead of saying, 'Oh, that's a nice octopus', parents marvel at the creativity behind the projects. 'What is this?' they might ask, and the children eagerly explain:

> *This is a deep-sea creature I made because*
> *I love how they glow in the dark.*
>
> *I wanted to make a creature that could fly*
> *and swim at the same time.*

The pride in their voices is palpable. As if by magic, the act of working becomes more than just producing a final product, but the freedom to think, create and explore on their own terms. They weren't finishing an assignment, they were crafting something meaningful that belonged to them.

> *'The principal goal of education is to create people who*
> *are capable of doing new things, not simply repeating*
> *what other generations have done.'*
> *—Jean Piaget, Swiss psychologist*

Growth-driven learning makes this possible. In this kind of environment, learning is about nurturing originality, encouraging curiosity and fostering individuality. In doing so, we help children develop the essential skills they'll need for the future—critical thinking, creativity and a love of learning.

For adults, the key is to step back and remove ourselves from the equation. We're there as facilitators, helping children take those steps in their own way. If we fail to let go, then learning becomes a chore, a box-ticking exercise focused on grades and perfection. **Textbooks, worksheets, rigid rubrics and mandated standards can be the true thieves of educational joy.** When children are in that kind of learning structure, the magic of curiosity and exploration gets lost.

They say, 'If you love them, let them go'. If we want our children to succeed, we must give them the space to explore, make mistakes and find their own way. Letting them lead their learning journey and letting their individuality shine are two of the most powerful gifts we can give them.

## Bringing the real world into education

Education is meant to prepare our children for the real world, so we need to create activities and experiences that make learning tangible and meaningful. The way we teach, activities we plan and discussions we have all shape how children will understand and respond meaningfully to the world around them.

In 2016, I was teaching a Year 6 class about democracy. To make this abstract concept come alive, we started with the ancient Greeks—the birthplace of democracy—and moved through history to modern times, before diving into the Australian democratic system. Then, I encouraged the children to create their own political parties. The Clinton–Trump election in the USA was making headlines at the time, providing the perfect opportunity to draw parallels between our classroom and the outside world.

Just like the candidates in the US election, the children got creative. They made campaign posters, rallied for support and presented their policies in the hope of being elected. If they succeeded, they would be responsible for delivering on their promises. We talked about the importance of keeping promises, transparency and accountability. Their ideas were brilliant—more books in the library, an after-school club for extra work, outdoor learning opportunities, even the right to wear baseball hats in class.

The candidates gave speeches, debated and campaigned tirelessly. When election day finally came, everyone was excited and slightly nervous. Who would be elected and which policies would shape our classroom? We set up secret voting booths and anonymous ballots—just like a real Australian election.

When the votes were counted, we announced the new class leadership team. There were smiles of joy on some faces and disappointment on others. The policies clearly mattered to them. But we had discussed fairness in the process, so they accepted the decision and moved on.

Two weeks later, however, the new leadership team still hadn't implemented many of their promises. Predictably, their voters were unhappy:

*What happened to the outdoor seating you promised us?*

*And what about the baseball hats?*

The complaints started rolling in—directed both at me and the elected leaders—and rightly so. The class leader quickly realised they needed to honour their promises, and fast. But for some students, the damage was already done. One child even remarked:

*I wish I had voted for the Nature Society instead.*

Throughout our discussions leading up to the vote, we emphasised the responsibilities that come with leadership. Being in charge isn't just about authority—it's about meeting people's needs, answering tough questions and being accountable. If we treat others poorly, we lose friends. If we break rules, there are consequences. And if a political leader fails to keep promises, they must be held accountable.

The next day, we all sat and watched the US election live in class. The children understood exactly what was happening. They had felt the disappointment of having their elected leader break promises and experienced firsthand what it was like to see policies they cared about being sidelined. They'd seen the importance of being honest, transparent and having a dedicated group of supporters.

As the votes rolled in, the children watched the sadness and frustration on the faces of Democrats, and the elation and triumph on the faces of Republicans. They understood exactly how each side felt because they'd felt those emotions during their own election.

We talked about the importance of integrity in leadership and how, regardless of the size of the election, honesty and transparency build trust. They understood why some people might feel let down and how important it is for a leader to deliver on their promises, whether in a classroom or on a national stage. They weren't just learning about democracy, they were experiencing it.

If there's one thing I want my students to take away, it's the importance of critical thinking. Real-world learning, like our classroom democracy, teaches lifelong lessons. Children need to become critical thinkers, able to make informed decisions and consider multiple perspectives. Which party had the best policies? Who could be trusted to deliver? These questions matter.

## Purposeful learning and critical thinking

When children take on meaningful tasks—especially those connected to the outside world—they build critical-thinking skills. Jerome Bruner, an American psychologist, emphasises that learning is most effective when children actively construct new ideas, rather than just passively absorb information. They see a problem, work towards a solution and gain perspective—all of which helps them better understand the world around them. As they solve problems, they learn to adapt, reflect and grow—becoming adaptable, empathetic young people who can navigate complexities.

Purposeful learning encourages children to see beyond the surface. They learn to recognise manipulation—like how cereal boxes are designed to catch their attention or how tech executives send their children to schools without screens while marketing technology to others. Once children see through these tactics, they're less likely to be fooled.

Our job is to give children the tools to explore, understand and connect the dots before they become voters and consumers. We can empower them to make better choices that serve humanity, not hidden agendas.

*'Education is not the learning of facts,*
*but the training of the mind to think.'*
*—Albert Einstein*

There has never been a more important time for children to learn to think critically. Our task is simple: help them open their eyes so they can see the world for what it really is.

## Where there's purpose, there's hope!

Hope is a powerful word. But what does hope really mean, and how does it fit into our children's education? Hope is more than having a positive outlook—it's much deeper than that. According to a 2024 survey by the Human Flourishing Lab:

*Hope is about believing in one's own power to create change, which impacts both individual and collective success.*

When children realise they have the power to make changes, they become more hopeful. They stop seeing challenges as impossible obstacles and start seeing them as opportunities—stepping stones that lead to a better, brighter world.

But not everyone feels this way. The Human Flourishing Lab's survey showed that only 44 per cent of Americans are optimistic about humanity making real progress on major global challenges, such as climate change, inequality and political instability. While many people feel hopeful about their own lives, they have much less confidence in our collective ability to tackle these challenges. Factors like political division, economic instability and a constant stream of negative news contribute to shaping this outlook.

That's why we must empower our children, even in the face of big global issues. They need to believe they can play an active role in solving these problems, working together with others to make a difference. Our goal is to nurture a hopeful, forward-thinking generation of people who are confident and capable of taking on the challenges of tomorrow. The question is: what can we do to increase our children's hope?

Since starting Upschool.co, I've been able to work with some of the world's largest school networks. Beaconhouse in Pakistan educates 315,000 children; City Montessori School in India, run by Professor Geeta Gandhi Kingdon, has 60,000 students; and Ryan Schools International in India, run by the incredible Dr Snehal Pinto, educates more than 250,000 children globally. The Upschool framework is centred around our motto: *Purposeful education for a better tomorrow.* With such a vast reach, it would be a missed opportunity not to explore how our purposeful learning framework could impact these children's levels of hope.

To capture this data, I approached Dr Snehal Pinto with a big proposal. I suggested creating a series of courses where 50,000 children from her school network could work on achieving each of the seventeen UN SDGs through real-world learning. The process was straightforward: children would first learn about a specific SDG, then choose a hands-on action to address that goal and carry it out.

Afterwards, they would write to some of the world's leaders, including Mark Zuckerberg, Ursula von der Leyen and Prime Minister Modi, sharing their thoughts on what they had done and what these leaders could do to help improve the world, too.

The objective of these letters wasn't necessarily to get a response but to make sure their voices were heard. After completing each SDG, the children would create a digital resume based on their achievements. By the end of the course, their resume would document who they had become and what they had accomplished through their efforts to meet all seventeen SDGs.

Dr Pinto was thrilled about the project. In April 2024, we launched it for more than 50,000 children across India. Recent research shows that hope is at an all-time low globally. The oceans are rising, wars are ongoing, species are becoming extinct and forests are burning. With all the negative news bombarding our homes and classrooms, it's no surprise our children are feeling less hopeful about the future.

We wanted to see if we could change that. If we gave children the chance to actively make the world a better place, in ways they chose themselves, would their hope for the future improve?

To measure this, Professor Jason Skues, my colleague at Upschool, and I developed a modified version of the University of Kansas's Hope Scale. We would assess the children's levels of hope before and after their involvement with the SDG projects. This would indicate if the hands-on approach of making real positive changes in their community could change the way children felt about their future. The children were given statements to respond to before and after completing the SDG courses, including:

*I am doing just as well as others my age.*

*When I have a problem, I can come up with lots of ways to solve it.*

Once analysed, the results were astounding—and some of the things the children did to achieve the SDGs would leave you in tears.

Some children took recycled tyres, painted them and turned them into colourful furniture for their school. Others raised funds to bring doctors to remote schools, so children could receive free health checks. A group even visited local houses to educate residents about water conservation and sustainable waste-disposal techniques. But what stood out was how these actions helped the children realise their innate ability to improve the world around them—tackling major issues like recycling and healthcare, and building stronger communities in a hands-on way.

They began to see the world's problems not as issues for adults to handle or challenges to face later in life, but as things they could actively help change. And they wanted to start that journey immediately.

By giving the children the trust and belief that they could help tackle the world's biggest and most pressing issues, the students were deeply engaged, not just intellectually but emotionally and behaviourally. They developed critical skills like problem-solving, communication and empathy, and connected their learning to meaningful actions that tackled real-world challenges. Teachers consistently praised the course for its innovative and inclusive approach, which allowed students to explore their potential, feel a sense of purpose and step confidently into the role of global changemakers. Children began to see themselves as capable of driving real, lasting change—and feel hopeful about their ability to create a better future for everyone.

Of course, our children can't single-handedly stop wars, halt the Amazon deforestation or save endangered species in distant lands. But they can try, and that act of trying is what matters. The willingness to take action builds character, resilience and a hopeful spirit—especially when it's done as a group, with everyone working together towards a shared goal. When we undertake these kinds of projects collectively, each success is a victory for the whole group. **There's no need for competition and comparison because everyone is striving towards the same significant purpose.**

Despite what some might think, this type of purposeful learning doesn't hinder academic abilities—if anything, it enhances them. A 2012 study by Farrington and colleagues found that students who felt a greater sense of purpose in their learning were more engaged and performed better academically.

*'The function of education is to teach one to think intensively and to think critically. Intelligence plus character—that is the goal of true education.'*
*—Martin Luther King, Jr*

There is no better way to build character and intelligence than by having children come together, using their collective skills to create a brighter future for all.

## The playground extension

In 2018, when I was a school principal, I covered a class for several weeks, teaching children aged six to twelve across multiple classrooms. We'd been learning about letter writing and how emotive language can capture a reader's attention. Around the same time, the children were also asking for a playground extension to create more space for play. However, the school being situated in a national park made that extremely difficult.

To make the lesson purposeful and relevant, I asked for the children's help. I explained that I wanted to give them what they wanted, but my hands were tied. I couldn't get permission to move the playground boundary, nor could I get hold of the newly elected local council member. I said:

*You've all mastered letter writing. You know how to structure your letters and use emotive language to write from the heart. I know you want a bigger playground, but this is beyond my control. Do you have any ideas about how you could use your new skills to solve this problem?*

One young girl immediately raised her hand. She suggested that everyone write letters to the local council member, inviting her to come to the school and see the situation for herself. I was impressed at her brilliant suggestion and knowledge of local government. But truth be told, I was hoping someone would suggest exactly that.

Each child received an envelope and a stamp. I made it clear that I wouldn't read, check or grade their letters—they were theirs to send. I was writing one, too. We were in this as a team. Their mission was simple: persuade the council member to visit our school. I encouraged them to go all out—decorate their letters and make them stand out. I was adding flowers to my letter, some children suggested colourful borders and others talked about including drawings. One girl sprayed her letter with perfume, while another filled her envelope with petals. Grades and comments became irrelevant. The goal was for the council member to show up at the school.

Once completed, we sealed the letters, wrote the addresses on the front and off we went to post them. One by one, the children pushed their letters into the mailbox, and you could see it meant something personal to each of them. This would definitely be in the hippocampus later that night.

As we walked back to school, I overheard them wondering whether the council member would actually respond. Many doubted she'd even read them. I listened without saying much, sensing their scepticism about our political system.

Weeks went by and the playground still hadn't changed. The children kept asking if I'd received a response but, unfortunately, I hadn't. Frustrated, three girls decided to try again. They encouraged everyone to write a second letter, this time expressing their disappointment at not receiving a reply. I couldn't argue with their determination.

Out of curiosity, I read some of these new letters. They were well-written, expressing genuine frustration. It made me nervous about how the council member might react, but I believed their feelings were valid. Just as we were about to send the new batch, I received a call from the council member's office. She had received the original letters and wanted to arrange a visit.

When I shared the news, we had a long discussion about patience and giving people the benefit of the doubt. When the council member arrived, we spent two hours in conversation. She was gracious and impressed with the children's determination, and congratulated me for initiating such an effective way to bring learning to life. Before I could respond, a girl in Year 5 jumped in:

*It wasn't Gavin's idea; it was ours. We want a bigger playground and since Gavin can't move the fence without your permission, we decided to write to you. Gavin didn't even read the letters!*

The council member turned to me and my smile confirmed the truth. She was astonished. Later, as she stood in the school doorway, ready to leave, she said, 'There are some amazing children here. Did you really not read the letters?'

'I didn't,' I replied. 'The goal was to get you here. I told them that if their letters were powerful enough, you'd come. And here you are. They've achieved their mission and no grade or comment from me could replace how they feel right now.'

She smiled, shook my hand and left.

In the end, the playground didn't get any bigger—we were told that although the letters were very powerful and the children had achieved their collective objective, the rules in a national park are too strict.

But for me, the initiative was never really about the playground. It was about bringing learning to life. The children had learned one of life's most valuable lessons:

*When you work collectively towards a shared goal, amazing things can happen (but not when it comes to national parks).*

The children had clearly learned how to structure a letter, use emotive language and apply persuasive techniques. But now they understood how to use those skills to create real collective change and move mountains. This is what truly measures the greatness of any educational journey—empowering children to make a tangible difference in the world around them through the knowledge that we share.

## Let children solve the problems

We've all been there. You meet someone stranded on the side of the highway with a flat tyre or come across someone lost in the street. You help them jack up the car or find their way to the shops. When we help others solve their problems, our brain rewards us with a small dose of serotonin, the happiness chemical. We walk away proud, with shoulders back, head high and a spring in our step because we've just made the world a little bit better.

### The science of doing good

This uplifting feeling is deeply rooted in our biology. A 2006 study by neuroscientist Jorge Moll and colleagues explored this phenomenon using MRI scans. They asked participants to make decisions about donating to charity while monitoring their brain activity. The results showed that, when people chose to help others, hormones like serotonin and oxytocin—both strongly linked to happiness and wellbeing—were released, and brain regions associated with pleasure and trust were activated. Our brains are therefore wired to reward altruistic behaviour, encouraging us to keep doing good.

So, if our children's brains reward them with happiness, a sense of belonging and calm every time they help another person, surely we should be using this mechanism as a way to encourage our children to do great things—rather than giving them ticks, stickers or extra iPad time. The reward for their work is the feeling they get from making the world better, and that's really all they need.

I was recently in the UK visiting friends and family. One evening, I was sitting on the sofa with a cup of tea when the eldest child came over to talk about his day. He's a thoughtful and enthusiastic nine-year-old, and like any child at that age, with the right questioning, he's full of interesting stories, especially regarding school. As we chatted, he said their teacher had given out classroom jobs to some of the children to help with responsibilities like managing the library or organising materials. I'm sure we can all agree this is a great way to involve children and give them ownership over running the classroom and even the school.

Unfortunately for him, he hadn't been assigned a job. Despite expressing to his teacher how much he wanted to help, especially in the class library (he loves books), there weren't enough roles to go around. Like any child who feels left out, he was disappointed.

But instead of dwelling on the disappointment, he decided to come up with a solution himself. The next day, as soon as he arrived home from school, he went straight up to his room. At first, no one thought much of it—perhaps he was playing with Lego? But after a while, curiosity got the better of me. I decided to check on him.

When I opened the door, there he was, completely focused at his little desk surrounded by Lego pieces on the floor. He glanced at me then got back to what he was doing without saying a word. Upon inspection, he was designing a poster for something he called the Climbing Club. His idea was simple but clever: a club for anyone who loved climbing, with meetings at the playground's climbing frames during lunch breaks. He'd even made small membership cards to hand out to new members. The effort and thought he'd put into it were impressive, especially for someone his age.

What stood out most was his initiative. Faced with a situation that wasn't going his way, he didn't give up or rely on adults to fix it for him. He found his own way to make a difference and give himself a meaningful role. As his pseudo-uncle, I was very proud of him. Even if he didn't have any members yet, I let him know how amazing I thought his idea was.

He took his poster to school and put it up in the corridor. By lunchtime, five children had joined his club, and he'd handed out all his membership cards—with a waiting list for more! The Climbing Club was officially up and running. That evening, he came home brimming with excitement.

Moments like these remind us of the importance of fostering children's independence and resilience. They need opportunities to face challenges, think critically and act without us stepping in too quickly to solve the problems for them. When they do, the confidence and skills they gain will serve them well, no matter what life throws at them.

## The Ganges River dolphin

In 2024, I visited the Chitwan jungle in the south of Nepal. I'd been climbing to Everest Base Camp to record lessons on Sherpa culture when I was kindly offered the chance to explore the Chitwan jungle in search of rhinos and their offspring. When an opportunity like this comes up, I never look a gift horse (or rhino) in the mouth. I hopped on a jungle jeep, took two buses and a plane ride, and soon enough, we were there.

Chitwan National Park is one of the only places in the world where you can walk freely in the jungle with wild rhinos and their babies without needing someone with a gun by your side. You might ask, 'What happens if they charge?' Well, according to my local guide, rhinos almost always do a mock charge before they attack, so you get one warning. To be on the safe side, we also had a wonderful Asian elephant with us during the trek, because they offer protection while you're in the jungle.

Over the days I spent searching for rhinos, I became quite close to one of the elephants. Amazingly, she seemed to have taken a shine to me. Alongside her mahout (her human big brother), we walked through the jungle together, her trunk resting on my shoulder as she carefully selected leaves to ease a stomach-ache or roots to give her energy. I seized the chance to film some lessons of this incredible experience.

Back in Australia, my team and I edited the footage for Upschool. As usual, I wanted to ensure children could apply what they learned to make the world a better place. After much thought, I decided to use the elephant video as the catalyst for a course titled *How to Save an Animal Species*. In the course, children would watch the video to learn about the threats to their habitat and then choose an endangered animal to try to save.

Now, you might be thinking, *Children stopping an animal from becoming extinct? Surely not!* But as you know, I like to go big and I love children to go big, too. To help the children choose, I created a simple booklet featuring sixteen endangered animals. They could pick one, research it, understand the statistics of how many were left in the wild and, using a suggestion board of real-life activities, try to help save it.

Of course, it's a tough challenge, especially for children. But when I launched the course, hundreds of schools joined my online onboarding session, fully embracing the confidence it showed in children's ability to make a difference. My advice to the schools and teachers was simple:

*Don't dictate what the children do. Let them go big and don't worry if some of their plans fail.*

To help the children get started, the course included ideas like writing to a local television station to raise awareness or creating posters to put up around the community to educate people about the importance of the chosen animal. Ultimately, though, I wanted the children to come up with their own ways to tackle this almost impossible project. As the course ran worldwide, I got feedback on how children were approaching this mission of change. While many schools did incredible work, one school—Tagore International School in India—took the project to the next level, showing just what children can do when they believe in what they're doing.

Unlike other schools, where lots of small groups of children worked on different animals, the children at Tagore School decided to work together to save a local animal: the Ganges River dolphin. The Ganges River dolphin is under threat from human development and river pollution. Only about 60 of these dolphins are believed to remain in the wild. As soon as the children became aware of this, they felt they needed to take action.

The children started by writing letters to Prime Minister Modi, alerting him to their concerns. Each child sent emails and handwritten letters to his office, sharing their thoughts on the dolphin's possible demise, the reasons behind it and what they believed could be done. Next, the children held an eco-fashion show for parents, with clothes made from recycled materials to demonstrate how fast fashion contributes to river pollution. They even invited parents into the school to turn old, recycled clothes into new ones that could then be sold.

Following that, they made placards and marched into the community to raise awareness about the dolphin's plight, gathering support from local business owners and community leaders who shared their concerns. Finally, the children held a movie night at their school, screening films about dolphins—especially the Ganges River dolphin—and selling popcorn and drinks to raise money to push their campaign even further. These children weren't giving up; the future of this creature was in their hands.

They organised a massive social media campaign to share their work with the world. They even appeared at international conferences attended by the UN, where they presented on the issues facing the dolphin and what we can all do to help.

But as we know, change doesn't happen overnight and, several months later, the dolphin is still under threat. But now, many people (maybe even you) who had no idea the Ganges River dolphin even existed are aware of how much danger it's in. The children also learned that everyday actions, like buying fast fashion or dumping waste or chemicals into local waterways, aren't helping the dolphin's plight. With the awareness raised and local businesses getting behind their mission, people in the community have begun changing their habits.

Saving the Ganges River dolphin from extinction will take much longer than it takes for this story to reach you. But for these children, the wheels of change have begun to turn. The seeds of love, empathy and empowerment have been planted. Now, they will need persistence and determination to keep the momentum going and create lasting, meaningful change—for this amazing creature or any other issue these children may face.

Will the children succeed? In my opinion, they already have. The minute they decided to work with purpose, chose something that mattered to them and strived to make the world a better place, they succeeded far beyond what any exam or test score could measure.

## A real education, a real difference

The magic of education lies in its ability to change the world, one child at a time. When we align our teaching with purpose, when we connect the classroom to the outside world, we give children the chance to make a real impact.

Whether it's writing to a prime minister, redesigning a school playground or saving the Ganges River dolphin, when children tackle meaningful problems, they do more than learn—they transform. They become individuals who understand their place in the world and realise that their actions matter and they have the power to shape a better tomorrow.

For us—the parents and teachers who have the role of guiding our youngest citizens—the advice is clear. Know why you are teaching what you teach. Help children understand why it's worth their time and how their work can change the world. Ask them for help with big-picture problems and never underestimate their ability to think outside the box and put those thoughts into action. There's no better time to start than today. If you haven't already begun, now is the time.

Real learning is purposeful. It's messy and unpredictable, takes time, and requires patience from the adults involved. It's often far from perfect. But through that imperfection lies growth, creativity and character—traits that tests and exams can't measure. When we understand why we're teaching certain topics and allow children to connect what they learn to the outside world, we guide them towards finding their purpose. We help them experience the consequences of making a positive difference and give them the hope that they can face any challenge the world throws at them.

*The equation is simple: education + purpose = change.*

## Step 6

# Connection before curriculum

Back in the summer of 2004, after some careful planning and a lot of saving up, I headed out on an epic journey through Asia with a group of my closest friends. We travelled around Malaysia on motorbikes, caught trains in China and took a boat to Japan. Six months later, the time came to return to reality—we had to start earning money instead of endlessly spending what little we'd saved.

Sitting in a youth hostel in Tokyo, we discussed our next steps. Our funds were dwindling but going home was not an option. We hadn't left England to return so soon—there was still so much of the world we wanted to explore.

After a long discussion (and a few glasses of sake), we made a bold decision—we were going to move to Australia. As we waited for our visas to be approved, we scoured the internet for potential jobs in Sydney. I gravitated towards the teaching opportunities, searching for a role that would fit my experience and skill set.

Luckily for me, my teacher training in Sheffield had prepared me for something quite specific. Sheffield has a large Pakistani community and my first-ever job was at a local primary school in the heart of it. It was a wonderfully diverse and close-knit community, filled with warm, welcoming families.

During my time there, I was introduced to the Quran. While I couldn't claim to be an expert, I'd sat in on lessons run by the local sheikh and gained a basic understanding of the religion. Along the way, I'd picked up a few Arabic phrases from the hadiths.

As I browsed through the job listings in Sydney, one caught my eye. It was for a Year 5 teaching position at an Islamic school on the outskirts of the city. The ad mentioned that while being Muslim wasn't a requirement, a basic understanding of the religion would be preferred. Given the experience I'd gained in Sheffield, it felt like the perfect fit.

After arriving in Sydney a few weeks later, I lined up a job interview. Lo and behold, after speaking a few words of Arabic and sharing my experiences in Sheffield's Pakistani community, I got the job. It was such a relief to finally have a steady income and see money coming into my bank account instead of watching it disappear.

The school of 600 children was a beautiful place full of rich diversity, with so many different cultures and nationalities gathered in one setting. I was the only male non-Muslim teacher there, which meant I stood out like a sore thumb, but nobody seemed to care and I soon began to feel like a part of the community.

The school had strict policies regarding poor behaviour, rudeness, or not completing homework and class tasks—these were not tolerated. Children were often sent to the principal's office for such issues, and while she was a kind woman, the children dreaded it.

After several years of working at the school, I was given a Year 6 class. Part of my role was to select the Student Representative Council (SRC). This group would lead the school during outings, debates and ceremonics, and would receive special badges. Being chosen to join the SRC meant a great deal to the children and their families. It was a position of real responsibility and pride.

As I looked through the list of my new students with the principal, she gave me a heads-up about one girl. Apparently, she'd almost been expelled three times for bad behaviour, spent countless hours in the principal's office and earned herself the label of 'naughty child'. When the principal shared the girl's reputation with me, I immediately knew what had to be done. I decided to offer her the role of school captain—the leader of the SRC.

On the first day, as I stood in front of my new class, I greeted the children, told them about the year ahead and made the announcement that this girl would be our new school captain. She looked like she was about to faint from the shock. The rest of the class glanced around the room as if they were waiting for the punchline, convinced it was some kind of prank. But it was no joke. And as you can probably imagine, I had a reason behind my decision.

At the end of the school day, I asked her to stay behind. I said, 'I know you've had a rough few years and you've been labelled the "naughty child", but I believe in you. I believe you do the things you do to get noticed, but they're noticing you for all the wrong reasons. I want people to notice you for the good things you can bring to this school, not the bad. Do you think you can turn it around and lead the school?'

She smiled a smile like I'd never seen before—her eyes, her ears and her mouth all smiled at once. Someone believed in her, just like Mr McKenny had once believed in me.

'Yes, of course,' she said, and ran out of the classroom with such pride in her steps, like a weight of negativity had been lifted.

As I packed up my things for the day, the principal came into my room, curious about my decision. After a few moments, she let it go and trusted I knew what I was doing. That night, she received a few complaints from parents. But the principal, to her credit, kindly defended my decision.

From that moment on, the girl came to school a changed person. She became calm, content and incredibly helpful. I nurtured her transformation with words of praise and gratitude, and the more I encouraged her, the better she got. She started helping others, leading groups of younger children, and giving speeches at formal ceremonies on topics such as kindness and love. She was proving everyone wrong, and it was wonderful to see. At the end of the year, she graduated having done an amazing job.

Fast forward ten years. I'd left the school, retrained as a Montessori teacher and, to be honest, completely forgotten about that student.

Then I was invited by an old colleague to attend an Islamic festival in the city's west. It was a lovely night with stalls selling sweets, speeches, singing and even rollercoaster rides. As I wandered around the festival, I heard my name being called from behind me.

I turned around to see a group of young women, all wearing hijabs, smiling.

'Are you Mr McCormack?' one of them asked.

'Yes, I am,' I replied, a bit puzzled.

'You probably don't remember me, but I was in your class.'

I smiled, taken aback. 'Wow, I'm really sorry, but I don't remember you.'

'I was in your class in Year 6. I was the naughty kid and was about to be expelled, but you made me school captain and believed in me. I'm now in law school. I'm going to become a lawyer.'

My eyes filled with tears. My whole face smiled, just like hers had the day I made her school captain. The emotional circle of learning had come back to reward me with a heart full of happiness and hope. It was, hands down, one of the greatest gifts teaching has ever given me. To this day, I'm so grateful I bumped into her.

## Shaping the world, one child at a time

For parents, the journey with children is generally lifelong. You can see the fruits of your labour and watch as your once little baby slowly but surely morphs into a mature and responsible human being. For teachers, that relationship is obviously different. We may only see them for twelve months, but we pour our heart and soul into educating the children in our care. We stay up all night planning lessons, marking books, and writing positive comments to boost their self-esteem and nurture their confidence, so they can grow into the best versions of themselves.

Teaching is a beautiful profession, filled with joy and hope. The bittersweet part is that every year we say goodbye to these wonderful humans who we've spent hundreds of hours with. Suddenly, they're gone, and we're left not knowing if the effort we made,. the sleepless nights and the lessons we taught actually made a difference. That is, until you bump into them at an Islamic festival and find out they're going to become a lawyer.

Teaching, like parenting, is an opportunity to shape the world, one child at a time. And while we might not always get to sit in the shade of the trees we plant in the classroom as seeds, someone else will, and that's the beauty of it.

Over the last 25 years as a teacher, I've tried taught hundreds—if not thousands—of children. I've observed so many classes and visited schools all over the world. Even though plenty of teachers have been at this job longer than I have, it feels like I've been living and breathing education non-stop, 24/7, since I was in primary school myself.

In this time, I've gathered a collection of strategies, stories and resources I believe can help every teacher, parent and adult who works with children make an impact. My hope is that these can reshape education—and the lives of the children in our care—for the better.

In this chapter, I'm pulling together some of my favourite ideas for you to try. Some are tried and tested, others less so, but they all share the same purpose: **to make education a more human, nurturing process that reflects the skill set our children will need out in the world**. As I always say in my teacher training sessions: take what you need, leave what you don't.

## The connected species

Humans learn remarkably easily. Just one of our senses needs to be stimulated for our brain to start absorbing new information. But our brain, designed to keep us safe and alive for as long as possible, is also pretty selective about who it chooses to learn from.

We've been wired to learn from members of our tribe or community—people who care about our wellbeing. When we feel a bond with someone, we view their advice and teachings more positively. Conversely, when we lack that connection, our perception shifts and we're less receptive to what they have to say. Without trust or a sense of genuine care, we may become sceptical of their intentions or dismissive of their advice. Their words might feel hollow with their actions coming across as insincere or self-serving.

A 2019 study at the University of Cambridge used electroencephalography (EEG) to measure brain activity in students and their teacher. The research revealed that when children trusted and felt connected to their teacher, their brain activity synchronised with the teacher's. This brain-to-brain synchrony was directly linked to better retention and understanding of the material being taught. This demonstrates the profound impact of a strong teacher–student relationship on learning outcomes.

Similar results were found in a 2020 study from New York University. It showed that brain-to-brain synchrony between students and teachers occurred with a delay of about 300 milliseconds—the time it takes to process spoken language. This synchrony was a strong predictor of how well the students would understand and remember the lesson, emphasising how crucial trust and connection are in the learning process.

So, what does this mean for us as teachers and parents?

If we want our children to learn from us, to listen and take in what we're saying, we need to prioritise connection first. For parents, we can build this connection through physical touch, love, care and attention. But for teachers, it's more challenging. The different nature of this relationship means we must find creative ways to connect.

To assist teachers with the challenging task of connecting with the children in our classrooms, here are ten ways I believe will foster that bond with students to allow everyone's brains to work in harmony.

1. **Greet every child.** When children arrive, greet them by name, look them in the eye, shake their hand and smile. Ask them how they're feeling. This simple act sets the tone for a day where they feel seen and valued.

2. **Create a welcoming space.** Arrange the classroom with natural materials and calming decor. Remove clutter, avoid overdecorating and create cosy spaces where children feel safe and relaxed.
3. **Listen at their level.** When a child speaks, get down to their level, look them in the eye and listen until they've finished talking. This shows them their words matter and helps build trust.
4. **Ask about their home life.** During one-on-one moments, ask children about their family or home life. Simple questions like 'How's your pet guinea pig?' or 'What did you have for dinner last night?' show you care about their whole world, not just what happens at school.
5. **Give them ownership.** Give children options for their activities, like choosing between a puzzle or drawing task. Having control over their learning means they feel respected and empowered.
6. **Collect something together.** Engage in a class project, like asking every child to bring in one plant and care for it over the term. This not only brightens up your classroom, but also promotes a sense of equality and inclusivity.
7. **Let them choose a job.** Provide a list of classroom jobs, such as Class Librarian and Head of Excursions, and let each child select one they'd like to take on for the term. This encourages taking ownership and having pride in the classroom community.
8. **Always use kind words.** Instead of focusing on negatives, say, 'I can see how hard you worked! Let's think about how to improve this together.' Using positive and respectful language reinforces a safe learning space focused on collective growth.
9. **Ask their opinion.** Before making decisions about excursions or which books to buy for the new library, ask for children's opinions and respect their input.
10. **Model kindness and be real.** Be empathetic and respectful towards everyone in the classroom, and be honest when you need their help. When children see you treating others kindly and acting naturally, they feel safe.

**Figure 23.** Connecting with children in the classroom

Once we establish these connections and become part of the children's trusted inner circle, they begin to trust and learn from us without hesitation. *When our children trust us and feel connected to us, their brains synchronise with ours and learning becomes almost seamless.* But if we skip this step because we feel the lessons can't wait or the scheduling is too tight, then we might as well save our breath. The children will either not be listening or may be perceiving our words as negative, meaning no real learning will occur anyway.

## Make safe spaces

Until about age fifteen—when they decide hanging out with their friends is the most important thing in the world—our children spend most of their time in one of two places: the home or the classroom. Because we want them to look back on these years with fondness and joy, we must ensure they are safe spaces devoid of fear or anxiety. Anxiety can wreak havoc on a child's ability to learn, play and sleep. As adults, one of the most important things we can do to nurture growth in our children is to create spaces where they feel safe enough to open up, communicate freely, be themselves and experiment without fear of humiliation or retribution.

When children feel safe, their brains release oxytocin, or the bonding hormone. Oxytocin fosters feelings of trust, safety and connection, which are essential for a child's development. In a secure environment, their brains won't be in 'fight-or-flight' mode (which is regulated by cortisol, the stress hormone) but a state where they can engage fully with learning and social interactions.

## How environment affects children's development

In 2010, a group of researchers at Harvard's Center on the Developing Child set out to discover how a secure and supportive environment affects children's brain development. In a series of observational studies, neuroimaging techniques and experiments, researchers observed children in various environments—some safe and nurturing, others filled with stress and chaos—to see how these settings impacted their behaviour.

First, the researchers created safe environments that were calm, predictable and supportive by using familiar toys and materials, allowing free play under attentive guidance, and incorporating positive reinforcement to build trust and confidence. Then, to induce feelings of stress, they crafted scenarios that mimicked unpredictability and threat, introducing sudden loud noises or unexpected changes, setting problem-solving tasks under time pressure, and role-playing challenging social interactions.

The researchers used MRI scans to monitor brain activity while children performed tasks requiring executive functions. Their findings revealed that when the children felt safe and nurtured, their prefrontal cortex (which manages decision-making, self-regulation, problem-solving and planning) became highly active.

> This part of the brain is associated with higher-order thinking, learning effectively and exploring new ideas with curiosity.
>
> On the flip side, when the children were exposed to environments filled with stress, unpredictability or threat, their amygdala (the brain's emotional and fear-processing centre) became active, triggering the 'fight-or-flight' response and prioritising survival over learning. In this response, the brain reallocates resources from the prefrontal cortex, making it harder to focus, retain information, think creatively and solve problems.
>
> The study concluded that when children feel safe, their capacity to learn, understand and solve problems is significantly enhanced.

The question is: how do we create safe spaces?

The key lies in positioning ourselves as allies—we're always on their side. Remember, children are shaped by their environment and much of their behaviour is learned. So, can we hold them solely responsible for their actions? Our role is to guide and support them, helping them unlearn harmful patterns and develop healthier, more positive ways of navigating the world.

Children aren't looking to rebel for rebellion's sake—they just want to understand where the boundaries lie. When we explain what the rules are and why they're are needed, and enforce them consistently while following them ourselves, they're more likely to follow them themselves. They know what to expect, which gives them a strong foundation from which to explore, learn and grow, thus making them feel safe.

Just like touching a hot stove teaches a child immediately about consequences, clear rules and consistent responses provide a similar understanding. The key is consistency. Don't worry about the sad faces or tears when rules are enforced—it's a natural reaction, much like how they'd cry after burning their hand on the hot stove. It's part of their development. Even if they tell you they hate you and storm off to their bedroom, we know that's not the truth, so don't take it to heart.

Our role is to decide on the rules together, communicate them openly, then enforce them and reflect. If those tears cause you to waver, then that's where things go awry. Children quickly learn they can shift the line with enough sadness or resistance, then there's no real boundary at all.

Early in my career, I made the mistake of prioritising popularity with the children by easing up on consequences for their behaviour, hoping to avoid upsetting or discouraging them. I quickly learned that consistency is better. While it's a challenging path, the rewards are profound and long term. Our children soon realise there is a line and we're willing to hold it firm for their sake.

Dr Daniel Siegel, a renowned expert in interpersonal neurobiology and co-author of *The Whole-Brain Child*, notes:

> *Children who feel safe, loved, and accepted are more willing to take risks, explore new ideas, and build meaningful connections with others.*

When children feel secure, they're empowered to engage in their learning journey, developing critical emotional and social skills without the looming fear of punishment or unpredictability. While they may not always express gratitude in the moment—especially when you are enforcing boundaries or navigating difficult conversations—trust me, both you and your children will come to appreciate the importance of setting clear limits and holding firm. The foundation you establish and the boundaries you uphold will prepare them for a world filled with rules, regulations and limitations that they must learn to navigate.

## Ask them about their expectations of you

We've all heard the term 'student voice', right? It makes us think of kids posting updates on the school website or writing articles for the newsletter. The *UN Convention on the Rights of the Child* (1989) says that children have the right to express their views on matters that affect them. When we give them that opportunity, we help boost their self-esteem and engage more in their learning.

British education researchers Carol Robinson and Carol Taylor argue that fostering student voice can transform school environments. In their 2007 paper, 'Theorizing Student Voice: Values and Perspectives', they highlight how genuinely engaging students in decision-making fosters a more inclusive and participatory school culture. When students feel heard, it strengthens their sense of belonging, leading to more positive relationships with teachers and increased motivation in their learning. Their research suggests that when we listen to children and involve them in shaping their educational experiences, the entire school community benefits—creating an atmosphere where students feel valued, respected and empowered.

While there are many ways to help kids master this skill, I believe it all starts with something I like to call the 'terrific teacher survey', which I found online many years ago through an educationalist by the name of Daniel Sobel.

For parents reading this, you can try something similar at home:

*What do your children expect from you as their parent?*

*What makes a 'terrific parent' in their eyes?*

Just like in school, this could foster an incredible level of openness and trust. You might be surprised by the insights your children offer.

When children feel they have a say, they're more likely to engage in the learning process, take ownership of their education and thrive in anything they do. This simple act of asking children to tell you what they expect from a terrific teacher is a direct way to build that trust and engagement. You're creating a culture of mutual respect, where both teachers/parents and students/children feel respected and valued, and hold each other accountable in a positive, growth-oriented way.

## The terrific teacher survey

For teachers reading this, here's how it works. At the start of each term, you place the following card in front of small groups of students. The children then work together to discuss and formulate answers to some important questions, such as:

*What does a terrific teacher do?*

*What does a terrific teacher say?*

*What is a terrific teacher like?*

*What does a terrific teacher never do?*

It's a simple exercise, but the impact is powerful.

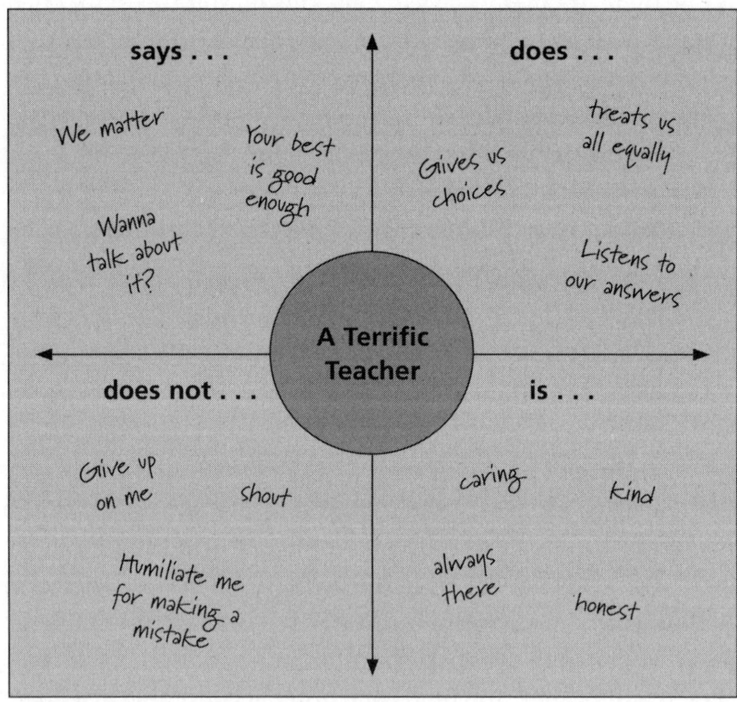


**Figure 24.** What does a terrific teacher do?

Encourage the children to be open and honest, without any fear of getting in trouble. They collaborate to come up with three points for each section. Once they're done, collect the cards and read them. The next day, share feedback with the class, which may sound like this:

*I've read your feedback. Thank you for being honest. I'm going to do my best to be the best teacher I can be. I saw that a terrific teacher never shouts or humiliates children, and that a terrific teacher says things like 'you matter' and 'your best is good enough'.*

*My pledge to you is that I'll do my best to follow this.*

*But remember, I'm human, and I make mistakes. If I do, I'll apologise, and I want you to hold me accountable just as I do with you. If I make a mistake, let me know. You can either tell me in person or pop it in your diaries, and I'll say sorry and try my best to do better.*

From that moment on, something incredible happens. Every child feels heard. They know their opinions matter, and they've helped set the tone and expectations for the classroom. You now know exactly what your children expect from you and where they've set the bar.

Also, by discussing the feedback openly, you're modelling the powerful life lesson of accountability. You're not just an authority figure, but a learner, growing and improving alongside them. You suddenly become human. This kind of openness helps to create a more collaborative environment where everyone feels comfortable to share, reflect and learn from mistakes.

## Make everything a collective decision

In my early years as a teacher, I'd spend the holidays rearranging the classroom—moving shelves and tables and redecorating the walls. I wanted the children to return to an exciting, fresh start. But when the children returned on the first day of term, I'd face at least two weeks of chaos.

It felt like all the work we'd done in the previous term on classroom values and rules had been thrown out the window. Every day of those first two weeks was pure frustration, with children appearing disorganised and unsettled, and I couldn't figure out why. Initially, I attributed it to the children's home environments, where the rules were looser and the atmosphere felt more like a playground than a classroom. But I was wrong and, to any past parents of my classes, I apologise for even thinking that.

After speaking to a psychologist friend of mine, I realised it was my fault. You see, the children were used to the classroom as it was. They knew where everything was—where they hung their coats, where the cardboard and scissors were kept, and where the maths materials were. But I'd changed everything.

Upon returning, the room looked foreign to them. They didn't know where anything was, and so it took them two weeks to settle into this new environment and feel comfortable again. The parents weren't tossing out the rulebook at home, I was disrupting their sense of order and feelings of being safe and connected.

Regardless of the changes we wish to make in our schools or home, our children need to be involved in the process. Not only because it empowers them and gives them a sense of ownership and responsibility, but because they won't need to become reacquainted with the new environment or change of routine.

And to any teachers planning on rearranging the classroom for the next term, get the children involved in that, too! Ask them to help create a plan for where things should go. Then, before the term ends, let them move the furniture alongside you and their classmates. Trust me, you'll notice the difference when school starts again.

## Let them know they matter

Life can be a whirlwind. As parents, it feels like a million things are demanding our attention: work, folding clothes, emails, errands and picking up the kids to drop them off again somewhere else, like a non-profit Uber. It can feel like time is constantly slipping through our fingers, so it's tough to carve out time for the children. But when we stop to think about what truly matters, we know our children need us more than any of those distractions, and how we spend our time with them can literally shape their world.

According to research from the American Time Use Survey and global lifestyle studies, in an average day you spend:

- 33 per cent sleeping
- 33 per cent working
- 17 per cent on screens (e.g. emails, Netflix and social media)
- 5 per cent eating
- 4 per cent in the bathroom or taking care of personal hygiene.

That's 92 per cent of our day already spoken for. That leaves just eight per cent (about 1.9 hours) for everything else, including quality time with our children.

It's a sobering vision. Considering that many children are in after-school clubs and go to bed much earlier than we do, I'm assuming that the time we actually have with them is much less. Therefore, if we don't make an intentional effort to carve out moments to connect, these precious opportunities may be lost in the rush and our children may feel they simply don't matter.

The idea of 'mattering' perfectly captures the importance of this connection. Dr Gregory Elliott, a sociology professor at Brown University, has spent years researching how feeling valued impacts wellbeing. He says:

> *When people feel that they matter to someone, their psychological wellbeing is significantly enhanced.*

For children, feeling seen, heard and valued nurtures their self-esteem, emotional security and motivation to grow and learn.

This concept of mattering is simple yet profound. When children feel they matter because we show interest in their world, listen to their stories and make time for them, they feel secure and loved. Whether it's placing a heartfelt note in their lunchbox like 'I believe in you' or 'You are amazing', or dedicating time to hear about their day, these actions send this powerful message:

*You are important. I see you. You matter.*

The washing can wait and emails will still be there tomorrow. But these small, ordinary moments with our children—sharing laughter over bubbles at the sink or exchanging stories while folding the laundry—are the moments that weave the fabric of their childhood. They create memories that will stay with them long after the chores are forgotten. These simple acts of connection leave a lasting imprint, far more profound than any task we might cross off a list.

**Figure 25.** Show your kids they matter

## Give them your time

I once had a girl in my school who had become very sad. Her hair was unkempt, her shoulders hunched and her enthusiasm for learning seemed non-existent. Concerned for her wellbeing, I had a conversation with her and discovered she felt overlooked, especially at home. When I asked if she read with anyone before bed, she told me she went to bed alone, saying: 'I tuck myself in.'

After reaching out to her parents, we hatched a plan: Wednesday night would become 'Daddy–Daughter Night'. One night each week just for her. Lo and behold, when she found out she'd have one-on-one time with her father every Wednesday, her attitude changed. Her hair was in pigtails and she practically skipped into school. It was that simple—she just needed to know she mattered.

Dr John Gottman, renowned for his research on relationships and emotional intelligence, says consistent, quality time with your child builds a strong emotional connection and fosters a sense of security:

*Children feel loved and important when we are emotionally and physically present with them, which helps lay the foundation for their future relationships and emotional health.*

If you notice signs of disengagement or emotional distress in your child, perhaps it's time to designate every Wednesday as Parent–Child Night. Picture a simple evening where you pick up your child from school and head to their favourite café or take a walk along the beach with ice creams in hand. No phones, no distractions—just quality time together. Once you schedule and lock in this time, your child will look forward to it all week and it can help carry them through the rough days. Not only will your bond grow stronger, but those simple moments will become cherished memories they'll carry into adulthood. And those memories? They'll serve as bridges to help both of you navigate future challenges, no matter how difficult.

The key is to stick to it. Whether it's Daddy–Daughter Night on Wednesdays, a Mum–Son Night on Thursday or a Daddy–Son Night on Tuesdays, make sure it becomes sacred, especially for your child. No matter what happens, don't break it.

## Hold student conferences—those sacred 30 minutes

In 2023, I created a teacher-training course for Upschool called *Education for the 21st Century.* Working alongside the brilliant Professor Mark Williams, we spent months figuring out how to best represent everything I'd learned and observed about education. And while the course was fun to curate, one of the most challenging parts was designing the section on assessment. I wanted something that could fit seamlessly into schools worldwide, and that focused on whole-child development. After some thought, I decided to use a method I'd already tested in a previous school, which worked well and yielded great results.

As I've mentioned before, the school I ran didn't rely on grades, points or comparisons between children. Like most Montessori schools globally, we didn't use exams. The only comparison we ever made was between the child and who they were yesterday. But we also did something special, and that's what I'd like to share with you.

At the start of each term, we'd outline the subjects ahead, giving the children a clear idea of what to expect. We'd also invite them to contribute their own ideas on how they could be involved in their learning journey. As the term progressed, we'd observe, mark their books, and keep track of their work at home and in school, making sure they were meeting the government's curriculum outcomes. But the real magic happened at the end of term—something many Montessori schools call 'student conferences'.

In each classroom, teachers created a booking chart on the wall where students could sign up for a 30-minute one-on-one chat in the last week of term. The children chose a time that matched their schedule. This wasn't your typical teacher–student meeting. It was designed to find out how the term's experience had been for the child, but also how we teachers had done. Each teacher received a template to help guide the 30-minute conversation, which was something like the following, although I have adapted it since:

## Student Conference  Name ______________________

| Area | Questions | Student Responses |
|---|---|---|
| **Reflection on Experience** | 1. What has been your favourite part of school this term and why? | |
| | 2. Can you share a moment or activity that made you really happy in class? | |
| | 3. Was there anything that you found challenging this term? How did you deal with it? | |
| | 4. Is there something we did in class that you'd like to do more often? | |
| | 5. How do you feel about the way we work together in class? Is there anything we can do to make it even better? | |
| **Academic Learning** | 6. What's one thing you've learned in English that you found really interesting? | |
| | 7. Can you tell me about a maths problem or concept that you enjoyed working on? | |
| | 8. What's a science experiment or topic we covered that you found fascinating? Why? | |
| | 9. In history, what story or event have your learned about that you would like to explore more? | |
| | 10. Is there a subject or topic you wish we could spend more time on? | |
| **Well-being and Feelings** | 11. How do you usually feel during the day at school? Are there times when you feel particularly excited, anxious, or curious? | |
| | 12. Do you feel comfortable asking for help in class when you need it? Why or why not? | |
| | 13. What are some ways you like to relax or have fun when you're not in school? | |
| | 14. Do you have any worries about school or learning that you'd like to talk about? | |
| | 15. What's one thing you're looking forward to in the next term? | |

**Figure 26.** Student conference template

In the last week of term, the teacher would emphasise the need for the children to demonstrate independence and collaboration, while individual students met with them in a quiet corner of the classroom. During the first part of the session, the conversation was heavily focused on reflection. We'd ask the children how they thought we'd done as teachers:

*Did we meet your expectations?*

*What could we have done better?*

At first, the children were hesitant, worried that being honest might lead to getting in trouble. But over time, they learned this was a safe space. Some children said things like:

*You shouted at the class in week four, and it upset me.*

We'd apologise, reflect and promise to improve—it was a powerful way to build trust and mutual respect. Other children requested that we go outside more or include more videos in our lessons, which was all valuable feedback.

**Figure 27.** The student–teacher conference

In the second half of the conversation, we focused on the subjects they'd studied. We'd ask questions like:

*What can you tell me about volcanoes?*

*What's a proper noun?*

Because we'd been monitoring their progress throughout the term, the point wasn't just to assess their knowledge. Instead, we'd pay close attention to their body language, tone, intonation and confidence—those subtle but important educational skills that aren't covered in tests.

Finally, we'd touch on their wellbeing:

*Is school enjoyable for you?*

*What could we do to make learning more enjoyable or easier?*

Although the conferences were time-consuming, the children held them sacred. They looked forward to that 30-minute session where they could express how they felt and share what they had or hadn't enjoyed. They felt heard and valued. And if held during 'Big Work' week, teachers will find the rest of the class so engrossed in their activities that the pressure on the teacher is almost non-existent.

I'm often asked, 'How can we measure what a child learns without tests?' First, I'm confident that any teacher can tell you what their children can and cannot do without the need for a test. And second, I often think of all the qualities that thrive outside the boundaries of any exam. A test can't capture a child's empathy when they inform you they're worried that some of their friends feel lonely on the playground, or the confidence to tell you they require more hands-on projects to enhance their learning, or convey their dreams for the future of the planet.

Real learning isn't to acquire facts but to learn how to think, and develop curiosity, connection and growth. **We want children who are skilled but also thoughtful, resourceful and resilient.** No silent test riddled with anxiety can ever show us these traits, but a simple 30-minute uninterrupted conversation can.

## The wheel of reflection

Self-reflection is a major factor when it comes to assessing children. Can our children monitor their own progress? The answer is yes! To support the idea of termly conferences, I've recently developed the 'Wheel of Reflection'. This simple tool lets children reflect on the skills they've demonstrated each day. It works like this: as the day comes to a close, each child takes out their wheel, turns to a partner and says:

*Today, I tried to be brave/honest/kind when …*

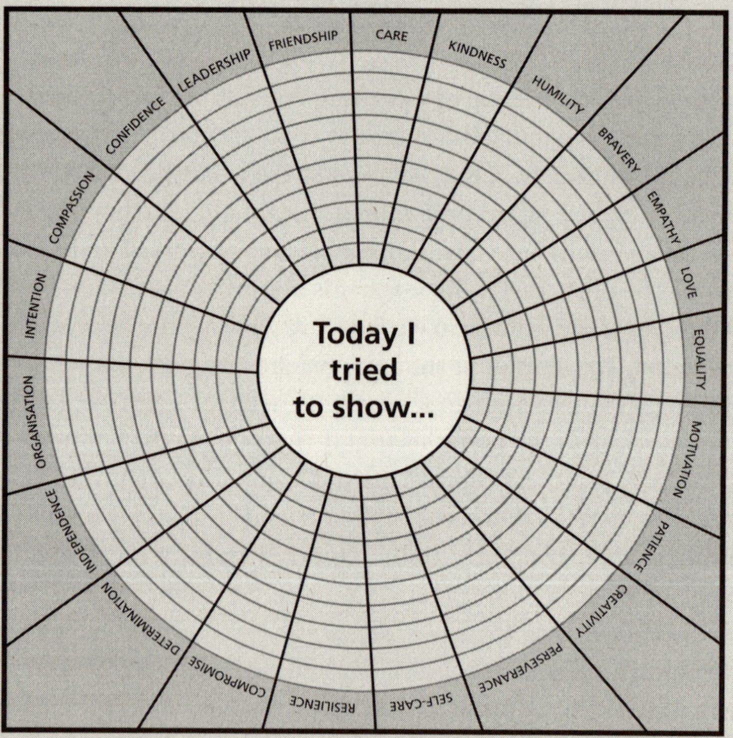


**Figure 28.** Wheel of Reflection

Then they explain a scenario from that day where they feel they've demonstrated that skill. For example, a child may turn to another and say, 'Today, I tried to show bravery when I asked the principal if he was willing to ban school uniforms because I thought they were outdated.' If they can explain how they showed that skill and their partner agrees, they get to colour in a segment of their wheel.

Over time, this visual chart becomes a beautiful representation of the child's progress regarding the 40 skills listed around the circumference of the circle. It demonstrates their progress towards being more kind, confident and empathetic. It's also a great starting point for reflective discussions with both teachers and parents during the child's journey.

The value of the Wheel of Reflection and termly conferences isn't just anecdotal. In 2002, Zimmerman found that students who engage in regular self-reflection and self-regulation strategies have greater academic success and personal development. This process fosters autonomy and helps children develop a sense of ownership over their learning.

With the conferences and the Wheel of Reflection working together, the children get a clear picture of what to work on next term, and what amazing progress they've made academically and personally. And by offering multiple opportunities for reflection—both daily and termly—we're not just assessing what children know, we're helping them develop critical self-awareness and lifelong skills. And although I've never done these two activities with children at home, I'm sure if parents could find time for these, they'd provide valuable insights into what our children are thinking, how they're feeling and what progress they've made beyond the tests, points and scores we usually use to monitor and measure their attainment.

## Find their hook

I first heard the term 'educational hook' from my mentor Sue, back in my early years as a teacher, and it's become one of my favourite phrases. Educator and author Dave Burgess, who popularised it in 2012, describes it as that magical moment when we capture a child's interest so deeply it pulls them into a state of focused learning. Best known for his book *Teach Like a Pirate*, Burgess highlights that tapping into students' natural interests is one of the most powerful ways to engage them in the learning process. I completely agree.

When we spend time to observe, notice and find their hook, we'll witness a child's enthusiasm, creativity and curiosity come to life. One of the most important tasks parents and educators can do is recognise that spark of enthusiasm. And once you spot it, fan it until it becomes a raging inferno.

Remember, it's not our journey, it's theirs, so don't try to navigate the journey for them or tempt them to take an alternate route. They've made their choice, and we must respect it. From that moment on, our job is to cultivate that passion. For example, if they show a desire to make endless comic books, we buy them drawing pencils, sketch pads and paints. We dive into comic book collections together, visit museums to learn more about manga and watch documentaries on comic book creators. By doing this, we're showing them that we've noticed who they are and what they're passionate about, and that we fully support their journey.

In turn, something magical happens. They don't just become more skilled at their chosen passion—their character grows, their confidence blossoms and our bond with them strengthens. We don't have to fill their spare time with activities we pull from a hat because they're busy chasing their dreams, shaping themselves into the person they're destined to become—all because we noticed and acted on their *hook*.

Whether at home or in school, instead of only following the rigid path provided by the curriculum or projects determined by others, they're now driven by their own interests. And yes, they'll still have to meet the mandated syllabus outcomes and do homework, but the reason behind their work is different. Everything becomes connected because they're working towards a bigger goal.

By taking time to notice their passion and not putting our own ideals onto them, we give them the tools to discover who they are and what they can achieve. It becomes about *who* they become, not *what*.

## Keep calm and don't take it personally

We've all done it. We've let our emotions get the better of us, shouting in frustration or using words we wish we hadn't said. And yes, we're tired, work is stressful, and time is short, but our children—whether in the classroom or at home—should never be on the receiving end of that. We need to remain consistent, fair and just. **What we say, we do. We follow the rules we set, and we keep the promises we make.**

When a child breaks the rules or misbehaves, don't take it personally. It's rarely an intentional challenge or an attack on us. More often, it's a signal—a cry for help, a need for connection or an indication that communication has broken down. As neuroscientist Professor Mark Williams often points out, 'All children are born as empaths.' They don't set out to upset or harm. They're a product of their environment or they've learned the behaviour elsewhere. Their behaviour usually reflects a deeper need, and it's our job to take time to understand and address the cause. Sometimes, that means recognising our own part in the situation. Whatever the approach, in my experience, maintaining a calm and consistent manner yields the best long-term results.

One of the most valuable lessons I've learned is this: unless there's an emergency, never raise your voice at a child, especially not in anger. Yelling can damage the trust we work so hard to build, and often leads to regretful words that can't be taken back and are long remembered. Children don't forget it when we use harsh words or threaten them.

No matter the situation, pause before responding. Take a breath, assess the context and seek out the deeper cause. Often, the issue isn't the behaviour itself but underlying feelings like frustration, confusion or disconnection. Children who act out often need the most love and understanding.

When addressing misbehaviour, do so calmly and gently, using a soft voice. If you're a parent, a gentle touch can help reinforce your care and support. Correct children privately if possible, to spare them embarrassment and prevent escalation. Sometimes, a quiet conversation, a meaningful new responsibility or one-on-one time can address the root cause of the behaviour far more effectively than loud reprimands.

Yelling may bring short-term compliance, but it seldom resolves the deeper issue. For genuine, long-lasting improvement, take a calm, thoughtful approach and offer consistent support. As Dr Laura Markham, author of *Peaceful Parent, Happy Kids*, reminds us:

> *Children often model their emotional responses on the adults around them. By remaining calm and composed, we teach them how to handle frustration and conflict in a healthy way.*

Although sometimes hard, staying calm builds trust. It's better for everyone's mental health and reinforces the foundations of our current and future relationship with them. When children know we'll respond fairly and predictably, they feel secure in the relationship. They learn their boundaries and understand that, even when they make mistakes, we're there to support them. And that's what truly matters.

## Be on their team

In 2021, the UK's Mental Health Foundation and Swansea University conducted a study involving 2349 British teenagers aged thirteen to nineteen. Their research revealed that 69 per cent of the participants reported feeling alone 'often' or 'sometimes' in the previous fortnight, and 59 per cent felt they had no one to talk to during that time.

These stark findings, alongside other international research, tell us that although many children have 30 other kids in their class, a teacher at school and parents at home, childhood can be a lonely place. Our children often feel alone, especially as they move into adolescence.

Of course, they have friends, but friendships can shift from week to week, or even day to day. These sudden changes, along with all the other challenges childhood delivers, can be terribly stressful. Children need a reliable support network behind them—like the pit crews at a Formula 1 race. Whether the driver finishes first or last, their team is always there, cheering them on, backing them up, and pushing them to be better with positivity and unwavering support.

As parents and teachers, we have a huge impact on our children's future. The best thing we can do is let them know we're on their side. There'll be times when they need their 'tyres pumped up', and we might be the only ones consistently showing up for them. To do that, we must be actively present, offering words of encouragement and support, making sure they never feel alone no matter how difficult life may seem.

In the classroom, this means recognising each child's individuality, and making sure everyone gets their fair share of attention, responsibility and care. No child should ever feel left out, no matter how they make us feel. We must make sure they feel seen, heard and valued.

At home, this support is even more intimate. These are *your* children, and the love and care you give them carries more weight. You must build that deep, emotional connection so they know they're never alone. Because, no matter how bad the world outside may seem, you're always there with a hug, a kiss and the message that everything will be okay and that we love them, no matter what.

I've seen both sides of the spectrum: some children are dropped off at school every day with a kiss and 'I love you very much and I'm proud of you', while others are sent by an Uber with no parent present, day in, day out. And the truth is that these small daily acts build over time and have a long-term effect on how children feel.

By consistently showing them we're on their team, and by offering gentle encouragement and reminders of our unconditional love, the foundation we build will help them navigate almost anything, because they know that if they fall, we'll be right there to catch them.

## 10 things to always tell your child

Here are ten things I believe every parent should consistently whisper into their child's ear before bedtime. These words are simple reminders that, no matter what, they'll never face life's challenges alone. There's always someone ready to lift them up, recharge their spirit or be there to catch them on the hardest days.

1. **I'm so proud of you.** 'Even when things don't go perfectly, I love how you try your best.'
2. **You can always talk to me.** 'I'm here to listen. No matter what's on your mind, big or small, there's never a bad time.'
3. **It's okay to make mistakes.** 'Everyone make mistakes, even grown-ups. What matters is that you learn and keep trying.'
4. **I'll always have your back.** 'No matter what, you can count on me to be there whenever you need me.'
5. **You make my life better.** 'Just having you around makes every day more special for me.'
6. **Be kind to yourself.** 'You're doing your best, and that's enough. Treat yourself the way you'd treat a good friend.'
7. **It's cool to be different.** 'The world needs people like you, with your unique ideas and dreams. Being yourself is what makes you special.'
8. **You're loved, no matter what.** 'Even if we argue or have tough days, my love for you never wavers.'
9. **It's okay to feel sad or angry sometimes.** 'Everyone feels sad or angry sometimes. I'm here if you want to talk about it or just need a hug.'
10. **I love spending time with you.** 'Whether we're doing something fun, chores or just hanging out, it's always my favourite part of every day.'

**Figure 29.** Ten things to always tell your child

## Use communication to lower their anxiety

Many children's fears come from the uncertainty of the unknown. A lack of clarity about their day can turn small worries into big stressors, impacting their ability to focus and thrive. Questions like these can race through their minds:

*What lessons are happening today?*

*Who will I sit with at lunch?*

*Will my teacher be there?*

*Who's picking me up after school?*

Now, think about how similar questions affect us as adults in our work or home life:

*What's the agenda for today's meeting?*

*Who will be there?*

*Will I have enough time to finish my tasks?*

*Who's picking up the kids?*

These uncertainties can leave us ALL feeling anxious, distracted or overwhelmed. If it's challenging for adults to navigate this unpredictability, imagine how much harder it must be for children, who lack the life experience and coping mechanisms we've developed. But don't worry—I've discovered several fantastic ways to ease these anxieties, which will make everyone's life a lot less stressful.

For parents, one of the simplest steps is to be on time for school. Of course, life happens, and being late occasionally is inevitable—especially with multiple children in a busy city. But aim to be at the classroom door on time. Although it may seem like nothing if we arrive a few minutes late, when you're a child, it's quite the opposite.

On countless occasions, I've seen what happens when a child arrives late to class. First, they walk in, feeling vulnerable and out of place. The other children have already chosen their seats, figured out who they're playing with at lunchtime and caught up on the latest gossip. Whether it's the latest Pokémon card or the new song by Taylor Swift, it all matters and your child feels like they've missed out—much like walking into an important executive meeting late with everyone turning to look. Being on time helps your child start the day with equality and inclusion.

At home, having a weekly family meeting can work wonders for everyone in your household. If this feels like I'm turning your entire existence upside down, remember, take what you like with these ideas and leave what you don't. If you do like the idea of a family meeting, however, maybe start with a scheduled check-in where everyone talks about their week ahead.

To complement this idea, you might have a calendar on the wall where everyone adds their plans:

*Who's picking up the kids on Thursday?*

*When is Daddy-Daughter Night?*

*What homework is due?*

Once again, sticking to the plan as much as possible is key. Of course, life changes and plans shift—that's natural. But communicating any changes well in advance helps children feel secure and included. Children are highly perceptive. They'll notice if they're consistently being overlooked or if the plan changes at the last minute without warning.

In the classroom, with 30 children or more looking to find out what the week ahead is all about, preparation is just as important, if not more so. Teachers can outline the term's subjects, projects, excursions and expectations from Day 1. If you've made your medium-term planning documents, then why not share a simplified version with your students? One they can stick in their books or even take home. Children can then refer back to the plan as the term progresses and tick off events, signifying progress; it's something solid to rely on.

For teachers who wish to take this idea of communication one step further, a simple but effective strategy is to have a board by the classroom door that lists 'the daily plan'. Before the children arrive at school, you write up the plans for the day for everyone to see, with times and even the 'educational void' or 'free time' allocation, which many children look forward to the most.

For younger children, you can make it more visual and include pictures rather than words. Either way, breaking down the day like this helps children know what to expect as soon as they walk in and discussing this plan during your morning meeting or circle time gives them the chance to ask questions and feel in control before the day kicks off.

Although this may seem time-consuming, research shows that structure and routine foster a sense of safety and reduce anxiety in children, especially those who are neurodivergent. A study by Selman et al. (2024) found that consistent routines and clear communication significantly reduced stress and improved emotional regulation in children with autism, as well as those living in foster care or refugee settings. For all children, however, having a clear sense of what's coming next helps them stay focused and feel secure, allowing them to engage more fully in learning.

Plus, when children are aware of the schedule, they often become the guardians of time, reminding you if you stray from the plan by saying things like, 'Sir, I think we're ten minutes late for the whole school assembly.' With this kind of efficiency, Google Calendar may soon become a thing of the past!

## Leave space for free time

As we've discussed throughout this book, independence is one of the greatest skills our children can develop. At home and in school, we should give children multiple opportunities to *choose* how they spend their time. As we discussed in Chapter 4, not every moment needs to be filled with curriculum content or structured activities. Some of the most valuable learning happens in unplanned moments.

These spaces are what I call the educational void or, as others call it, free time or golden time. This is a period in the classroom or at home where nothing is scheduled—no assignments, no clubs, no structured lessons, no expectations. When this free time is intentionally built into a child's routines, something powerful happens. Space is created for independence to thrive, where children can explore who they are and what they enjoy, without the pressure of deadlines or adult expectations.

Free time doesn't mean time wasted—it's time for exploration. It's an opportunity for children to engage in self-directed activities, pursue their interests and develop their autonomy. According to a 2014 study published in *Frontiers in Psychology* by Dr Yuko Munakata, a professor of psychology, children who have more time to engage in unstructured activities are more likely to develop stronger executive functioning skills, including planning, decision-making and self-regulation. How about that!

Many of the skills and qualities we've been emphasising—problem-solving, creativity, resilience and self-discipline—can emerge during these moments of unscheduled time. When children are left to their own devices, they must figure things out for themselves.

They may invent new games, create their own projects or simply daydream. All these experiences are valuable and contribute to their development as independent thinkers.

At home, this might mean cutting back on a few after-school clubs to allow children time to play in the garden, house or even in their room. This can feel uncomfortable at first, especially in a culture where every minute seems to need a purpose. But giving children the freedom to choose what they do with their time teaches them how to manage it.

In the classroom, teachers can explicitly list free time on the daily planning calendar, like this:

| | |
|---|---|
| **9.00–10.00 am** | Science activity on volcanoes |
| **10.00–10.45 am** | Mathematics (3D Shapes) |
| **10.45–11.30 am** | Free time |
| **11.30–12.00 pm** | Reading comprehension |

During this designated time, children are invited to choose what they want to do and with whom they wish to collaborate. To keep them on track, set some gentle limitations, such as requiring that the activity be linked to a topic the class is currently studying or has recently explored.

Although these ideas may seem abstract, by creating these 'educational voids', you can spend time observing your students' essential skills while also letting them follow up on something that has captured their interest, dive into a personal project or work collaboratively on an idea with a friend. And as children grow older, the free time can gradually be extended, fostering greater independence, until they're working with minimal guidance needed.

To some teachers, this idea might feel impossible or unattainable, but I'm convinced that if we integrate it into our timetable from an early age, the long-term benefits will far outweigh any initial adjustments. Through this approach, children learn to trust their instincts, make decisions and adapt when things don't go as planned. Yet our heavily structured timetables, mandated subjects, and constant interruptions from bells and announcements are limiting their opportunities to take ownership of their learning and develop those essential skills. Honestly, the sooner we can start implementing this, the better.

## The diary and the 15-minute morning

*'The most important thing in communication is hearing what isn't said.'*
*—Peter Drucker, author*

One of the most effective ways I've found to encourage communication with children is by giving each child their own diary. This diary becomes something special and almost sacred to them. Everyone receives a blank diary that they'll update for up to ten weeks and maybe keep for a lifetime. On the first day of term, the children decorate the diary however they like—with colourful pictures, patterns, logos or words. This personalisation is unique, it reflects who they are and, whether it's unicorns or poetry on the cover, the diary becomes theirs.

There are just two simple rules:

1. The diary must be looked after.
2. It must go home every day.

For the first fifteen minutes of each school day, the children have a clear objective: to independently choose their seat, gather their resources, check the daily plan on the whiteboard and write down the schedule. They also note who they plan to work with and what they aim to do during free time or passion project periods—whether they're planning to collaborate on a big project with a friend, start something new or just read quietly. The diary is a powerful tool to help children manage their time and develop executive functioning skills.

Throughout the day, they keep their diaries safe, ticking off things they've completed and jotting down anything that may be relevant. Each day, they use just one page. As the day comes to an end and the classroom is readied for tomorrow, they're asked to reflect—not on what they achieved but on how they felt. Maybe they write:

*I felt happy today when Thomas included me in his game.*

*I felt anxious because Mr McCormack forgot about the school assembly and he made us all rush.*

This kind of reflection encourages emotional awareness—something that can be difficult for children to express verbally or in person.

To further improve the impact of this tool, the teacher's desk has a box where children can place their diaries if they have a message they want the teacher to read. Sometimes there's something happening at home or school that they don't feel ready to talk about out loud—whether it's feeling left out, struggling with bullying, or even something positive but personal. This optional, secure method of communication gives them a way to share their thoughts without the pressure of face-to-face conversations, knowing their words will be treated with care. If needed, the teacher can silently intervene or offer support, while respecting their privacy.

The diary also plays a significant role in keeping parents in the loop about their child's day at school. It opens up opportunities for deeper conversations at home, moving beyond the standard 'What did you learn at school today?' Instead, parents can engage with their child's feelings, experiences and reflections on a more meaningful level, prompting conversations that build connection and understanding.

The diary fosters a culture of communication, personal responsibility, reflection and personal growth. More than just a tool for organisation, it can be incorporated from the very beginning of school life to become a bridge connecting children, teachers and parents in a meaningful way. According to a study published in *Frontiers in Psychology* in 2019:

*Emotional expression is crucial for children's social and emotional development, as it enables them to communicate their needs and feelings, facilitating support from caregivers and peers.*

I've seen this firsthand in my own classroom and in those I've managed. When we give children a voice, encouraging them to express their emotions and offering a safe space for sharing, we let them know that their thoughts and feelings matter. They have the power to communicate their needs and experiences in a way that feels right for them, safe in the knowledge that it will always be read and acted upon if required.

## Provide different ways to find the answer

As adults, it's easy to think we need to have all the answers. But if we want our children to grow into independent thinkers, we need to resist the urge to spoon-feed them answers. When they ask questions, our job isn't to know everything—how could we? Only ChatGPT knows everything, right? Instead of providing them with a quick answer, the best thing we can do is to guide them towards research and investigation. For instance, answering their question with a question:

*Why is the Moon round?*

*Is it round? I'm not sure. Let's find out together—*
*want to help me research it?*

Or guiding them to a way to find the answer:

*Can we write to the Prime Minister?*

*I'd love to write to him, too. If you can find his email address,*
*let's draft a letter together.*

While this is a great start, if we want our children to become seekers of knowledge, both at school and home, we need to provide as many avenues for research as possible. Relying solely on Google, ChatGPT or even what Grandad says just isn't enough. Critical thinking and deep learning come from digging deeper and gathering different perspectives, not just one or two sources. Encouraging them to consult at least three sources from three different media is a great way to set a standard. Honestly, this should be part of every school rubric.

Of course, when we think of research, computers are often the first things that come to mind. And I get it—I've been glued to my own computer for nearly a year while writing this book! But I've also spent endless hours talking to teachers and parents, observing my friends' children while they play, and having countless phone conversations. Research is so much more than just finding facts. As Professor Jason Skues of Swinburne University puts it:

> *To truly know something, you need to be able to have a conversation about it and draw from multiple sources of information and from multiple avenues. You can't just list a bunch of facts and expect people to take you seriously.*

So, the question is, in an age where fake news fuels uncertainty and requires media literacy and critical thinking skills, are we providing our children with enough opportunities—starting at an early age—to gather and evaluate information from diverse sources?

Ultimately, research shouldn't be limited to computers. Plenty of other valuable resources are available for children to gather information. Perhaps they have a classmate who's a dinosaur expert, or maybe the school principal or other teachers have insights to share. Even a small classroom library, if available, can be a treasure trove of information.

But my two favourite resources (which you don't see often enough in schools) are these:

## 1. The humble telephone

Imagine giving children access to a telephone. Allowing them to call anyone in the world to get answers to their questions opens up endless possibilities. Of course, you'll need a booking system and a child-safe protocol, with the teacher making the call or listening in, but the potential is incredible. Children could call the National

History Museum to ask about dinosaurs or reach out to an international animal welfare charity for advice on how to save an injured bird they've found. It brings the world right into the classroom and children develop a plethora of life skills along the way.

## 2. The parent skills database

At the start of the year, the teacher asks parents in their class to fill out a survey about their jobs and hobbies, then compiles all that information into a handy chart. Whenever children are working on a project and require further research or expertise, they can refer to this chart and reach out to a parent with expertise in a specific area. For example, if a group is researching dinosaurs, they could consult one of the mums in the class, who happens to be a palaeontologist at the local university. Or if they need help designing a website or poster, they could ask a parent who works in web design. With a little encouragement, that parent might even visit the school to help build the website, making the experience even more engaging and hands-on. The school community comes together in a meaningful way, with children learning from someone they already know and trust. It's a win-win, and the need for a 'working bee' is immediately null and void.

# If they're busy, leave them alone

In many Montessori schools, it's almost unheard of for a child—or even a teacher—to disrupt someone who is deeply absorbed in their work. No matter what's next on the schedule, or how pressing the next lesson might seem, the golden rule is:

*If people are busy working, we leave them alone.*

Ever been absorbed in reading a book only to be startled by the doorbell, then you realise you can't remember the last three pages of the story? The same thing happens to our children as they learn.

Unfortunately, even in schools celebrated for being future-focused and progressive, we still hear bells and announcements, disturbing the peaceful hum of deep learning. These interruptions—announcing a parcel waiting at reception or reminding everyone about an upcoming after-school bake sale—might seem minor. But these disruptions can have a profound impact on how our children learn.

When children learn something new, they rely heavily on what's called 'working memory'. Alan Baddeley, a leading researcher in cognitive psychology, describes it beautifully as a system with compartments that temporarily hold and manage information until the brain either moves it into long-term memory or lets it go. Most people can hold about five to seven pieces of information in their working memory at once. However, with today's constant distractions—like social media reels or instant updates—children struggle to keep even those few slots available for learning new concepts.

When an unnecessary interruption shatters their focus, that carefully managed information can be lost in an instant, making it harder for children to retain or fully engage with what they were learning.

Imagine a child completely absorbed in their work. At school, some children might be doing maths, others might be writing stories or building models. At home, they might be busy crafting a castle out of cardboard boxes or weaving an elaborate tale in their notebook. Their working memory is running smoothly, and they're in a beautiful state of flow, where learning feels natural and everything clicks. Then an announcement bursts through the speakers: 'Jonathan, please come to reception to collect your sports uniform, your mum just dropped it off.' Or at home, you call out to ask if they've fed the dog yet.

Here's where the problem lies.

In that moment, the child's focus is shattered. The conveyor belt of information grinds to a halt and everything they've just been learning vanishes. Research by Kraft and Monti-Nussbaum in 2021 demonstrated that interruptions like these result in up to 10–20 days of lost learning time over a school year. When the interruption ends, children take a while to get back on track. They might have to reread the last few lines of their story or mentally reconstruct where they left off on that cardboard model and it's a time-consuming process to get the memory conveyor belt running at full speed again.

So, if we want to maximise our children's ability to achieve flow and engage in deep learning, we must avoid unnecessary disruptions. At school, that means turning off bells and announcements that aren't for emergencies. At home, it means waiting for a natural pause before asking questions or giving reminders. If Jonathan needs to know his sports uniform has arrived, let's find a more subtle way to get the message to him.

## Everyone has a job

Children love doing the work of adults and classroom jobs are no different. The concept of classroom jobs bring a sense of collective responsibility to the children who share the space, while also fostering a culture where everyone pitches in to keep the environment ready for learning.

To do this effectively and make sure the classroom is ready each day, the teacher can ask the children to brainstorm a list of tasks they think are essential. Then assign each child a job for the week, which rotates throughout the year. At the end of the day, before doing their daily reflection and heading home, the class spends five minutes on their designated jobs. You can play some gentle music—maybe Mozart or Bach—in the background, creating a calm atmosphere. Whether it's sharpening pencils, organising library books or restocking paper for the next day, each child contributes. And you do too. That's right, you'll have a job as well! When the music starts, you'll model what teamwork looks like and get involved in preparing the room for another day of independent learning.

The best part? When the children leave for home, the room is set for the next day, and they have a beautiful sense of collective responsibility and cohesion. Plus, you won't have to stay behind to tidy up, sharpen pencils or restock supplies! You can head home, put your feet up and relax—well, almost. You'll still have to plan the nest day's lessons, mark books and write reports. But hey, at least the classroom is ready, and heading straight home sounded nice, didn't it?

# Let them sit where they like

When I travel around the world meeting children in schools, I always ask them one simple question about the school they go to:

*Can you sit where you like?*

More often than not, the answer is 'no'. In many traditional classrooms worldwide, children are seated in neat rows, often with the goal of minimising chatter or keeping so-called 'unruly' children apart. While the intention might be well-meaning, this rigid setup often stifles how children are inclined to learn and engage with their environment.

Every classroom is filled with a range of learning styles. Having all desks facing forward might seem efficient, ensuring all eyes are on the teacher, but it reinforces a teacher-centred approach to learning. By letting children choose where they sit each day, we signal that we trust them to decide where they'll learn best, based on how they feel or their mood that day.

First, however, set up the rules of engagement and ensure the space caters to different types of learners. This means creating distinct areas—individual tables for those who prefer working solo, paired tables for cooperative learners and group tables for collaborative work. Some children may also prefer working on the floor, while those who are easily distracted may need a quieter space.

Once the environment is ready and your classroom values and expectations are in place, you'll notice these different types of learners begin to emerge as they choose where to sit based on the following traits:

## 1. The isolated learner

This child thrives when working alone, fully focused. They like to come in, sit by themselves, work diligently and leave, producing high-quality work without needing much interaction with others.

## 2. The parallel learner

These are pairs of children who work almost in sync. They sit side by side, often doing the same task at the same time, providing moral support by being together.

## 3. The cooperative learner

Similar to parallel learners, cooperative learners work in pairs but aren't always working on the same thing. They help each other, chat while they work, and offer friendship and encouragement along the way.

## 4. The collaborative learner

These children gravitate towards group tables, often forming a team to tackle larger projects. Their workspace is filled with chatter, movement, and ideas flying back and forth. Natural leaders usually emerge within the group. It's a hive of activity where each child brings their strengths to achieve a shared goal.

**Figure 30.** Different learning types

## A taste of the real world

Traditional 'everyone facing forward behind desks of two' classrooms were designed to enforce conformity in industrial Britain, but we're a long way from there now, and I find quiet classrooms to be stagnant and stale.

Think of hot-desking or co-working spaces in modern companies. Offices like Canva in Sydney or Airbnb in San Francisco operate in much the same way. Employees are free to choose their workspaces based on their tasks or personal preferences. So why shouldn't our classrooms function in the same way?

A lively, engaging and dynamic classroom feels like a real-world environment—full of individuality, background noise, movement and collaboration. The children are learning in a natural way, and the space hums with progress, trust and productivity.

With an emphasis on movement and choice, this model of learning is anything but quiet. It involves chatting, debate and a gentle hum of conversation. So, for those who might ask, 'What about those children who need silence to concentrate?' For them, a basket of noise-cancelling headphones in the corner can easily solve that issue.

# The power of positivity

I know it's not realistic to be positive all the time, but the impact of positivity on how children feel about school, learning and life is huge. Our goal should be to get children excited to come to school every day. But how do we make that happen? Well, simple gestures matter, like greeting them with a smile, encouraging their ideas, or (for parents) giving them a hug after school and showing real interest in what they have to share.

An often overlooked area is how parents and schools communicate with each other. Too often, parents only hear from the school via the weekly newsletter or when there's a problem. But what if we flipped that? What if we made it a priority to share the good things children are doing, not just when there's a problem to solve?

I once worked with a teacher who was struggling with a difficult class and constant negative feedback from parents. Looking into it, I discovered she was desperately trying to involve parents in improving the class but was only sending home messages about problems: 'Please talk to Alex—he was very chatty in class today.'

I suggested she shift the focus and start highlighting the great things her students were doing. She agreed. Within weeks, the energy in the classroom changed and parents became more supportive. It was amazing how a simple change could make such a huge difference.

Imagine opening an email that celebrates Sunita helping younger children or working hard on her Vikings project during free time. Instead of a scolding, Sunita comes home to 'I'm so proud of you!' This kind of recognition can transform how a child feels about school, making it a place where their best side is seen and celebrated.

Daily emails would be too much, but a quick, encouraging word at pick-up time or an occasional note can work wonders. A simple compliment can lead to a high-five or hug, leaving everyone feeling uplifted. This small change helps strengthen the bonds between parents, teachers and students, creating a thriving school community.

## Reignite your sense of wonder

When our children are young, we often find ourselves waiting (sometimes not so patiently) as they stare up at the sky or gently stroke a leaf. We're in a hurry, so we say, 'Come on, we're going to be late for school!' But if we just stop for a moment, we can remember that the world is pretty incredible—especially when you're seeing it through fresh eyes.

Take the Moon, for instance. It formed around 4.5 billion years ago when a Mars-sized object called Theia smashed into Earth. The debris from that collision eventually came together to form our Moon, which stabilises Earth's tilt and controls the tides, allowing life to thrive on land. At about 400 times smaller than the Sun and 400 times closer to Earth, it's the perfect size and distance to cover the Sun perfectly, causing solar eclipses. But the Moon is slowly drifting away from us at 3.8 cm per year, so those breathtaking eclipses won't last forever—enjoy them while you can!

Or how about this? Blue whales, the biggest creatures on Earth, used to live on land millions of years ago! Their ancestors slowly evolved to return to the sea, taking their fur and their lungs with them, and eventually growing into the giants we know today.

And what about the concept of sound? Music, thunderstorms, birds chirping? None of these exist! Your brain just interprets waves of air hitting the bones in your ear, which creates the illusion of sound. The universe is dead silent. The same goes for smells and colours—they're crafted by your brain to help make sense of the world. So, when someone asks, 'If a tree falls in the forest and no one is around to hear it, does it make a sound?' Nope. Sound isn't real; it's all in our heads.

You might be wondering, why does this feel like a chapter from *100 Amazing Facts You Didn't Know*? Well, these fascinating little nuggets of knowledge are memorable. Now imagine the impact of hearing them as a curious seven-year-old.

Our children need to be excited about the world we live in again. Too often, they're glued to YouTube or TikTok videos. But the real world is where the magic happens—splashing in puddles, digging in the dirt or feeling the wind in their hair. And as their guides, we have to inspire them to want to explore it.

If we stop in the street to notice the Moon and talk about how incredible it is, our children will notice it, too. They'll sense our awe, hear the excitement in our voice and soak it all up. It could be a butterfly in your garden, a rock at the park or a flower blooming through a crack on the pavement—there's wonder everywhere.

And yeah, I get it. It's easy to get bogged down by work, the news, interest rates or the economy. But right outside your door is a planet full of wonder, which can spark an unstoppable sense of curiosity in our children.

If you've sadly lost that sense of wonder, it's time to get it back. If you still have it, make sure you keep it alive. Your curiosity will light the way for your children to see everything and everyone as an opportunity to learn something new.

## What is it all about?

As we've explored throughout this book, the cracks in our understanding of what defines a successful educational journey stem from a fundamental mismatch: our schools and homes are slowly drifting apart. The same is happening with our children. They're learning from behind screens, which many think is a future-focused approach. But it's quite the opposite. The expectations we place on our children and the environments in which we teach them are nothing like what they'll encounter in the real world.

Our homes and classrooms don't always align with what schools demand, and vice versa. The education system seems obsessed with competition—children against children, schools against schools. We prioritise curriculum over connection, focusing more on grades and outcomes than on building relationships and teaching real-world skills. Teachers, under immense pressure from time constraints and performance targets, often aren't allowed to be the educators they dreamed of being—ones who signed up to change the world. Instead of fostering creativity and connection, they're forced to chase attainment and data.

Isn't the whole point of education to prepare our children to be compassionate, capable humans? As Professor Mark Williams says, 'We're a connected species' which thrives on collaboration and experiences that bring us together. What makes us unique among all known species is our ability to work together, care for each other and share responsibilities through trust.

Consider ants. They're industrious and organised, building complex colonies with intricate tunnels, and working together in synchrony to gather food and protect their queen. They can carry up to 100 times their own body weight—that's like you carrying a large school bus. They can also communicate with each other through chemical signals and carry out incredible feats, like forming bridges with their own bodies to cross gaps. But you won't find ants helping out a neighbouring colony when their food stores run low, or sharing resources with other insect species in need. Only humans can look beyond our immediate circles to care, collaborate and extend kindness across boundaries, building connections that make the world a more compassionate place.

It's through empathy, a willingness to help and connect beyond our own tribe that we find success—not just in education but in life. Our classrooms and homes should reflect the world we want to build: one filled with understanding, trust and shared purpose. My hope is that the stories, ideas and strategies shared in this book inspire you to rethink how we educate our children, what we expect from them and what we view as educational success.

Here's my challenge to you:

- Try some of these ideas in your classroom or at home.
- Give every child a diary to plan, record and reflect on their day.
- Have a family meeting tonight.
- Rearrange your classroom to cater to all four types of learners.
- Delete parts of your timetable and replace them with 'free time'.

Once you've started, reflect on the new energy and direction that your class, home and community begins to embrace.

We may not be able to fly or see ultraviolet light, but we can work together, trust each other, and show empathy and understanding. And those are exactly the things we should be focusing on if we want to build a better, more compassionate education system—one that emphasises not just what our children are achieving but who they are becoming.

## Step 7

# Trust is key

Back in 2009, I bought a car. I'd never owned one before—only a motorcycle. But as I got older and life started to feel a bit more finite, I figured my days on two-wheeled transportation were coming to an end.

Not having much money but loving unique things, I found a beat-up 1974 Datsun 260Z online for a few thousand dollars. It had been one of my favourite cars since childhood, so I decided to buy it. Over the next few years, I slowly brought it back to life—changing the seats to leather, repainting it with a friend's help and making it look fantastic. The car became my pride and joy. I drove it to school every day and took it on road trips all over Australia.

Fast forward ten years. I arrived at school only to find my usual parking spot taken. So I parked in another spot close to the corner of a quiet junction. As I did so, I got a strange feeling in my stomach. Something was telling me not to park there. I had no idea where the feeling came from, but it was strong, right down in my gut.

I didn't listen. I hopped out, locked the door, shook off the feeling as ridiculous and went to class.

After a long day in school, I returned to my car to head home. But as I put the key in the door to open it, something wasn't quite right. To my dismay, someone had smashed into the front corner, denting it badly, and tearing off the bumper and right headlight. I was devastated. Not only was my beloved car damaged, but I regretted that I hadn't trusted my instincts. I knew I shouldn't have parked there, but I ignored my gut—and look what happened.

Since that day, I've always trusted my gut, or intuition. It's not some mystical sixth sense; rather, it's the ability to tap into a deep well of subconscious knowledge. For example, perhaps my mind had catalogued memories of that corner being a tricky spot—drivers taking it too fast, the road curving precariously. We know more than we realise, and listening to that quiet, inner nudge can make all the difference.

Trusting our instincts helps us make choices that feel right and safe. Trust isn't just internal—it's what binds us to others and fuels our ability to inspire and support each other, but it's often riddled with doubt.

As adults, self-doubt is something we all face from time to time. We wonder if we're doing enough, if others are judging us or if we're falling short. But here's the thing: we're not alone in this feeling. Teachers, parents, professionals—everyone has moments where they're just winging it and learning as they go. And that's okay. We're all doing our best, growing with each challenge and, often, we're doing far better than we give ourselves credit for.

If we want our children to believe they can do amazing things, take risks and chase their dreams, we need to start believing in ourselves—and each other. Trusting others is important, but trusting ourselves goes so much deeper.

- **For teachers**, trusting yourself means leaning into your gut instinct when you feel a lesson isn't landing quite right. That's your cue to pivot, to make it personal and engaging. You're there on the front lines, picking up on children's emotions and adapting to their needs in real time. Trust that voice inside saying, 'Let's try something different.' Your intuition, experience and care help you meet them where they are and give them exactly what they need to thrive.
- **For parents**, there's no guidebook or degree to prepare you for the tough moments. But here's the good news: you know your child better than anyone else. Trust that little voice inside telling you what they need—a bit of patience, an extra hug or just more of your time. We've all felt that pang of regret after raising our voices or getting caught up in a screen at the exact moment our child needed

us most. Trust those feelings—they're there for a reason—and act on them.

- **For parents and teachers together**, the key is working as a team. Trust each other and come together to define what success looks like for your children. You're the role models and guides and the ones with the power to shape their futures. When your values and expectations are in sync, everything becomes smoother—for everyone. That shared trust and commitment make all the difference in helping to build a supportive community.
- **For school principals, heads of departments and government officials**, this is where trust is key. Teaching is a profession for a reason. We don't second-guess a doctor prescribing medication for tonsillitis or a solicitor drafting a property contract—we trust them to be the skilled professionals they are. Teachers deserve that same respect.

When teachers are trusted to do the job they've worked so hard to master, their passion shines through. No one thrives under micromanagement: being told which textbook page to turn to or worksheet to hand out. Every teacher brings something unique to the classroom—their own stories, experiences and perspectives—and those personal touches ignite the passion we all hope to see in schools.

When teachers feel trusted, their lessons come to life, filled with creativity, pride and excitement. That energy ripples out, inspiring children, families and the wider community. And when schools are filled with empowered, passionate teachers, the potential for what children can achieve becomes limitless.

Throughout this book, I've handpicked many personal stories to show what teaching and parenting can look like, and evoke the possibilities in raising resilient children. It was incredibly difficult to choose which stories to tell.

I could have told you about the children in India who planted a forest of 25,000 trees, hoping to attract their first bird, or the children in Australia who wrote a song about climate change that went viral on Spotify. There simply aren't enough pages to include them all.

But there's one story I haven't told you yet. It's the kind of story that shows what happens when we model the behaviours we want to see in our children. It demonstrates the power of human connection over curriculum and highlights how the true measure of educational success has nothing to do with points or scores but everything to do with the impact we have on the world. It's a story of hope for a better tomorrow.

## Backpacks of hope

It was mid-2021. I'd been a principal for about four years and, by this point, I had a remarkable team of teachers working with me. They weren't just smart, well-travelled and open-minded—they genuinely cared about each child and their individual needs. I trusted them. The school had become a beautiful place filled with innovation, fresh ideas and a strong sense of freedom.

The parents were also incredibly supportive. We'd worked hard to establish shared values and practised what I've described throughout this book. Home and school had a real sense of alignment, and everyone knew we were in this together. It was an environment where children thrived and it was a joyful place to be.

Four girls in Year 6 had booked an appointment to see me at 11 am with an idea they wanted to run by me. They were all eleven years old, extremely independent and close friends.

They had been studying continents with their teacher, who introduced them to Spain because that's where she was from. Through tactile and engaging content, she linked Spain to Europe then invited the children to choose a continent that interested them and research a country within it—using the 'emotional circle of learning'.

They explained that they had chosen to study Asia, specifically Myanmar. Through their independent research they discovered that a war was happening and that many refugee children would soon be arriving in Australia. They'd lost their families and had nowhere else to go. One of the girls said:

*We couldn't stop thinking about what it would feel like to be in a strange country, all alone. If we can do something—anything—to help them feel welcome, we want to try.*

My eyes lit up hearing this. It meant the system we had in place was working. Listening to the depth of their understanding and foundational knowledge, alongside their determination to make a difference, was music to my ears.

Then they asked if they could borrow $500 from me.

'$500? What for?' I asked.

They wanted to use the money to buy backpacks they'd researched online. They planned to give these backpacks to the parents in our school community and ask them to fill them with items the families no longer needed—things that might help refugee children settle into school and life in Australia.

It was a brilliant idea, but I wasn't just going to hand them $500. I didn't want to dampen their enthusiasm, so I said:

*There are plenty of ways to raise $500 in a community like ours. Come back to me once you've figured out the first step—raising the funds.*

The next day, they were back—this time with a poster they'd created. It announced a bake sale. They'd already gone around to the other classes, letting everyone know that on Thursday, all the students would bring homemade treats and cakes for parents to buy. This money would go towards buying the backpacks. Now, with fewer than 100 children in the primary campus at the time, it would take an impressive bake sale to raise $500! But I added their poster to the school newsletter. Soon enough, Thursday rolled around.

At the end of the day, I wandered out to the playground to see the bake sale in full swing. I heard the girls calling out:

*Every cookie saves a refugee!*

*Chocolate has never tasted so sweet!*

With some cookies priced at $10 each and their persuasive powers in action, plus the support of the community, the girls struck gold.

When the families all left, their arms filled with chocolate cookies and freshly baked fairy cakes, the girls had raised $514 and it was time for the project to begin.

The next morning, we met in my office. I congratulated the girls on their creativity and determination. We ordered the backpacks to be delivered to the school.

The girls showed me a PowerPoint presentation they'd put together the night before, documenting their plan for the project. It included some heartbreaking statistics about what the young refugees had endured and the long distances they'd need to travel to reach their new home in Australia. The girls had a clear goal for their well-organised slideshow—to use it as leverage.

They asked if they could present their story to some influential mums in our community to gain their support. Naturally, I agreed. The next morning at 10 am, the three mums in question appeared at my door. The girls had prepared a big screen in my office, set up their laptop, and shared their compelling story and plan.

By the time they'd finished, one of the mums was in tears—not just of sadness for the children, but also of pride for the young people our community was producing. With that, the girls secured the full support of these mums and, in turn, the whole community.

Soon, the backpacks arrived. The girls were beyond excited. As they planned the next phase of the project—distributing the bags to families—I gave them one piece of advice. Having organised fundraisers and collections before, I knew that parents sometimes used these occasions as a chance to offload unwanted items. So, I gently warned the girls, with no disrespect to the parents, that they might end up with bags of random items the refugee children wouldn't find useful.

Not to worry, the girls assured me. One of them handed me a typed and printed list of acceptable items for the backpacks. It included dictionaries, rulers, pencil cases, sunscreen, shoes and even cuddly toys. Stunned by their thoroughness, I asked how they came up with it. One replied:

*You always give us freedom within limits, so we're doing the same with the parents.*

I laughed out loud at that.

The next day, the girls stood outside both school campuses, canvassing families to take a backpack home and fill it with the specified items. They spoke with so much passion. Even when parents hesitated, they turned on the charm, saying, 'How would you feel if you had to leave your country without your family?' I wouldn't have gone that far myself, but it clearly worked! Before long, all 100 backpacks were gone—some families even took three.

Two weeks later, all the filled backpacks had returned to the school library. The girls asked for the morning off class to check all the bags and, of course, the teachers and I approved this Big Work.

At lunchtime, I went to the library to check on them. They'd been busy all morning, sorting through every single item. I asked what they'd been up to. They explained:

> *We emptied all the bags onto the floor and made sure each one had a fair share of items. And because we bought three different-coloured bags, the green ones are for three to six-year-olds, the blue for six to twelve, and the black for twelve and older.*

I was stunned. How could they have organised this so well? Their thoughtfulness and preparation were remarkable.

We took a photo of the girls standing proudly in front of their backpacks, fists in the air, celebrating their hard work.

But afterwards, I brought them back to reality. 'Girls, I'm so proud of you. You've accomplished so much, but we have a problem. The refugees are arriving in Darwin and we're in Sydney—that's about 3000 kilometres away. And we're out of money. We're still a long way from success.'

I expected them to look puzzled or discouraged, but I was wrong.

One girl pulled a piece of paper from her pocket and said, 'No problem, Gavin. We have a plan for that. Can we use the telephone in your office, please?'

'My telephone? What for?'

*We have the phone numbers of two charities in Australia that help refugees from Myanmar and we want to call them to tell them our story to see if they can help us get the backpacks there for free.*

Once again, I was floored. Of course, I said yes.

I took the piece of paper with the phone numbers, called each organisation to let them know about the calls they'd be receiving, and asked the girls to come back to my office after lunch.

That afternoon, the girls returned. Gathering around my desk, one of them dialled the first number and put it on speaker. I had no idea what they were going to say, so I let them take the lead. The girls didn't just ask for help; they invited the charity representatives to visit our school and meet them in person. One agreed immediately and the other invited us to meet them on the grounds of another school.

When the call ended, I asked the girls why they didn't just accept help from the first organisation. They replied, they wanted to interview both groups first, then decide which one they liked best. I almost fainted at their audacity and thoughtfulness.

Over the next week, the girls met with both organisations. Eventually, they chose to partner with a charity called The House of Sakinah, a wonderful group run by Muslim women.

'Why did you choose this charity in particular?' I asked. Their response?

*It's a charity run by women, and we're girls, so we want to support women in business.*

Who was I to argue? I was just a man standing in the way of their vision!

When a bus arrived at the school from The House of Sakinah, the girls loaded the 100 bags onto it. We took some photos and the bus set off on its epic journey. It was a momentous day.

Weeks passed. The girls got busy with other projects and their usual classwork, but they constantly asked if there was any word from the ladies at the charity. But nothing came through ... until one Thursday, just before the end of term.

I received an email from the CEO of the charity that said:

*Dear Gavin, your children have changed the world.*
*Make sure you're sitting down, have some tissues*
*handy and press play on the video below.*

As the video began to play, I saw a group of young girls seated in what looked like a transit room, the fluorescent lights casting a cool glow over everything. Their hijabs—some pastel, some bright—contrasted with the blandness of the room, and though their faces looked weary, their eyes were wide with anticipation. Each girl held a backpack; black, blue and green—the very ones our students had filled so carefully, item by item.

The girls opened their bags slowly, almost reverently, pulling out dictionaries, lunchboxes and small plush toys—koalas and teddies. They hugged their new belongings, clutching the soft toys to their chests. Some whispered in their own language, while others looked down, smiling. The room was filled with an almost sacred quiet. Watching it, I felt my eyes well up. By the time the last backpack had been opened, my shirt was soaked. I felt such pride and gratitude, knowing this simple act had brought so much comfort.

I called the girls into my office. They entered silently, already sensing the emotion in the room. They stood around my desk, eyes wide and expectant. I pointed to the tissues I'd set out on the table and told them they might want to keep them close. As I pressed play, we fell into silence, watching as the refugees carefully explored their bags. The girls were transfixed, faces softening with each new item being pulled from the backpacks.

Tears began streaming down their faces—not from sadness, but from something deeper. These were tears of hope, of connection, of seeing firsthand that their kindness had crossed continents and touched lives.

I opened my mouth to tell them how proud I was, but the words wouldn't come. The lump in my throat was so big, I could hardly breathe, let alone speak. So we stood in shared silence, watching the impact of their actions ripple across the screen.

After we'd watched the video twice, one of the girls wiped her cheeks, looked up and said, 'I want to do it again.' The others nodded in agreement. They put their arms around each other, sharing a quiet sense of accomplishment, then made their way home for the day.

That night, I wrote an email to our community about what the girls had achieved. It was the most meaningful email I've ever written, capturing everything I believe is missing in much of today's education. Those four brave, confident girls had shown us all that when we empower students to take on meaningful, purposeful work, they can achieve anything. It was my proudest moment for our school community. From board members to parents, teachers to students, we'd all worked together to define what educational success could look like. The proof was in the smiles of those refugee girls in Darwin—girls who thought they'd been forgotten but now knew they mattered.

A few days later, the school holidays began. During that time, I must have told this story 50 times—to friends at parties, on hikes and in passing conversations.

When the holidays ended, I arrived back at school around 7 am, hoping to get a head start before the children and teachers arrived. As I unlocked my office door, I saw the same four girls already waiting for me, excitement shining in their eyes.

I laughed and asked, 'What are you doing here so early? School doesn't start for another hour.'

One stepped forward and said:

> *We saw on the news that women are suffering from abuse by their husbands during COVID-19, and we want to help them.*

In that moment, I realised they had fully internalised the spirit of education, compassion and action. These girls, once just curious students, had become changemakers, driven by a purpose that went beyond any curriculum.

'Well,' I said, feeling a surge of excitement. 'What's the plan?'

Their faces lit up. They had a plan, alright. And I had no doubt they'd carry it through.

*

Why is this story so important? First, it's a powerful reminder of what children can achieve when we trust them and step back. Second, it highlights what's so often missing in conversations about how to improve our education systems.

When we talk about the future of education, the conversation often drifts towards advancements like AI, virtual classrooms, or immersive tools like augmented reality and virtual reality. And while these innovations are transformative, they're just tools. Tools to spark curiosity, help children explore and make learning exciting. But tools alone can't shape the hearts and minds of the next generation.

Education has to reach into the essence of what schools and homes stand for—sanctuaries where humanity is nurtured. Schools aren't just places for academic instruction, they're spaces where children absorb the values that define who they are: kindness, empathy, resilience, integrity and a sense of purpose. These qualities will prepare them to thrive in a rapidly changing world.

And the home? Values are equally important. It's in the shared dinners, bedtime stories and meaningful conversations where children first learn about love, trust and compassion. Education starts in those small, warm moments at home and grows in the classroom.

The future of education isn't about chasing technological mastery, having the top grades or attending the best school. It's about raising resilient children and fostering the human connections between students and teachers, children and parents, and individuals and their communities. The true measure of a successful education is the kind of human beings we raise—humans filled with empathy, wisdom and the determination to leave the world better than they found it.

# Chapter references

## Chapter 1


Adamson, L. B., & Frick, J. E. (2003). The still face: A history of a shared experimental paradigm. *Infancy, 4*(4), 451–473. https://doi.org/10.1207/S15327078IN0404_01

Bandura, A. (1977). *Social learning theory.* Prentice-Hall.

Braune-Krickau, K., Schneebeli, L., Pehlke-Milde, J., Gemperle, M., Koch, R., & von Wyl, A. (2021). Smartphones in the nursery: Parental smartphone use and parental sensitivity and responsiveness within parent–child interaction in early childhood (0–5 years): A scoping review. *Infant Mental Health Journal, 42*(2), 161–175. https://doi.org/10.1002/imhj.21908

Harris, R. (2011). *The happiness trap: How to stop struggling and start living.* Shambhala.

Ismail, N. A. S., Mageswaran, N., Bujang, S. M., & Awang Besar, M. N. (2022). Beyond words: Analyzing non-verbal communication techniques in a medical communication skills course via synchronous online platform. *BMC Medical Education, 22,* 1–9.

Kemp, S. (2022, January 26). *Digital 2022: Global overview report.* Data Reportal. Retrieved from https://datareportal.com/reports/digital-2022-global-overview-report

Mehrabian, A. (1971). *Silent messages: Implicit communication of emotions and attitudes.* Belmont, CA: Wadsworth Publishing Company.

Mezulis, A. H., Hyde, J. S., & Abramson, L. Y. (2006). The developmental origins of cognitive vulnerability to depression: Temperament, parenting, and negative life events in childhood as contributors to negative cognitive style. *Developmental Psychology, 42*(6), 1012–1025. https://doi.org/10.1037/0012-1649.42.6.1012

Rizzolatti, G., Fadiga, L., Gallese, V., & Fogassi, L. (1996). Premotor cortex and the recognition of motor actions. *Cognitive Brain Research, 3*(2), 131–141. https://doi.org/10.1016/0926-6410(95)00038-0

Shipp, Josh. Every kid is one caring adult away from being a success story. TEDx Talks, 2017. Available at: https://www.youtube.com/watch?v=Kf3_KvWJpQA

Tronick, E., Als, H., Adamson, L., Wise, S., & Brazelton, T. B. (1978). The infant's response to entrapment between contradictory messages in face-to-face interaction. *Journal of the American Academy of Child Psychiatry, 17*(1), 1–13. https://doi.org/10.1016/S0002-7138(09)62273-1

Twenge, J. (2017). *iGen: Why today's super-connected kids are growing up less rebellious, more tolerant, less happy—and completely unprepared for adulthood.* Atria Books.

Vogel, S., & Schwabe, L. (2016). Learning and memory under stress: Implications for the classroom. *NPJ: Science of Learning, 1,* 16011. https://doi.org/10.1038/npjscilearn.2016.11

Witters, D. (2023, May 17). US depression rates reach new highs. *Gallup.* Retrieved from https://news.gallup.com/poll/505745/depression-rates-reach-new-highs.aspx

## Chapter 2

Dweck, C. S. (2006). *Mindset: The new psychology of success.* Random House.

Einstein, A., cited in Viereck, G. S. (1929, October 26). What life means to Einstein. *Saturday Evening Post.* Retrieved from https://gwern.net/doc/philosophy/1929-einstein.pdf

Gilbert, P. (2010). *Compassion focused therapy: Distinctive features.* Routledge.

Hubbard, E. (1901, November). *The Philistine: A periodical of protest, June 1901 to November 1901.* Kessinger Publishing.

Hubbard, E. (1927). *The note book of Elbert Hubbard.* The Roycrofters.

Jinpa, T. (2015). *A fearless heart: How the courage to be compassionate can transform our lives.* Avery.

Kanov, J. M., Maitlis, S., Worline, M. C., Dutton, J. E., Frost, P. J., & Lilius, J. M. (2004). Compassion in organizational life. *American Behavioral Scientist, 47*(6), 808–827. https://psycnet.apa.org/doi/10.1177/0002764203260211

Lillard, A. S. (2021). *Montessori: The science behind the genius* (3rd ed.). Oxford University Press.

McCormack, G. (2020). *How education can save the world.* TEDxSydney. Retrieved from https://tedxsydney.com/contributor/gavin-mccormack/

Organisation for Economic Co-operation and Development (OECD). (2019). *PISA in focus #91: How is students' motivation related to their performance and anxiety?* Retrieved from https://www.oecd.org/content/dam/oecd/

en/publications/reports/2019/01/how-is-students-motivation-related-to-their-performance-and-anxiety_3aa99589/d7c28431-en.pdf

OECD. (2023). *PISA 2022 results*. Retrieved from https://www.oecd.org/en/publications/pisa-2022-results-volume-i_53f23881-en.html

OECD. (2024). *Programme for International Student Assessment (PISA)*. Retrieved from https://www.oecd.org/en/about/programmes/pisa.html

Robinson, K. (2006). *Do schools kill creativity?* TED Talk. Retrieved from https://www.ted.com/talks/sir_ken_robinson_do_schools_kill_creativity?trigger=15s

Sinek, S. (2014). *Leaders eat last: Why some teams pull together and others don't*. Penguin Publishing Group.

Sriram, R. (2020, June 24). *Why ages 2–7 matter so much for brain development*. Edutopia. Retrieved from https://www.edutopia.org/article/why-ages-2-7-matter-so-much-brain-development

Whitebread, D., Basilio, M., Kuvalja, M., & Verma, M. (2009). *The importance of play: A report on the value of children's play with a series of policy recommendations*. University of Cambridge. Retrieved from https://www.csap.cam.ac.uk/media/uploads/files/1/david-whitebread---importance-of-play-report.pdf

Whitebread, D., Coltman, P., Pino Pasternak, D., Sangster, C., Grau, V., Bingham, S., & Demetriou, D. (2009). The development of two observational tools for assessing metacognition and self-regulated learning in young children. *Metacognition and Learning, 4*(1), 63–85. https://doi.org/10.1007/s11409-008-9033-1

## Chapter 3

Al-Khwarizmi, Muhammad ibn Musa. (1831). *Al-Kitab al-Mukhtasar fi Hisab al-Jabr wal-Muqabala*. Circa 820 AD. Translated and edited by F. Rosen in *The algebra of Muhammad ibn Musa Al-Khwarizmi*. The Oriental Translation Fund.

Cameron, W. B. (1963). *Informal sociology: A casual introduction to sociological thinking*. Random House.

China Daily. (2023, November 2). Pressure, expectations lead to student depression. Retrieved from https://www.chinadaily.com.cn/a/202311/02/WS6542fd2da31090682a5ec042.html

Darling-Hammond, L., et al. (2020). Implications for educational practice of the science of learning and development. *Applied Developmental Science, 24*(2), 97–140. https://doi.org/10.1080/10888691.2018.1537791

Elman, B. A. (2013). *Civil examinations and meritocracy in late imperial China*. Harvard University Press.

Goldstein, H., & Leckie, G. (2008). School league tables: What can they really tell us? *Significance, 5*(2), 67–69. https://academic.oup.com/jrssig/article-abstract/5/2/67/7029800

Kaya, M., & Erdem, C. (2021). The relationship between students' well-being and academic achievement: A meta-analysis study. *Child Indicators Research, 14*(3), 981–1007. https://doi.org/10.1007/s12187-021-09821-4

Miseliunaite, B., Kliziene, I., & Cibulskas, G. (2022). Can holistic education solve the world's problems: A systematic literature review. *Sustainability, 14*(15), 9737. https://doi.org/10.3390/su14159737

Organisation for Economic Co-operation and Development (OECD). (2017). *PISA 2015 results (volume III): Students' well-being.* https://doi.org/10.1787/9789264273856-en

Piaget, J. (1973). *To understand is to invent: The future of education.* Grossman Publishers.

World Economic Forum. (2020). *The Future of Jobs Report 2020.* Retrieved from https://www3.weforum.org/docs/WEF_Future_of_Jobs_2020.pdf

## Chapter 4

Dweck, C. S. (2006). *Mindset: The new psychology of success.* Random House.

Groves, S. (2016). *Strategies to remove unwanted information: A comparison between negating and forgetting* (PhD dissertation). Swinburne University of Technology.

Krueger, C., Holditch-Davis, D., Quint, S., & Decasper, A. (2014). Recurring auditory experience in the 28- to 34-week-old fetus. *Infant Behavior and Development, 37*(4), 537–543. https://doi.org/10.1016/j.infbeh.2004.03.001

Kuhl, P. K. (2011). Early language learning and literacy: Neuroscience implications for education. *Mind, Brain, and Education, 5*(3), 128–142. https://doi.org/10.1111/j.1751-228X.2011.01121.x

Lewandowsky, S., Ecker, U. K. H., Seifert, C. M., Schwarz, N., & Cook, J. (2012). Misinformation and its correction: Continued influence and successful debiasing. *Psychological Science in the Public Interest, 13*(3), 106–131. https://doi.org/10.1177/1529100612451018

Mann, S., & Cadman, R. (2014). Does being bored make us more creative? *Creativity Research Journal, 26*(2), 165–173. https://doi.org/10.1080/10400419.2014.901073

Mason, M. F., Norton, M. I., Van Horn, J. D., Wegner, D. M., Grafton, S. T., & Macrae, C. N. (2007). Wandering minds: The default network and stimulus-independent thought. *Science, 315*(5810), 393–395. https://doi.org/10.1126/science.1131295

Montessori, M. (1949). *The absorbent mind.* Holt, Rinehart & Winston.

Penfield, W., & Boldrey, E. (1937). Somatic motor and sensory representation in the cerebral cortex of man as studied by electrical stimulation. *Brain, 60*(4), 389–443. https://doi.org/10.1093/brain/60.4.389

Taycher, L. (2010, August 5). *Books of the world, stand up and be counted! All 129,864,880 of you.* Retrieved from https://booksearch.blogspot.com/2010/08/books-of-world-stand-up-and-be-counted.html

Tseng, J., & Poppenk, J. (2020). Brain meta-state transitions demarcate thoughts across task contexts exposing the mental noise of trait neuroticism. *Nature Communications, 11*(1), 3480. https://doi.org/10.1038/s41467-020-17255-9

Wilkes, A. L., & Leatherbarrow, M. (1988). Editing episodic memory following the identification of error. *Quarterly Journal of Experimental Psychology, 40*(2), 361–387. https://doi.org/10.1080/02724988843000168

## Chapter 5

Aristotle. (1908). *Nicomachean ethics.* Translated by W. D. Ross, Book II, 1103b.

Dewey, J. (1938/1998). *Experience and education* (60th anniversary ed.). Kappa Delta Pi.

Moll, J., Krueger, F., Zahn, R., Pardini, M., de Oliveira-Souza, R., & Grafman, J. (2006). Human fronto-mesolimbic networks guide decisions about charitable donation. *Proceedings of the National Academy of Sciences, 103*(42), 15623–15628. https://doi.org/10.1073/pnas.0604475103

Piaget, J. (1976). *To understand is to invent: The future of education.* Penguin Books.

Robinson, K. (2009). *The element: How finding your passion changes everything.* Penguin Books.

Routledge, C., & Abeyta, A. (2024). *Hope in America: Visions of the future.* Human Flourishing Lab. Retrieved from https://humanflourishinglab.org/wp-content/uploads/2024/01/HFL-Hope-in-America-2024.pdf

Thomas, J. W. (2000). *A review of research on project-based learning.* Autodesk Foundation.

Zimmerman, B. J. (2002). Becoming a self-regulated learner: An overview. *Theory into Practice, 41*(2), 64–70. https://doi.org/10.1207/s15430421tip4102_2

## Chapter 6

Ba, S. & Hu, X. (2023). Measuring emotional synchrony in the classroom using wearable devices: A systematic review. *Computers & Education, 200,* 104797. https://doi.org/10.1016/j.compedu.2023.104797

Baddeley, A. (1992). Working memory. *Science, 255*(5044), 556–559. https://doi.org/10.1126/science.1736359

Bevilacqua, D., Davidesco, I., Wan, L., et al. (2020). Brain-to-brain synchrony and learning outcomes vary by student–teacher dynamics: Evidence from a real-world classroom electroencephalography study. *Journal of Cognitive Neuroscience, 31*(3), 401–411. https://doi.org/10.1162/jocn_a_01274

Black, P., & Wiliam, D. (1998). Inside the black box: Raising standards through classroom assessment. *Phi Delta Kappan, 92*(1), 81–90. https://doi.org/10.1177/003172171009200119

Burgess, D. (2012). *Teach like a pirate: Increase student engagement, boost your creativity, and transform your life as an educator.* Dave Burgess Consulting, Inc.

Drucker, P. F. (1999). *Management challenges for the 21st century.* HarperBusiness.

Drucker, P. F. (2009). *The essential Drucker: The best of sixty years of Peter Drucker's essential writings on management.* HarperCollins.

Elliott, G. C. (2009). *Family matters: The importance of mattering to family in adolescence.* Wiley-Blackwell.

Ginsburg, K. R. (2014). The importance of play in promoting healthy child development and maintaining strong parent–child bonds. *Frontiers in Psychology, 5*, 1–6. https://doi.org/10.1542/peds.2006-2697

Gottman, J. M. (1997). *Raising an emotionally intelligent child: The heart of parenting.* Simon & Schuster.

Harvard Center on the Developing Child. (2010). *Toxic stress: The facts.* Retrieved from https://developingchild.harvard.edu/key-concept/toxic-stress

Innis, G. (2012, May 6). Boundaries and expectations are important parenting tools. *Michigan State University Extension.* Retrieved from https://www.canr.msu.edu/news/boundaries_and_expectations_are_important_parenting_tools

Kraft, M. A., & Monti-Nussbaum, M. (2021). The big problem with little interruptions to classroom learning. *AERA Open,* 7. https://journals.sagepub.com/doi/10.1177/23328584211028856

McDonald, B., & Boud, D. (2003). The impact of self-assessment on achievement: The effects of self-assessment training on performance in external examinations. *Assessment in Education: Principles, Policy & Practice, 10*(2), 209–220. https://doi.org/10.1080/0969594032000121289

Markham, L. (2012). *Peaceful parent, happy kids: How to stop yelling and start connecting.* Penguin.

Maxwell, J. C. (2007). *The 21 irrefutable laws of leadership: Follow them and people will follow you.* HarperCollins Leadership.

Mental Health Foundation. (2021, July 13). Signs of hope for British teenagers' mental health but loneliness and anxiety remain high: New findings from long-term study. Retrieved from https://www.mentalhealth.org.uk/about-us/news/signs-hope-british-teenagers-mental-health-loneliness-and-anxiety-remain-high-new-findings-long-term

Robinson, C., & Taylor, C. (2007). Theorizing student voice: Values and perspectives. *Improving Schools, 10*(1), 5–17. https://doi.org/10.1177/1365480207073702

Schunk, D. H., & Zimmerman, B. J. (1994). *Self-regulation of learning and performance: Issues and educational applications.* Routledge.

Selman, S. B., & Dilworth-Bart, J. E. (2024). Routines and child development: A systematic review. *Journal of Family Theory & Review, 16*(2), 1–20. https://onlinelibrary.wiley.com/doi/full/10.1111/jftr.12549

Siegel, D. J., & Bryson, T. P. (2011). *The whole-brain child: 12 revolutionary strategies to nurture your child's developing mind.* Delacorte Press.

United Nations. (1989). *Convention on the Rights of the Child.* Retrieved from https://www.unicef.org/child-rights-convention/convention-text

Wiggins, G. (1998). *Educative assessment: Designing assessments to inform and improve student performance.* Jossey-Bass.

Zimmerman, B. J. (2002). Becoming a self-regulated learner: An overview. *Theory into Practice, 41*(2), 64–70. https://doi.org/10.1207/s15430421tip4102_2

# About the author

Gavin McCormack is the co-founder of Upschool.co, a platform that inspires children to develop real-world skills and take action that creates genuine impact. With more than 25 years of experience in education – including a decade as a trained Montessori teacher – Gavin has taught in classrooms across the globe and championed innovative, purposeful learning. He is the Montessori Australia Ambassador, a TEDx speaker, and the author of numerous children's books, including a biography of legendary Liverpool manager Sir Kenny Dalglish. Gavin has built schools, libraries, and teacher training centres in Nepal and was recently awarded the 2024 Outstanding Global Contribution to Education Award at the GESS Awards in Dubai. For the past five consecutive years, he has been recognised by *The Educator* magazine as one of Australia's Most Influential Educators.